CW00376877

TREASURY

of the

CATHOLIC CHURCH

TREASURY

of the

CATHOLIC CHURCH

Two Thousand Years of Spiritual Writing

❧ ❧

Compiled by

Teresa de Bertodano

DARTON · LONGMAN + TODD

First published in 1999 by
Darton, Longman and Todd Ltd
1 Spencer Court
140–142 Wandsworth High Street
London SW18 4JJ

ISBN 0–232–52294–4

A catalogue record for this book is available from the British Library.

Designed by Sandie Boccacci
Phototypeset in 12/16pt Bernhard Modern by Intype London Ltd
Printed and bound in Great Britain by
The Cromwell Press, Trowbridge, Wiltshire

For
those who have carried this anthology
in their prayers
and
in thanksgiving
to Mater Admirabilis

Laurence was one among the seven deacons who served the Roman Church; this was a charge of great trust, to which was annexed the care of the goods of the Church and the distribution of its alms among the poor.

When the Prefect of Rome was informed of these charities, imagining that the Christians had hid considerable treasures, he wanted to secure them: for he was no less a worshipper of gold and silver than of Jupiter and Mars. With this in view he sent for St Laurence, and said to him, 'Bring out your treasures, the Emperor has need of them for the maintenance of his forces. I am told that according to your doctrines you must render to Caesar the things that belong to him.'

Laurence went all over the city, seeking out the poor who were supported by the Church. On the third day he gathered together a great number of them, and placed them in rows, the decrepit, the blind, the lame, the maimed, the lepers, orphans, widows and maidens; then he went to the Prefect and invited him to come and see the treasure of the Church. The Prefect, astonished to see such an assembly of misery and misfortune, turned to the deacon with threatening looks, and asked him what all this meant, and where the treasures were which he had promised to show him. St Laurence answered, 'What are you displeased at? These *are* the treasure of the Church.'

St Laurence (d. 258)

CONTENTS

ACKNOWLEDGEMENTS

A very great debt is due to Professor Donna Orsuto of the Gregorian University and David Dawson Vasquez of the Catholic University of America. I would also like to thank Herbert Alphonso SJ, Donna Orietta Doria Pamphilj, Michael McNulty SJ, Gerald O'Collins SJ, the Rev. Gregory Mustaciuolo and Nicholas Schofield.

I am indebted to the International Academy of Marital Spirituality (INTAMS) in Brussels and its director Mrs Aldegonde Brenninkmeijer-Werhahn. Also to Hans Storm and Elvira Roncalli of the Library for the Interdisciplinary Study of Marriage (LIBISMA) and to Julia Archer, Helen Archer, Stratford Caldecott, Mary Corbett and Angela Dunlea of Marriage Care, and to Peter Grimer, Edith Dominian, Hilary and Richard Grey, Professor Mary Grey, William Johnston SJ and Barbara Wood.

I am very grateful to the Benedictine Community of Stanbrook Abbey and particularly Dame Felicitas Corrigan, Dame Philippa Edwards, Dame Teresa Rodrigues and Dame Margaret Truran. Dame Maria Boulding has very kindly allowed me to use her translation of *The Confessions of St Augustine*.

The following have been unfailingly generous in sharing their wisdom: Fr Bernard O. Cart. of Parkminster, Fr Robert Llewelyn, Fr Iain Matthew OCD, Petrina Morris, Madeleine Judd, Mary Stewart, Sally Trench, Benedict Vanier OCSO, Jean Vanier and Dr Thérèse Vanier.

John Atkinson, Librarian of the Franciscan Study Centre in Canterbury, Elizabeth Basset, Sr M. Bernard PCC, Jeanne Bisgood CBE, Sr Pia Buxton IBVM, Sr Emmanuel Orchard IBVM, Mr George Bull, Justin Coo, Heather Craufurd, The Rev. Douglas Dales, Chaplain of Marlborough College, Paddy Daly of the Catholic Media Office in Glasgow, Canon John Devane, Sr Pamela Dillon OP of the Dominican Monastery of Langeac, Cynthia Donnelly of the Madonna House Community in Combermere, John Dove SJ, Sr Emmanuelle OP of the Dominican Monastery of Bouvines, Thomas More Eyston, Andrew Forshaw OP of Blackfriars, Oxford, Dr Esther de Waal, Shirley du Boulay, Jim Forest, David Gibbs SJ, Jane Gore-Booth, Francesca, Countess of Gosford, Sr Frances Teresa

OSC, Win Harrison, Gerard Hughes SJ, Lord Hylton. To Louis Jebb, Lady Helen Asquith and Lord Oxford for kindly allowing me to use Hilaire Belloc's letter to Katharine Asquith, The Hon. William Jolliffe, Professor Edwin Judge of Macquarie University, Sydney, Sr M. Benedetta of the Sisters of St Joseph of the Sacred Heart in Sydney, Dom Philip Jebb OSB and Dom Boniface Hill OSB of Downside Abbey, Mark Le Fanu OBE and the Society of Authors, Angela Lewis, Mr Aidan Mackey of the Chesterton Study Centre, Sr Frances Makower RSCJ and Sr Eileen Coke RSCJ, Thomas M.McCoog SJ, Dom Donald McGlynn OCSO, Abbot of Nunraw, Dom John Moakler OCSO, Abbot of Mount St Bernard, Brigid McEwen, June McAllister, Caroline Morson, Edward O'Connor CSC of the University of Notre Dame, Pat O'Leary of *The Irish Catholic*, Eileen O'Reilly of the Legion of Mary in Dublin, Sister Susan Richert, Provincial Team Leader of the Sisters of the Presentation of the Blessed Virgin Mary, Canon Timothy Russ, Dom Cyprian Smith OSB of Ampleforth Abbey, Kathryn Spink, Barbara Swanekamp, Sr Diane Szarfinski OCD, Sr Teresa Patricia and Sr Cecilia of the Little Sisters of Jesus, Jenny Thom of Chichester Cathedral Visitors Office, Fr Roland Walls, Sr Benedicta Ward SLG, James Wicksteed.

Mrs Joan Bond of the Catholic Central Library in London has never failed to trace a document or a source – no matter how obscure.

My debt to the Benedictine community of the Adorers of the Sacred Heart of Montmartre is very great and particularly to Mother Xavier McMonagle, Mother Edmund Campion and Mother John Baptist.

My brother Martin de Bertodano and my sisters Joanna Hylton and Isabel Scott have given me unstinting help.

Morag Reeve has been the most helpful and supportive of editors. I am very grateful to her for inviting me to compile this anthology. Kate Webster kindly cleared the permissions. I am most grateful to her and to Helen Porter, to all at DLT, and especially to Sandy Waldron for her meticulous copy editing, and to Sandie Boccacci for designing the text. I am very grateful to the late Cardinal Hume for writing the Foreword.

FOREWORD

What is it that makes life worth living? For most of us the answer is likely to be loving relationships – caring for others and being cared for by them. Here lies the path to human wholeness – and wholeness is very much a part of holiness.

The men and women we meet in *Treasury of the Catholic Church* are both whole and holy – life-givers and life enhancers. If we were to ask any of them the meaning of life, I think they might tell us that life is about being fully alive, both here and in the hereafter. Some of those we meet here are widely known – Augustine, Julian of Norwich, Teresa of Avila. Others we may be meeting for the first time – Kateri Tekakwitha from America and Mary MacKillop from Australia.

On a personal note, I am pleased to see that so many fellow Benedictines have found their way into this book. The collection moves from St Benedict and his sister St Scholastica to St Anselm and down to Christian de Chergé who was martyred in Algeria with his six companions in 1996.

They have very different stories to tell us but the thread that binds them is a passionate love of God and a willingness to be still, to 'waste time with God' (often in the midst of hectic lives) and allow God to love them. These men and women invite us to allow God to love us in the same way. They are not 'different'. Some may be canonised saints but, more importantly, they are our brothers and sisters, closer to us than we can imagine and inviting us into an intimacy with Father, Son and Holy Spirit which we perhaps never dared to believe possible. They have much to teach us and to share with us. *Treasury of the Catholic Church* is an introduction to some outstanding individuals who may become our lifelong friends.

Basil Hume.

16 April 1999

INTRODUCTION

In bringing together examples of our remarkable spiritual heritage, it quickly becomes clear that there are many ways in which the 'cake' can be cut. The material could certainly be dealt with in a strictly chronological fashion, but overall it has seemed more helpful to group passages thematically, maintaining the chronology within themes.

The publishers specifically requested that this book should bring together writings from ancient and modern authors in communion with the Bishop of Rome. The result has been an inevitable impoverishment in terms of the great writings of other traditions. If, however, I had been given a totally free hand in the selection of material, the anthology would never have been completed and it would have been even more difficult to decide what to omit.

I did not originally intend to include the work of living writers, but this became impossible when compiling the section on marriage. I am told that spiritual writing on the subject has made rapid strides over the past thirty years and that such improvement was long overdue! Two of the writers whose material appears in this section are therefore very much alive and I thank William Johnston and Barbara Wood for allowing their work to be included.

If I have had a personal concern it has been to choose passages that counteract the unspoken assumption that God is boring. Should childhood experience of religion have consisted of hours spent listening to tedious and incomprehensible sermons it is perhaps inevitable that the subject of such homilies will seem boring. In *Best of Both Worlds*[1] by Bernard Basset one of the characters accuses her learned theologian son of the serious shortcoming of 'making religion dull'. Some readers may be familiar with Gerard Hughes' book *God of Surprises*[2] with its portrayal of 'Uncle George' – the elderly relative bent on hurling into the furnace of the damned those who fail to visit him once a week or act in other ways likely to displease Uncle George. 'We observe what we are told are his wishes and dare not admit, even to ourselves, that we loathe him'.

1 *Best of Both Worlds* by Bernard Basset (Burns & Oates, 1963).
2 *God of Surprises* by Gerard W. Hughes (DLT, 1985 and 1996).

If Uncle George is the god in whom we 'believe', a healthy dose of agnosticism may put us on the road to being discovered by the 'God of Surprises' – the God who shows a marked preference for those whose actions would have Uncle George lining them up for the furnace.

'Why does your Master eat with tax collectors and sinners?' asked the scribes and Pharisees of the disciples. Perhaps in part because sinners are better company than scribes and Pharisees. There seems little doubt that dubious characters revelled in the company of Jesus, otherwise they would not have gone on inviting him to their disreputable parties.

Theirs is the God whom the saints and mystics discover, the God who first discovers them. In *Treasury of the Catholic Church*, passages from their writings are taken from the earliest centuries to the present day. Many of those included have died as martyrs – some of them very recently. This age could indeed be described as 'the age of martyrs'. While it is impossible to be accurate, it is widely believed that of the tens of thousands of martyrdoms suffered over the past two millennia, more than half have taken place during the past century.

I am very greatly in debt to those who have spent so much of their time advising and helping me with this collection. Although the final result inevitably reflects personal preference, I have tried to spread the net broadly by including material from many countries.

I am still more in debt to those who have carried this undertaking in their prayers. The anthology is dedicated to them in the knowledge that the book would not have been completed without their support. The shortcomings are my own and while every effort has been made to trace the source of each passage, these efforts have not always been successful. I ask the indulgence of those concerned and that they will get in touch with me so that appropriate acknowledgement may be made in any future edition.

TERESA DE BERTODANO
1 March 1999

LOVE,
DIVINE AND HUMAN

Father, Son and Holy Spirit

When the Paraclete comes,
whom I shall send to you from the Father,
the Spirit of truth who issues from the Father,
he will be my witness.
And you too will be witnesses,
because you have been with me from the beginning.

John 15:26–7

Like to God

Who is there who can hear the names of the Holy Spirit and not feel exaltation in his soul, not lift up his thoughts to that supreme nature? For he is called the Spirit of God, the Spirit of truth, who proceeds from the Father, the upright Spirit, the guiding Spirit. His chief and distinguishing name is Holy Spirit.

To the Spirit all creatures turn for their sanctification; all who live virtuously seek him, and are, by his influence, refreshed and helped towards their own natural end. . . .

Even as bright and shining bodies, once touched by a ray of light falling on them, become even more glorious and themselves cast another light, so too souls that carry the Spirit, and are enlightened by the Spirit, become spiritual themselves and send forth grace upon others.

This grace enables them to foresee the future, to understand mysteries, to grasp hidden things, to receive spiritual blessings, to have their thoughts fixed on heavenly things, and to dance with the angels. So is their joy unending, so is their perseverance in God unfailing, so do they acquire likeness to God, so – most sublime of all – do they themselves become divine.

St Basil the Great (c. 330–79)

Seek God by Faith

Who then is God? He is Father, Son and Holy Spirit, one God. Seek no farther concerning God; for those who wish to know the great deep must first review the natural world. For knowledge of the Trinity is properly likened to the depths of the sea, according to that saying of the Sage. And the great deep, who shall fathom it? Since, just as the depth of the sea is invisible to human sight, even so the godhead of the Trinity is found to be unknowable by human senses. And thus if, I say, a man wishes to know what he ought to believe, let him not think that he understands better by speech than by believing; because when he seeks it, knowledge of the godhead will recede farther than it was.

Therefore seek the supreme wisdom, not by verbal debate, but by the perfection of a good life, not with the tongue but with the faith which issues from singleness of heart, not with that which is gathered from the guests of a learned irreligion. If then you seek the unutterable by discussion, he will fly farther from you than he was. If you seek by faith, wisdom shall stand in her accustomed station at the gate, and where she dwells she shall at least in part be seen. But then is she also truly in some measure attained, when the invisible is believed in a manner that passes understanding; for God must be believed invisible as he is, though he be partly seen by the pure heart.

St Columbanus (d. 615)

Father, Son and Holy Spirit

To the Trinity be praise!
  God is music, God is life
  that nurtures every creature in its kind.
Our God is the song of the angel throng
  and the splendour of secret ways
  hid from all humankind,
But God our life is the life of all.

※

The Holy Spirit is life that gives life,
Moving all things.
It is the root in every creature
And purifies all things,
Wiping away sins,
Anointing wounds.
It is radiant life, worthy of praise,
Awakening and enlivening
All things.

St Hildegard of Bingen (1098–1179)

The Love of the Trinity [I]

For when two persons who mutually love embrace each other with supreme longing and take supreme delight in each other's love, then the supreme joy of the first is in intimate love of the second, and conversely the excellent joy of the second is in love of the first. As long as only the first is loved by the second, he alone seems to possess the delights of his excellent sweetness. Similarly, as long as the second does not have someone who shares in love for a third, he lacks the sharing of excellent joy. In order that both may be able to share delights of that kind, it is necessary for them to have someone who shares in love for a third.

When those who love mutually are of such great benevolence that, as we have said, they wish every perfection to be shared, then it is necessary, as has been said, that each with equal desire and for a similar reason seek out someone with whom to share love, and that each devotedly possess such a one, according to the fullness of his power.

Richard of St-Victor (d. 1173)

The Love of the Trinity [II]

When one person gives love to another and he alone loves only the other, there certainly is love, but it is not a shared love. When two love each other mutually and give to each other the affection of supreme longing; when the affection of the first goes out to the second and the affection of the second goes out to the first and tends as it were in diverse ways — in this case there certainly is love on both sides, but it is not shared love. Shared love is properly said to exist when a third person is loved by two persons harmoniously and in community, and the affection of the two persons is fused into one affection by the flame of love for the third. From these things it is evident that shared love would have no place in Divinity itself if a third person were lacking to the other two persons. Here we are not speaking of just any shared love but of supreme shared love — a shared love of a sort such that a creature would never merit from the Creator and for which it would never be found worthy.

Richard of St-Victor (d. 1173)

The Paradiso

O Light Eternal fixed in Self alone,
known only to Yourself, and knowing Self,
You love and glow, knowing and being known!

That circling which, as I conceived it, shone
In You as Your own first reflected light
when I had looked deep into It a while,

seemed in Itself and in Its own Self-colour
to be depicted with man's very image.
My eyes were totally absorbed in It.

As the geometer who tries so hard
to square the circle, but cannot discover,
think as he may, the principle involved,

so did I strive with this new mystery:
I yearned to know how could our image fit
into the circle, how could it conform;

but my own wings could not take me so high –
then a great flash of understanding struck
my mind, and suddenly its wish was granted.

At this point power failed high fantasy
but, like a wheel in perfect balance turning,
I felt my will and my desire impelled
by the Love that moves the sun and the other stars.

Dante Alighieri (1265–1321)

God, Father and Mother

Jesus Christ, who does good to overcome evil, is our true mother. We take our lives from him, which is the start of motherhood, together with all the loving care that follows on, without end.

As truly as God is our father, so, just as truly, God is our mother. And he showed this in everything, especially in those sweet words when he said:

'It is I'. That is to say,
'It is I, the strength and goodness of fatherhood.
It is I, the wisdom of motherhood.
It is I, the light and grace of holy love.
It is I, the Trinity.
It is I, the unity.
I am the sovereign goodness in all things.
It is I who teach you to love.
It is I who teach you to desire.
It is I who am the lasting fulfilment of all true desires.'

Julian of Norwich (c. 1342–after 1416)

Eternal Trinity [I]

O eternal Trinity, eternal godhead! This godhead, your divine nature, made immensely precious the blood of the only-begotten Son. Eternal Trinity, you are like a deep sea, in which the more I seek, the more I find; and the more I find, the more I seek you. You fill the soul, yet somehow without satisfying it: in the abyss which you are you so fill the soul that it ever continues to hunger and thirst for you, desiring you, eager in your light to see you, who are the light.

With the light of my understanding, in your light I have tasted and seen the abyss which you are, eternal Trinity, and the beauty of your creation. Then looking at myself in you, I have seen that I am your image; this is a gift that I receive from you in your power, eternal Father, and in your wisdom, which is attributed to your only-begotten Son. The Holy Spirit who proceeds from you, Father, and from your Son has prepared me, giving me a will to love you.

St Catherine of Siena (c. 1347–80)

Eternal Trinity [II]

Eternal Trinity, you are the Creator, I the creature. I have come to know, in the new creation you made of me in the blood of your Son, that you are in love with the beauty of your creature.

O eternal Trinity, God, you are an abyss, a deep sea; you have given yourself to me – what greater could you give? You are a fire, ever burning and never consumed, consuming in your heat all the self-love of the soul, taking away all coldness. By your light you enlighten our minds, as by your light you have brought me to know your truth.

In this light I know you, and I picture you to myself as the supreme good, the good beyond all good, the blessed good, the incomprehensible good, the inestimable good, beauty beyond all beauty, wisdom beyond all wisdom. You are wisdom itself. You are the food of angels, who gave yourself to men in the fire of your love.

You are the garment which covers every nakedness. You feed the hungry in your sweetness, because you are gentle, without a trace of bitterness. O eternal Trinity!

St Catherine of Siena (c. 1347–80)

Trinity, Whom I Adore [I]

O my God, Trinity whom I adore, help me to forget myself entirely so as to be established in you, as changeless and calm as if my soul were already in eternity. May nothing disturb my peace or draw me forth from you, O my Unchanging Lord, but may every minute carry me further into the depths of your Mystery. Calm my soul, make of it your heaven, your beloved abode and the place of your rest. May I never leave you alone there, but may I be there entirely, wholly awake in my faith, all adoring and wholly yielded up to your creative action.

O my beloved Christ, crucified by love! I want to be a bride for your heart, I want to cover you in glory and love you – until I die of it! But I feel how powerless I am and I ask you to 'clothe me with yourself', to identify my soul with all the movements of your soul, to immerse me in yourself, to take possession of me, to substitute yourself for me so that my life may be but a radiance of your Life. Come into me as Adorer, as Restorer and as Saviour.

Blessed Elizabeth of the Trinity (1880–1906)

Trinity, Whom I Adore [II]

O eternal Word, Utterance of my God, I wish to spend my life listening to you; I wish to make myself wholly teachable so as to learn everything from you. Then through all nights, all voids, all powerlessness, I wish to keep my eyes always upon you and live beneath your great light. O my beloved Star, fascinate me so that I may no longer be able to withdraw from your radiance.

O consuming Fire, Spirit of love, 'come upon me' so that there may be brought about in my soul a kind of incarnation of the Word: that I may be for him an additional humanity in which he renews the whole of his Mystery.

And you, O Father, bend down towards your poor little creature, 'overshadow' her, see in her only 'the Beloved in whom you are well pleased'.

O my Three, my All, my Beatitude, infinite Solitude, Immensity in which I lose myself, I yield myself to you as a prey. Bury yourself in me that I may bury myself in you, until I depart to contemplate in your light the abyss of your splendours.

Blessed Elizabeth of the Trinity (1880–1906)

God's Love for Us

I have loved you
just as the Father has loved me.
Remain in my love . . .
just as I have kept my Father's commandments
and remain in his love.
I have told you this
so that my own joy may be in you
and your joy may be complete.
This is my commandment:
love one another,
as I have loved you.

John 15:9–12

Your Life for My Salvation

Where do you pasture your flock, O good shepherd, you who take on your shoulders the whole flock, for the whole of human nature which you take on your shoulders forms one sheep? Show me the place of green pastures and the restful waters, lead me to the grass which nourishes, call me by name, so that I who am your sheep may hear your voice. Give me by your voice eternal life. Speak to me, you whom my soul loves.

This is how I name you, for your name is above every name and cannot be uttered or comprehended by any rational nature. Your name which reveals your goodness is the love my soul has for you. How can I not love you who loved me, even though I was black, so much that you laid down your life for the sheep whose shepherd you are? Greater love than this cannot be conceived, that you should purchase my salvation with your life.

St Gregory of Nyssa (c. 330–c. 395)

The Ever Adorable Trinity [I]

Her most loving Jesus seemed to draw her toward himself by the breath of love of his pierced heart, and to wash her in the water flowing from it, and then to sprinkle her with the life-giving blood of his heart (cf. Jn 19:34). With this action she began to revive, and from the smallest cinder she was invigorated and grew into a green tree, whose branches were divided in three, in the form of a fleur-de-lys. Then the Son of God took this tree and presented it with gratitude to the glory of the ever adorable Trinity. When he had presented it, the whole blessed Trinity with great graciousness bowed down toward the offering. God the Father, in his divine omnipotence, set in the upper branches all the fruit that this soul would have been able to produce, were she to correspond aright to divine omnipotence. In the same way, she saw the Son of God and the Holy Spirit setting in the other two sections of the branches the fruits of wisdom and goodness.

St Gertrude the Great (1256–c. 1302)

The Ever Adorable Trinity [II]

When she had received the body of Christ, she beheld her soul . . . in the likeness of a tree fixing its roots in the wound of the side of Jesus Christ; she felt in some new and marvellous way that there was passing through this wound, as through a root, and penetrating into all her branches and fruit and leaves a wondrous sap which was the virtue of the humanity and divinity of Jesus Christ. Thus, through her soul, the work of his whole life took on more splendour, like gold gleaming through crystal. Hereupon not only the blessed Trinity, but all the saints, rejoiced with delight and wonder. They all rose up in reverence and, as though on bended knee, offered their merits, represented like crowns, hanging them on the branches of the tree we have mentioned, to the praise and honour of him the splendour of whose glory now shone through her and gladdened them with fresh delight.

St Gertrude the Great (1256–c. 1302)

The Hazelnut

At this time our Lord showed me an inward sight of his homely loving. I saw that he is everything that is good and comforting to us. He is our clothing. In his love he wraps and holds us. He enfolds us in love and he will never let us go.

And then he showed me a little thing, the size of a hazelnut, in the palm of my hand – and it was as round as a ball. I looked at it with my mind's eye and I thought: 'What can this be?' and answer came: 'It is all that is made.' I marvelled that it could last, for I thought it might have crumbled to nothing, it was so small. And the answer came into my mind: 'It lasts, and ever shall, because God loves it.' And so all things have being through the love of God.

In this little thing I saw three truths. The first is that God made it. The second is that God loves it. And the third is that God looks after it.

Julian of Norwich (c. 1342–after 1416)

Love Was His Meaning

From the time it was shown, I often asked to know what was our Lord's meaning. And fifteen years after, and more, I was answered in inward understanding, saying this:

'Would you know your Lord's meaning in this?
Learn it well.
Love was his meaning.
Who showed it you? Love.
What did he show you? Love.
Why did he show you? For love.
Hold fast to this and you shall learn and know more
   about love, but you shall never know nor learn about
   anything except love for ever.'

So was I taught that love was our Lord's meaning.
And I saw full surely that before ever God made us, he
   loved us. And this love was never quenched, nor ever
   shall be.
And in this love he has done all his works.
And in this love he has made all things profitable to us.
And in this love our life is everlasting.
In our making we had beginning, but the love in which he
   made us was in him from without beginning.
In which love we have our beginning.
And all this shall we see in God without end – which Jesus
   grant us.

Julian of Norwich (c. 1342–after 1416)

You Gave Us Memory

You drew us out of your holy mind
like a flower
petaled with our soul's three powers,
and into each power
you put the whole plant,
so that they might bear fruit in your garden,
might come back to you
with the fruit you gave them.
And you would come back to the soul
to fill her with your blessedness.
There the soul dwells –
like the fish in the sea
and the sea in the fish.
You gave us memory
so that we might be able to hold your blessings
and so bring forth the flower of glory to your name
and the fruit of profit to ourselves.
You gave us understanding
to understand your truth
and your will –
your will that wants only that we be made holy –
so that we might bear first the flower of glory
and then the fruit of virtue.
And you gave us our will
so that we might be able to love
what our understanding has seen
and what our memory has held.

St Catherine of Siena (c. 1347–80)

Living Flame

Flame, alive, compelling,
yet tender past all telling,
reaching the secret centre of my soul!
Since now evasion's over,
finish your work, my Lover,
break the last thread, wound me and make me whole!

Burn that is for my healing!
Wound of delight past feeling!
Ah, gentle hand whose touch is a caress,
foretaste of heaven conveying
and every debt repaying:
slaying, you give me life for death's distress.

O lamps of fire bright-burning
with splendid brilliance, turning
deep caverns of my soul to pools of light!
Once shadowed, dim, unknowing,
now their strange new-found glowing
gives warmth and radiance for my Love's delight.

Ah! gentle and so loving
you wake within me, proving
that you are there in secret and alone;
your fragrant breathing stills me,
your grace, your glory fills me
so tenderly your love becomes my own.

St John of the Cross (1542–91)

Aware of God's Presence

By the supernatural virtue of Charity, Divine Love dwells in the soul and in a very personal, intimate relationship, for there are several different ways in which God can be present. First of all, God is present everywhere in the world, because He is the Power that made the world, the Wisdom that planned it, and the Love that executed it. God is also present — but personally — in the Eucharist, and in our souls so long as the Sacramental presence lasts. But there is still another Divine presence which is more abiding, and that is the presence of God in the soul through Charity. To be in the state of Grace through Charity does not mean that we *have* something, but that we *are* something. For one of the consequences of the Faith is that an extraordinary event happens to us: we receive a Gift. Many baptized souls are ignorant of this mystery, and remain ignorant of it throughout their lives; for just as it is possible for some families to live under the same roof and never communicate, so it is also possible for a man to have God in his soul and yet hold little intimate exchange with Him. The more holy souls become, and the more detached from the world, the greater their consciousness of God's presence.

Fulton Sheen (1895–1979)

Our Love for God

When they had eaten, Jesus said to Simon Peter, 'Simon son of John, do you love me more than these others do?' He answered, 'Yes, Lord, you know I love you.' Jesus said to him, 'Feed my lambs.' A second time he said to him, 'Simon son of John, do you love me?' He replied, 'Yes, Lord, you know I love you.' Jesus said to him, 'Look after my sheep.' Then he said to him a third time, 'Simon son of John, do you love me?' Peter was hurt that he asked him a third time, 'Do you love me?' and said, 'Lord, you know everything; you know I love you.' Jesus said to him, 'Feed my sheep.'

John 21:15–17

The Beauty of God

Having received a commandment – to love God – we possess the power to love implanted in us at the moment we were constituted. The proof of this is not external, but anyone can learn it from himself and within himself. For by nature we desire beautiful things though we differ as to what is supremely beautiful; and without being taught we have affection towards those near and dear to us, and we spontaneously show goodwill to all our benefactors.

Now what is more marvellous than the divine beauty? What thought has more charm than the magnificence of God? What yearning of the soul is so keen and intolerable as that which comes from God upon the soul which is cleansed from all evil and cries with true affection: 'I am wounded with love'? Ineffable wholly and inexplicable are the flashes of the divine beauty.

St Basil the Great (c. 330–79)

Late Have I Loved You

Late have I loved you, Beauty so ancient and so new,
late have I loved you!
Lo, you were within,
but I outside, seeking there for you,
and upon the shapely things you have made I rushed headlong,
I, misshapen.
You were with me, but I was not with you.
They held me back far from you,
those things which would have no being
were they not in you.
You called, shouted, broke through my deafness;
you flared, blazed, banished my blindness;
you lavished your fragrance, I gasped, and now I pant for you;
I tasted you, and I hunger and thirst;
you touched me, and I burned for your peace.

St Augustine of Hippo (354–430)

Possess My Heart

'Set me as a seal on your heart.' As though to say: Love me, as I love you; have me in your mind, in your memory, in your desire; in your sighing, your groaning, your weeping. Remember, man, in what state I fashioned you, how far I preferred you before the rest of creatures, the dignity with which I ennobled you; how I crowned you with glory and honour, made you a little less than the angels, and subjected all things under your feet. Remember not only the great things I did for you, but what harsh indignities I bore on your behalf; and see if you are not acting wickedly against me, if you do not love me. For who loves you as I love you? Who created you, if not I? Who redeemed you, if not I?

Lord, take away from me the heart of stone, a heart shrunken and uncircumcised – take it away and give me a new heart, a heart of flesh, a clean heart. You cleanse our heart and love the heart that is clean – possess my heart and dwell in it, both holding it and filling it. You surpass what is highest in me, and yet are within my inmost self! Pattern of beauty and seal of holiness, mould my heart in your likeness: mould my heart under your mercy, God of my heart and God my portion for ever.

Baldwin of Canterbury (d. 1190)

The Fountain of Life

Arise, then, bride of Christ, be like the dove that nests in the rock-face at the mouth of a cavern, and there, like a sparrow which finds its home, do not cease to keep vigil; there, like a turtle-dove, hide the fledglings of your chaste love; place your lips there to draw water from the wells of your Saviour. For this is the spring flowing from the middle of paradise; it divides and becomes four rivers, then spreads through all devout hearts, and waters the whole world and makes it fruitful.

O soul devoted to God, whoever you may be, run to this source of life and light with eager longing. And with the power of your inmost heart cry out to him: 'O indescribable beauty of God most high! O pure radiance of everlasting light! O life that gives life to all life! O light that illuminates every light, and preserves in its undying splendour the myriad flames that have shone before the throne of your godhead from the dawn of time!

'O water eternal and inaccessible, clear and sweet, flowing from the spring that is hidden from the eyes of all mortal men; the spring whose depths cannot be plumbed, whose height cannot be measured, whose shores cannot be charted, whose purity cannot be muddied.'

From this source flows the river which makes glad the city of God, so that with glad shouts and songs of thanksgiving we sing to you our hymns of praise, and by experience prove that with you is the fountain of life; and in your light we shall see light.

St Bonaventure (c. 1217–74)

Thy Love and Thy Grace

Teach us, good Lord, to serve Thee
as Thou deservest,
to give and not to count the cost;
to fight and not to heed the wounds;
to toil and not to seek for rest;
to labour and not to ask for any reward
save that of knowing that we do Thy will.

Take, Lord, and receive all my liberty,
my memory, my understanding, and my entire will,
all that I have and possess.
Thou hast given all to me.
To Thee, O Lord, I return it.
All is Thine, dispose of it wholly according to Thy will.
Give me Thy love and Thy grace,
for this is sufficient for me.

St Ignatius of Loyola (c. 1491–1556)

God Alone

The more God gives the more he makes us desire, until we are empty and he is able to fill us with good things.

The immense benefits of God can only be contained by empty and solitary hearts. Therefore our Lord, who loves you greatly, wishes you to be quite alone, for he desires to be your only companion.

You must needs apply your mind to him alone, and in him alone content yourself, that in him you may find all consolation. Although God is always with us, if we set our hearts on other things beside him we cannot be at peace.

God knows what is best for all, and orders affairs for our good. Think on this only, that all is ordained by God. And pour in love where there is no love, and you will draw love out.

St John of the Cross (1542–91)

Prayer of Abandonment

Father,
I abandon myself into your hands,
do with me what you will.
Whatever you may do, I thank you:
I am ready for all, I accept all.
Let only your will be done in me
and in all your creatures.
I wish no more than this, O Lord.

Into your hands, I commend my soul;
I offer it to you
with all the love of my heart;
for I love you, Lord,
and so need to give myself:
to surrender myself into your hands
without reserve and with boundless confidence:
for you are my father.

Charles de Foucauld (1858–1916)

God's Love Brings Joy

The love of the Lord is greater in realization than in desire. Here, it differs from worldly love, which is greater in anticipation than in realization. All the popular love songs tell us: 'How happy we *will* be!' Divine love, on the contrary, does not look at all enchanting or ecstatic before we have it: the Cross frightens us; the sacrifice of selfishness and sin seems like a little death; non-sensual love appears as lovelessness. But after one makes the surrender, gives up the field to win the pearl, then one is possessed of a joy that is ineffable, that beggars all description. The discovery makes a man act so differently that his friends think he has lost his mind; but actually, he has found his soul, which the believer would not now give up for anything in all the world.

Fulton Sheen (1895–1979)

Self-surrender

Being in love with God, as experienced, is being in love in an unrestricted fashion. All love is self-surrender, but being in love with God is being in love without limits or qualifications or conditions or reservations. Just as unrestricted questioning is our capacity for self-transcendence, so being in love in an unrestricted fashion is the proper fulfilment of that capacity.

That fulfilment is not the product of our knowledge and choice. On the contrary, it dismantles and abolishes the horizon in which our knowing and choosing went on and it sets up a new horizon in which the love of God will transvalue our values and the eyes of that love will transform our knowing.

Though not the product of our knowing and choosing, it is a conscious dynamic state of love, joy, peace, that manifests itself in acts of kindness, goodness, fidelity, gentleness, and self-control (Gal. 5, 22).

Bernard Lonergan (1904–84)

Known by Jesus

What does it mean to be known by Jesus? It means accepting that all should be unveiled, in full light, in his sight and before our own eyes: our weaknesses and limits, and the whole sum of infidelities, great and small, that constitute our existence. Even though, by the mercy of God, we may not be great sinners, nevertheless there are all sorts of things in our lives that we find it difficult to look at honestly. Immediately after committing a fault, especially, we are sometimes extremely unwilling to acknowledge in the presence of Jesus, honestly and frankly, and without masks, that we are no more than what we are. That is why we are afraid of the light.

Think, for example, of the story of the woman taken in adultery. Jesus simply says to her accusers: 'Let him who is without sin among you be the first to throw a stone at her' (John 8:7). And one after another, all of them flee from his sight. They run far away from him. The only one who remains in the presence of the Lord is the woman accused who has now become the woman forgiven, in the light, because she hid nothing of her poverty from him. This is the deepest secret of an intimate relationship with the Lord: we have to allow him to look at us unreservedly, even if his gaze seems indiscreet, for in reality it is overflowing with mercy alone.

A Carthusian

Love of Neighbour

'The King will say to those on his right hand, "Come, you whom my Father has blessed, take as your heritage the kingdom prepared for you since the foundation of the world. For I was hungry and you gave me food, I was thirsty and you gave me drink, I was a stranger and you made me welcome, lacking clothes and you clothed me, sick and you visited me, in prison and you came to see me." Then the upright will say to him in reply "Lord, when did we see you hungry and feed you, or thirsty and give you drink? When did we see you a stranger and make you welcome, lacking clothes and clothe you? When did we find you sick or in prison and go to see you?" And the King will answer, "In truth I tell you, in so far as you did this to one of the least of these brothers of mine, you did it to me."'

Matthew 25:34–9

Give to the Poor [I]

Would you honour the body of Christ? Do not despise his nakedness; do not honour him here in church clothed in silk vestments and then pass him by unclothed and frozen outside. Remember that he who said, 'This is my body', and made good his words, also said, 'You saw me hungry and gave me no food', and, 'in so far as you did it not to one of these, you did it not to me'. In the first sense the body of Christ does not need clothing but worship from a pure heart. In the second sense it does need clothing and all the care we can give it.

We must learn to be discerning Christians and to honour Christ in the way in which he wants to be honoured. It is only right that honour given to anyone should take the form most acceptable to the recipient not to the giver. Peter thought he was honouring the Lord when he tried to stop him washing his feet, but this was far from being genuine homage. So give God the honour he asks for, that is give your money generously to the poor. God has no need of golden vessels but of golden hearts.

I am not saying you should not give golden altar vessels and so on, but I am insisting that nothing can take the place of almsgiving. The Lord will not refuse to accept the first kind of gift but he prefers the second, and quite naturally, because in the first case only the donor benefits, in the second case the poor get the benefit. The gift of a chalice may be ostentatious; almsgiving is pure benevolence.

St John Chrysostom (c. 347–407)

Give to the Poor [II]

What is the use of loading Christ's table with gold cups while he himself is starving? Feed the hungry and then if you have any money left over, spend it on the altar table. Will you make a cup of gold and withhold a cup of water? What use is it to adorn the altar with cloth of gold hangings and deny Christ a coat for his back! What would that profit you? Tell me: if you saw someone starving and refused to give him any food but instead spent your money on adorning the altar with gold, would he thank you? Would he not rather be outraged? Or if you saw someone in rags and stiff with cold and then did not give him clothing but set up golden columns in his honour, would he not say he was being made a fool of and insulted?

Consider that Christ is that tramp who comes in need of a night's lodging. You turn him away and then start laying rugs on the floor, draping the walls, hanging lamps on silver chains on the columns. Meanwhile the tramp is locked up in prison and you never give him a glance. Well again I am not condemning munificence in these matters. Make your house beautiful by all means but also look after the poor, or rather look after the poor first. No one was ever condemned for not adorning his house, but those who neglect the poor were threatened with hell fire for all eternity and a life of torment with devils. Adorn your house if you will, but do not forget your brother in distress. He is a temple of infinitely greater value.

St John Chrysostom (c. 347–407)

Love Your Neighbour

You do not yet see God, but by loving your neighbour you gain the sight of God; by loving your neighbour you purify your eye for seeing God, as John says clearly: 'If you do not love the brother whom you see, how will you be able to love God whom you do not see?'

You are told: love God. If you say to me: 'Show me the one I am to love', what shall I answer, except what John himself says: 'No one has ever seen God'? Do not think that you are altogether unsuited to seeing God – no, for John states: 'God is love, and he who dwells in love is dwelling in God.' Love your neighbour therefore, and observe the source of that love in you; there, as best you can, you will see God.

So then, begin to love your neighbour. 'Share your bread with the hungry, and bring the homeless poor into your house; if you see the naked, cover him, and do not despise the servants of your kinsfolk.'

If you do this, what will you obtain? 'Then shall your light break forth like the morning.' Your light is your God; to you he is 'morning light', because he will come to you after the night of the world; he neither rises nor sets, because he abides always.

By loving your neighbour and being concerned about your neighbour, you make progress on your journey. Where is your journey, if not to the Lord God, to him whom we must love with all our heart, and with all our soul, and with all our mind? We have not yet reached the Lord, but we have our neighbour with us. So then, support him with whom you are travelling so that you may come to him with whom you long to dwell.

St Augustine of Hippo (354–430)

Love Manifested in Us

There are two kinds of mercy then, mercy on earth and mercy in heaven, human mercy and divine mercy. What is human mercy like? It makes you concerned for the hardship of the poor. What is divine mercy like? It forgives sinners. Whatever generosity human mercy shows during our life on earth divine mercy repays when we reach our fatherland. In this world God is cold and hungry in all the poor, as he himself said: 'As you did it to one of the least of these my brethren, you did it to me.' God then is pleased to give from heaven, but he desires to receive on earth.

What sort of people are we – when God gives, we want to receive, when he asks, we refuse to give? When a poor man is hungry, Christ is in need, as he said himself: 'I was hungry and you gave me no food'. Take care not to despise the hardship of the poor, if you would hope, without fear, to have your sins forgiven. My dear brethren, Christ is now hungry, he is hungry and thirsty in all the poor; and what he receives on earth he returns in heaven.

I put you this question, dearly beloved: what is it you want, what is it you are looking for, when you come to church? What indeed if not mercy? Show mercy on earth, and you will receive mercy in heaven. A poor man is begging from you, and you are begging from God: he asks for a scrap, you ask for eternal life. Give to the beggar, so that you may deserve to receive from Christ. Listen to his words: 'Give and it shall be given you'. What effrontery it is for you to want to receive what you refuse to give! And so when you come to church give whatever alms you can to the poor in accordance with your means.

St Caesarius of Arles (c. 470–542)

The Leper's Kiss

The lover of complete humility went to the lepers and lived with them, serving them all most diligently for God's sake. He washed their feet, bandaged their ulcers, drew the pus from their wounds and washed out the diseased matter; he even kissed their ulcerous wounds out of his remarkable devotion, he who was soon to be a physician of the Gospel. As a result, he received such power from the Lord that he had miraculous effectiveness in healing spiritual and physical illnesses. I will cite one case among many, which occurred after the fame of the man of God became more widely known. There was a man in the vicinity of Spoleto whose mouth and cheek were being eaten away by a certain horrible disease. He could not be helped by any medical treatment and went on a pilgrimage to implore the intercession of the holy apostles. On his way back from visiting their shrines, he happened to meet God's servant. When out of devotion he wanted to kiss Francis's footprints, that humble man, refusing to allow it, kissed the mouth of the one who wished to kiss his feet. In his remarkable compassion Francis, the servant of lepers, touched that horrible sore with his holy mouth, and suddenly every sign of the disease vanished and the sick man recovered the health he longed for. I do not know which of these we should admire more: the depth of his humility in such a compassionate kiss or his extraordinary power in such an amazing miracle.

St Francis of Assisi (c. 1181–1226)

A Vessel of God's Love

Oh my very dear and cherished son, I want you to imitate this Word who is our rule, and the saints who followed him. Then you will become one with him and will have a share in his greatheartedness to replace [your own] smallheartedness. I tell you again, unless you rise up, open your eyes, and take as your model the boundless goodness and love God has shown to his creatures, you will never attain such perfect greatness of soul but will be so smallhearted that you will have no room either for yourself *or* for your neighbours. This is why I want you, as I said, to be engulfed and set on fire in him, constantly gazing into the gentle eye of his charity, for then you will love perfectly what he loves, and hate what he hates. Lift up, lift up your puny heart, your small disordered conscience! Don't give any leverage to the wicked devil, who wants to prevent so much good and doesn't want to be thrown out of his city. No, I want you, with courageous heart and perfect zeal, to realize that the Holy Spirit's law is quite different from ours. Imitate that dear Paul, who was so in love, and be a vessel of affection that bears and proclaims the name of Jesus. It seems to me that Paul gazed into this eye and lost himself in it. And he was granted such a great soul that he was willing and even desired to be separated from God, an outcast, for the sake of his brothers and sisters. Paul was in love with whatever God was in love with. He saw that charity is never scandalized, is never confounded.

St Catherine of Siena (c. 1347–80)

Be Cordial to Others

So far as you can without offending God, try to be genial and to behave in such a way with those you have to deal with that they may take pleasure in your conversation and may wish to imitate your life and manners, instead of being frightened and deterred from virtue.

The more holy someone is, the more cordial should they be with others.

Although you may be pained because their conversation is not what you would wish, never keep aloof if you want to help them and win their love.

Try to think rightly about God, sisters. He does not look at such trifling matters as you suppose; do not alarm your soul or lose courage for you might lose greatly. Keep a pure intention and a firm resolve not to offend God, as I said, but do not trammel your soul, for instead of advancing in sanctity you would contract a number of imperfections and would not help others as you might have done.

St Teresa of Avila (1515–82)

The Poor as God's Son

We should not judge the poor by their clothes and their outward appearance nor by their mental capacity, since they are often ignorant and uncouth. On the contrary, if you consider the poor in the light of faith, then you will see that they take the place of God the Son, who chose to be poor. Indeed, in his passion, having lost even the appearance of man, foolishness to the Gentiles and a scandal to the Jews, he showed he was to preach the gospel to the poor in these words: 'He has sent me to preach good news to the poor.' Therefore we should be of the same mind and should imitate what Christ did, caring for the poor, consoling them, helping them and guiding them.

Christ chose to be born in poverty and took poor men as his disciples; he himself became the servant of the poor and so shared their condition that whatever good or harm was done to the poor, he said he would consider done to himself. Since God loves the poor, he also loves the lovers of the poor: when someone loves another, he loves too those who love or serve that other. So we too hope that God will love us on account of the poor. We visit them then, we strive to concern ourselves with the weak and the needy, we so share their sufferings that with the apostle we feel we have become all things to all men. Therefore we must strive to be deeply involved in the cares and sorrows of our neighbour and pray to God to inspire us with compassion and pity, filling our hearts and keeping them full.

St Vincent de Paul (1581–1660)

Give Yourself to the Present

To escape the distress caused by regret for the past or fear about the future, this is the rule to follow: leave the past to the infinite mercy of God, the future to his good providence; give the present wholly to his love by being faithful to his grace.

When God in his goodness sends you some disappointment, one of those trials that used to annoy you so much, before everything thank him for it as for a great favour all the more useful for the great work of your perfection in that it completely overturns the work of the moment.

Try, in spite of interior dislike, to show a kind face to troublesome people, or to those who come to chatter about their troubles; leave at once prayer, reading, choir Office, in fact anything, to go where Providence calls you; and do what is asked of you quietly, peacefully, without hurry and without vexation.

Should you fail in any of these points, make immediately an act of interior humility – not that sort of humility full of uneasiness and irritation against which St Francis de Sales said so much, but a humility that is gentle, peaceful and sweet.

Jean-Pierre de Caussade (1675–1751)

Leper with the Lepers

Picture to yourself a collection of huts with eight hundred lepers. No doctor; in fact, as there is no cure there seems no place for a doctor's skill. A white man, who is a leper, and your humble servant do all the doctoring work.

Every morning, then, after my Mass, which is followed by an instruction, I go to visit the sick, half of whom are Catholics. On entering each hut, I begin by offering to hear their confession. Those who refuse this spiritual help are not, therefore, refused temporal assistance, which is given to all without distinction. Consequently, everyone, with the exception of a very few bigoted heretics, looks on me as a father. As for me, I make myself a leper with the lepers, to gain all to Jesus Christ. That is why, in preaching, I say we lepers, not my brethren, as in Europe. . . .

The average of deaths is about one every day. Many are so destitute that there is nothing to defray their burial expenses. They are simply wrapt in a blanket. As far as my duties allow me time, I make coffins myself for these poor people.

Father Damien of Molokai (1840–89)

Likes and Dislikes

In the Gospel the Lord showed me clearly what his new commandment demands. I read in St Matthew: 'You have heard it said that you should love your neighbour and hate your enemy; but I say to you, love your enemies and pray for those who persecute you'.

We all have our natural likes and dislikes. We may feel more drawn to one person and may be tempted to go a long way round to avoid meeting another. Well, the Lord tells me that the latter is the one I must love and pray for, even though the manner shown me leads me to believe that the person does not care for me. 'If you love those that love you, what thanks are due to you? For sinners also love those who love them' (Luke 6:32).

Nor is it enough to love. We must prove our love. We take a natural delight in pleasing friends, but that is not love; even sinners do the same.

St Thérèse of Lisieux (1873–97)

The Final Word is Love

Early one morning on the steps of Precious Blood Church, a woman with cancer of the face was begging (beggars are allowed only in the slums) and when I gave her money (no sacrifice on my part but merely passing on alms which someone had given me) she tried to kiss my hand. The only thing I could do was kiss her dirty old face with the gaping hole in it where an eye and a nose had been. It sounds like a heroic deed but it was not. One gets used to ugliness so quickly. What we avert our eyes from one day is easily borne the next when we have learned a little more about love. Nurses know this, and so do mothers.

※ ※

The final word is love. At times it has been, in the words of Father Zossima, a harsh and dreadful thing, and our very faith in love has been tried through fire.

We cannot love God unless we love each other, and to love we must know each other. We know him in the breaking of bread, and we know each other in the breaking of bread, and we are not alone any more. Heaven is a banquet and life is a banquet, too, even with a crust, where there is companionship.

We have all known the long loneliness and we have learned that the only solution is love and that love comes with community.

Dorothy Day (1897–1980)

The Doorway to Joy

At Mtemwa leper colony outside Harare John Bradburne visited every leper every day just to make sure that all was well. If anybody needed any help, John was there to give it. He would bath those who needed bathing, build fires, make beds, change dressings and give out whatever he had received or bought for his people. At the beginning of the 'round' his wheelbarrow was always full – full of sugar, tea, sweets, onions, vegetables, nuts, tomatoes, bread, meat – anything he had to give out. By the time he reached the chapel for the midday Angelus, the barrow was empty and each leper had been helped in some small way.

After a period of quiet in the presence of The Lord the afternoon would be spent in much the same way – cutting firewood, cleaning out the cattle grid, collecting reeds for making hats, making tea or coffee for the sick or just popping in . . .

Sometimes he would simply crouch on his haunches and chatter away, trying to help and encourage.

At a death John was always present to give comfort to the dying and to all the lepers who were losing a dear friend. In a small community like Mtemwa a death affects everybody very deeply and John helped the lepers, even those who had no beliefs, to see that death was, in most cases, a blessed relief from many years of suffering and the opening of the door to joy, peace and happiness.

John Bradburne (1921–79)

CREATION AND REDEMPTION

God the Creator

When he fixed the heavens firm, I was there,
    when he drew a circle on the surface of the deep,
when he thickened the clouds above,
    when the sources of the deep began to swell,
when he assigned the sea its boundaries
    – and the waters will not encroach on the shore –
    when he traced the foundations of the earth,
I was beside the master craftsman,
    delighting him day after day,
    ever at play in his presence,
at play everywhere on his earth,
    delighting to be with the children of men.

Proverbs 8:27–31

Halcyon Days

The halcyon is a sea bird which nests by the shore, laying its eggs in the sand, and bringing forth its young in the middle of winter; when the sea beats against the land in violent and frequent storms. But during the seven days while the halcyon broods: for it takes but seven days to hatch its young: all winds sink to rest, and the sea grows calm. And as it then is in need of food for its young ones, the most bountiful God grants this little creature another seven days of calm: that it may feed its young. Since all sailors know of this, they give this time the name of the *halcyon days*.

These things are ordered by the Providence of God for the creatures that are without reason, that you may be led to seek of God the things you need for your salvation. And when for this small bird he holds back the great and fearful sea, and bids it be calm in winter, what will he not do for you made in his own image? And if he should so tenderly cherish the halcyon, how much more will he not give you, when you call upon him with all your heart?

St Basil the Great (c. 330–79)

Blessing of the Kindling

I will kindle my fire this morning
In presence of the holy angels of heaven,
In presence of Ariel of the loveliest form,
In presence of Uriel of the myriad charms,
Without malice, without jealousy, without envy,
Without fear, without terror of any one under the sun,
But the Holy Son of God to shield me.
    Without malice, without jealousy, without envy,
    Without fear, without terror of any one under the sun,
    But the Holy Son of God to shield me.

God, kindle Thou in my heart within
A flame of love to my neighbour,
To my foe, to my friend, to my kindred all,
To the brave, to the knave, to the thrall,
O Son of the loveliest Mary,
From the lowliest thing that liveth,
To the Name that is highest of all.
    O Son of the loveliest Mary,
    From the lowliest thing that liveth,
    To the Name that is highest of all.

Celtic Tradition (c. 500–c. 800)

Divine Love

You, all-accomplishing
Word of the Father,
are the light of primordial
daybreak over the spheres.
You, the foreknowing
mind of divinity,
foresaw all your works
as you willed them,
your prescience hidden
in the heart of your power,
your power like a wheel around the world,
whose circling never began
and never slides to an end.

⁂

Love
Gives herself to all things,
Most excellent in the depths,
And above the stars
Cherishing all:
For the High King
She has given
The kiss of peace.

St Hildegard of Bingen (1098–1179)

Brother Sun, Sister Moon [I]

Most High, all-powerful, good Lord,
Yours are the praises, the glory, the honour, and all blessing.
To You alone, Most High, do they belong,
and no man is worthy to mention Your name.
Praised be You, my Lord, with all your creatures,
especially Sir Brother Sun,
Who is the day and through whom You give us light.
And he is beautiful and radiant with great splendour;
and bears a likeness of You, Most High One.
Praised be You, my Lord, through Sister Moon and the stars,
in heaven You formed them clear and precious and beautiful.
Praised be You, my Lord, through Brother Wind,
and through the air, cloudy and serene, and every kind of
    weather
through which You give sustenance to Your creatures.
Praised be You, my Lord, through Sister Water,
which is very useful and humble and precious and chaste.

St Francis of Assisi (c. 1181–1226)

Brother Sun, Sister Moon [II]

Praised be You, my Lord, through Brother Fire,
through whom You light the night
and he is beautiful and playful and robust and strong.
Praised be You, my Lord, through our Sister Mother Earth,
who sustains and governs us,
and who produces varied fruits with coloured flowers and herbs.
Praised be You, my Lord, through those who give pardon for
   Your love
and bear infirmity and tribulation.
Blessed are those who endure in peace
for by You, Most High, they shall be crowned.
Praised be You, my Lord, through our Sister Bodily Death,
from whom no living man can escape.
Woe to those who die in mortal sin.
Blessed are those whom death will find in Your most holy will,
for the second death shall do them no harm.
Praise and bless my Lord and give Him thanks
and serve Him with great humility.

St Francis of Assisi (c. 1181–1226)

The Divine Goodness

Suppose a person entering a house were to feel heat on the porch, and going further, were to feel the heat increasing, the more they penetrated within. Doubtless, such a person would believe there was a fire in the house, even though they did not see the fire that must be causing all this heat. A similar thing will happen to anyone who considers this world in detail: one will observe that all things are arranged according to their degrees of beauty and excellence, and that the nearer they are to God, the more beautiful and better they are.

※ ※

Because the divine goodness could not be adequately represented by one creature alone, God produced many and diverse creatures, that what was wanting in one in the representation of the divine goodness might be supplied by another. For goodness, which in God is simple and uniform, in creatures is manifold and divided. Thus the whole universe together participates in the divine goodness more perfectly and represents it better than any single creature whatever.

St Thomas Aquinas (c. 1225–74)

The True Light

'We, the chiefs and braves of the Huron nation, on our knees before Your Holiness present to you a precious perfume, the perfume of the virtues of Reverend Mother Mary of the Incarnation. . . . She it was who called us from the depths of our forests to teach us to know and adore the true Master of life. Through her we learned to be meek. . . . Our mothers have kissed the imprint of her feet. With her hand she marked on our hearts the sign of the Faith and the Faith remained graven on our hearts. . . . Many a moon has passed since that first dawning of the true light upon us. Our nation, then great, is now threatened with complete extinction, but, Holy Father, we beg you to receive with the last wish and the last breath of the Huron Tribe the testimony of its profound gratitude to Reverend Mother Mary of the Incarnation.'

Blessed Marie of the Incarnation (1599–1672)

Pied Beauty

Glory be to God for dappled things –
  For skies of couple-colour as a brinded cow;
    For rose-moles all in stipple upon trout that swim;
Fresh firecoal chestnut-falls; finches' wings;
  Landscapes plotted and pieced-fold, fallow, and plough;
    And áll trádes, their gear and tackle and trim.

All things counter, original, spare, strange;
  Whatever is fickle, freckled (who knows how?)
    With swift, slow; sweet, sour; adazzle, dim;
He fathers-forth whose beauty is past change:
      Praise him.

Gerard Manley Hopkins (1844–89)

Thistles for Some

How much you can learn, as I myself have learnt, from watching cattle dreamily grazing and ruminating in their pastures! See how the sagacious creatures, without any theory or inflation of mind, instinctively select the herbs and grasses that suit and sustain them; and how they peacefully pass by what does not thus help them! They do not waste their time and energy in tossing away, or in trampling upon, or even simply in sniffing at, what is anti-pathetic to them. Why should they? Thistles may not suit *them*; well there are other creatures in the world whom thistles *do* suit. And, in any case, are they the police of this rich and varied universe?

Friedrich von Hügel (1852–1925)

In No Strange Land

O world invisible, we view thee,
O world intangible, we touch thee,
O world unknowable, we know thee,
Inapprehensible, we clutch thee!

Does the fish soar to find the ocean,
The eagle plunge to find the air –
That we ask of the stars in motion
If they have rumour of thee there?

Not where the wheeling systems darken
And our benumb'd conceiving soars! –
The drift of pinions, would we hearken,
Beats at our own clay-shuttered doors.

The angels keep their ancient places; –
Turn but a stone, and start a wing!
'Tis ye, 'tis your estrangèd faces,
That miss the many-splendour'd thing.

But (when so sad thou canst not sadder)
Cry – and upon thy so sore loss
Shall shine the traffic of Jacob's ladder
Pitched between Heaven and Charing Cross.

Yea, in the night, my Soul, my daughter,
Cry – clinging heaven by the hems;
And lo, Christ walking on the water,
Not of Gennesareth, but Thames!

Francis Thompson (1859–1907)

Night Meditation

Night, most beautiful of the things I have made, it is you that bring peace, you that bring rest to aching limbs, dislocated by the day's work; you that calm, pacify, bring rest to aching hearts, to bruised bodies – bodies bruised by work, hearts bruised by labour and distress and daily cares. O my black-eyed daughter, the only one who can be called my accomplice. You aid and abet me, for you and I – I through you – together we entrap man within my arms, taking him as if by surprise. O night that binds up all wounds at the well of the woman of Samaria, that from the profoundest well draws the profoundest prayer. Night, O my daughter Night, you know the art of silence, daughter of mine in your beautiful cloak. You dispense rest and forgetfulness, balm, silence and shade. O starlit night, I created you before all else, you that put to sleep, enshroud all my creatures in eternal darkness even now, you that put man to rest in the arms of my maternal Providence. Silence of the dark – such a silence reigned before the creation of unrest, before the start of the reign of unrest. A silence like this will reign – a silence though of light – when all this unrest shall have been expended, spent, when they shall have drawn all the water from the well, after the destruction, the consummation of all man's disquiet.

Charles Péguy (1873–1914)

A Dazzling Darkness

Lord Jesus, when it was given me to see where the dazzling trail of particular beauties and partial harmonies was leading, I recognized that it was all coming to centre on a single point, a single person: yourself. Every presence makes me feel that you are near me; every touch is the touch of your hand; every necessity transmits to me a pulsation of your will.

That the Spirit may always shine forth in me, that I may not succumb to the temptation that lies in wait for every act of boldness, nor ever forget that *you alone* must be sought in and through everything, you, Lord, will send me – at what moments only you know – deprivations, disappointments, sorrow.

What is to be brought about is more than a simple union: it is a *transformation*, in the course of which the only thing our human activity can do is, humbly, to make ourselves ready, and to accept.

Pierre Teilhard de Chardin (1881–1955)

Making Amends

The fundamental thing that has stayed with me has been the service of fellow men and women. As a young boy of five, I was given a very unusual opportunity of sharing for a time, the lives lived by shepherds, crofters, fishermen, grooms, fishwives, and hen wives. People who were illiterate, but were poets at heart. They filled my young life with ecstasy with their stories, songs, and dances. They were my tutors who opened a life to me that is unknown to most people. They prepared the way for me when I started off with my packsack full as I paddled across streams, climbed hills, gazed at the high mountains, and cherished the valleys, or caught something of the majesty and the mysteriousness of the oceans, the rivers, and the silence of the dense forests. . . .

The base of my commitment is thankfulness and reparation. A thankfulness for sensing beauty in so many different forms, for friendship, and for being in a position to help and to heal. Reparation to try in some way to make amends for the injustice and callousness that people of the western world caused to primitive peoples.

Tony Walsh (1898–1994)

Jesus Born

Suddenly the star they had seen rising went forward and halted over the place where the child was. The sight of the star filled them with delight, and going into the house they saw the child with his mother Mary, and falling to their knees they did him homage. Then, opening their treasures, they offered him gifts of gold and frankincense and myrrh. But they were given a warning in a dream not to go back to Herod, and returned to their own country by a different way.

Matthew 2:9–12

Blessed Be . . .

Blessed be the Child who today delights Bethlehem,
Blessed be the Newborn who today made humanity young again.
Blessed be the Fruit who bowed Himself down for our hunger.
Blessed be the Gracious One who suddenly enriched
   all of our poverty and filled our need.

Blessed be He whose mercy inclined Him to heal our sickness. . . .
Blessed is He whom freedom crucified, when He permitted it.
Blessed is He whom also the wood bore, when He allowed it.
Blessed is He whom even the grave enclosed, when He set
   limits to Himself.
Blessed is He whose will brought Him
   to the womb and to birth and to the bosom and to growth.
Blessed is He whose changes revived our humanity.
Blessed is He who engraved our soul and adorned
   and betrothed her to Him[self].
Blessed is He who made our body a Tabernacle for His hiddenness.
Blessed is He who with our tongue interpreted His secrets.

St Ephrem the Syrian (c. 306–73)

Strength Made Weak

The Maker of man was made man that the Ruler of the stars might suck at the breast; that the Bread might be hungered; the Fountain, thirst; the Light, sleep; the Way be wearied with the journey; the Truth be accused by false witnesses; the Judge of the living and the dead be judged by a mortal judge; the Chastener be chastised with whips; the Vine be crowned with thorns; the Foundation be hung upon a tree; Strength be made weak; Health be wounded; Life, die.

To suffer these and such like things, undeserved things, that he might free the undeserving, for neither did he deserve any evil, nor were we deserving of anything good, we who through him received such great good things; to suffer these, he who was before all ages, without any beginning of days, Son of God, deigned in these days to be the Son of man; and he who was begotten of the Father, not made by the Father, was 'made' in the mother whom he had made; that here and now he might spring from her, who, except through him could no-when and no-where have been.

St Augustine of Hippo (354–430)

This Marvellous Sharing [I]

It is of no avail to say that our Lord, the son of the Virgin Mary, was true and perfect man, if he is not believed to be man of that stock from which the Gospel tells us he came.

Matthew says: 'The book of the genealogy of Jesus Christ, the son of David, the son of Abraham.' He then follows the order of Christ's human origin and traces the line of his ancestry down to Joseph, to whom the Lord's mother was betrothed.

Luke, on the other hand, works backwards step by step and traces his succession to the first of the human race himself, to show that the first Adam and the last Adam were of the same nature.

The almighty Son of God could have come to teach and justify men with only the outward appearance of our humanity, exactly as he appeared to patriarchs and prophets. This he did when he wrestled with Jacob, or entered into conversation, or when he did not refuse hospitable entertainment, and even partook of the food set before him.

Those outward appearances pointed to this man. They had a hidden meaning which proclaimed that his reality would be taken from the stock of his fore-fathers.

St Leo the Great (d. 461)

This Marvellous Sharing [II]

Hence God's plan for our reconciliation, formed before all eternity, was not realized by any of these prefigurations. As yet, the Holy Spirit had not come upon the Virgin nor had the power of the Most High overshadowed her. Only then, would the Word become flesh within her inviolate womb, in which Wisdom would build a house for herself. Then, too, the creator of ages would be born in time and the nature of God would join with the nature of the slave in the unity of one person. He through whom the world was created would himself be brought forth in the midst of all creation.

If the new man, made in the likeness of sinful flesh, had not taken our old nature; if he, one in substance with the Father, had not accepted to be one in substance with the mother; if he who was alone free from sin had not united our nature to himself, – then men would still have been held captive under the power of the devil. We would have been incapable of profiting by the victor's triumph if the battle had been fought outside our nature.

But, by means of this marvellous sharing, the mystery of our rebirth shone out upon us. We would be reborn in newness of spirit through the same Spirit through whom Christ was conceived and born.

Consequently the evangelist speaks of those who believe as those 'who were born, not of blood nor the will of the flesh nor of the will of man, but of God'.

St Leo the Great (d. 461)

Under Your Wings

And you, Jesus, are you not also a mother?
Are you not the mother who, like a hen,
gathers her chickens under her wings?

Truly, Lord, you are a mother;
for both they who are in labour
and they who are brought forth
are accepted by you.

You have died more than they, that they may labour to bear.
It is by your death that they have been born,
for if you had not been in labour,
you could not have borne death;
and if you had not died, you would not have brought forth.
For, longing to bear sons into life,
you tasted of death,
and by dying you begot them.
You did this in your own self,
your servants by your commands and help.
You as the author, they as the ministers.
So you, Lord God, are the great mother.

St Anselm of Canterbury (c. 1033–1109)

The Nativity of Christ

Behold the father is his daughter's son,
The bird that built the nest is hatched therein,
The old of years an hour hath not outrun,
Eternal life to live doth now begin,
The Word is dumb, the mirth of heaven doth weep,
Might feeble is, and force doth faintly creep.

O dying souls, behold your living spring;
O dazzled eyes, behold your sun of grace;
Dull ears, attend what word this Word doth bring;
Up, heavy hearts, with joy your joy embrace.
From death, from dark, from deafness, from despairs,
This life, this light, this Word, this joy repairs.

Gift better than himself God doth not know;
Gift better than his God no man can see.
This gift doth here the giver given bestow;
Gift to this gift let each receiver be.
God is my gift, himself he freely gave me;
God's gift am I, and none but God shall have me.

Man altered was by sin from man to beast;
Beast's food is hay, hay is all mortal flesh.
Now God is flesh and lies in manger pressed
As hay, the brutest sinner to refresh.
O happy field wherein this fodder grew,
Whose taste doth us from beasts to men renew.

St Robert Southwell (1561–95)

To Stir Up the World

The prodigious expanses of time which preceded the first Christmas were not empty of Christ: they were imbued with the influx of his power. It was the ferment of his conception that stirred up the cosmic masses and directed the initial developments of the biosphere. It was the travail preceding his birth that accelerated the development of instinct and the birth of thought upon the earth. Let us have done with the stupidity which makes a stumbling-block of the endless eras of expectancy imposed on us by the Messiah: the fearful, anonymous labours of primitive man, the beauty fashioned through its age-long history by ancient Egypt, the anxious expectancies of Israel, the patient distilling of the attar of oriental mysticism, the endless refining of wisdom by the Greeks: all these were needed before the Flower could blossom on the rod of Jesse and of all humanity. All these preparatory processes were cosmically and biologically necessary that Christ might set foot upon our human stage. And all this labour was set in motion by the active, creative awakening of his soul inasmuch as that human soul had been chosen to breathe life into the universe. When Christ first appeared . . . in the arms of Mary he had already stirred up the world.

Pierre Teilhard de Chardin (1881–1955)

One Body

It is truly a marvellous exchange: the creator . . ., taking a body, gives us his Godhead. The redeemer has come into the world to do this wonderful work. . . . One of us had broken the bond that made us God's children, one of us had to tie it again and pay the ransom. This could not be done by one who came from the old, wild and diseased trunk; a new branch, healthy and noble, had to be grafted into it. He became one of us, more than this, he became one with us. For this is the marvellous thing about the human race, that we are all one. If it were otherwise, if we were all autonomous individuals, living beside each other quite free and independent, the fall of the one could not have resulted in the fall of all. In that case, on the other hand, the ransom might have been paid for and imputed to us, but his justice could not have been passed on to the sinners; no justification would have been possible. But he came to be *one* mysterious Body with us: he our head, we his members.

St Edith Stein (1891–1942)

The Circle of a Girl's Arms

The circle of a girl's arms
have changed the world
the round and sorrowful world
to a cradle of God.

She has laid love in His cradle.
In every cot,
Mary has laid her child.

In each
comes Christ.
In each Christ comes
to birth,
comes Christ from the Mother's breast,
as the bird from the sun
returning,
returning again to the tree he knows
and the nest;
to last year's rifled nest.

Into our hands
Mary has given her child,
heir to the world's tears,
heir to the world's toil,
heir to the world's scars,
heir to the chill dawn
over the ruin of wars.

She has laid love in His cradle,
answering for us all.
'Be it done unto me.'

Caryll Houselander (1901–54)

Matthew's Magi

The Matthean infancy story is not only gospel (the good news of salvation) – it is the essential gospel story in miniature. And so, when we look back at the history of Christianity, perhaps we can understand better now why this infancy narrative has been one of the most popular sections of the whole Jesus story, one of the best known and of worldwide appeal. This was due not only to the appreciation of a good story that was satisfying to emotion and sentiment; it also reflected a Christian instinct recognizing therein the essence of the good news – that is, that God has made himself present to us (Emmanuel) in the life of one who walked on this earth, indeed, so truly present that this one, Jesus, was his Son. This revelation was an offence and contradiction to some, but salvation to those who had eyes to see. Of the latter the magi are truly the forerunners, the anticipation of all those who would come to worship the risen Jesus proclaimed by the apostles.

Raymond Brown (1928–98)

Jesus Crucified and Risen

It was very early on the first day of the week and still dark, when Mary of Magdala came to the tomb. She saw that the stone had been moved away from the tomb and came running to Simon Peter and the other disciple, the one whom Jesus loved. 'They have taken the Lord out of the tomb,' she said, 'and we don't know where they have put him.'

So Peter set out with the other disciple to go to the tomb. They ran together, but the other disciple, running faster than Peter, reached the tomb first; he bent down and saw the linen cloths lying on the ground, but did not go in. Simon Peter, following him, also came up, went into the tomb, saw the linen cloths lying on the ground and also the cloth that had been over his head; this was not with the linen cloths but rolled up in a place by itself. Then the other disciple who had reached the tomb first also went in; he saw and he believed. Till this moment they had still not understood the scripture, that he must rise from the dead. The disciples then went back home.

John 20:1–10

The Exultet [I]

Now let the angelic heavenly choirs exult; let joy pervade the unknown beings who surround God's throne; and let the trumpet of salvation sound the triumph of this mighty King. Let earth, too, be joyful, in the radiance of this great splendour. Enlightened by the glory of her eternal King, let her feel that from the whole round world the darkness has been lifted. Let mother Church likewise rejoice, arrayed in the brilliance of this dazzling light; let these walls echo with the multitude's full-throated song.

Dear brethren who are present at this wondrous lighting of the holy flame, I pray you join with me and invoke the loving-kindness of almighty God, that he who, not for any merit of mine, has deigned to number me among his ministers, may shed his own bright light upon me and enable me to glorify this candle with fitting praise, through our Lord Jesus Christ, his Son, who lives and reigns with him in the unity of the Holy Spirit, God; for ever and ever.

It is indeed right and proper with all the ardour of our heart and mind and with the service of our voice to acclaim God, the invisible almighty Father, and his only-begotten Son, our Lord Jesus Christ, who repaid Adam's debt for us to his eternal Father, and with his dear blood erased the bond contracted through that ancient sin.

Pascal Proclamation

The Exultet [II]

This is the Paschal feast wherein is slain the true Lamb whose blood hallows the doorposts of the faithful. This is the night when, long ago, thou didst cause our forefathers, the sons of Israel, in their passage out of Egypt, to pass dry-shod over the Red Sea. This is the night which swept away the blackness of sin by the light of the fiery pillar. This is the night which at this hour throughout the world restores to grace and yokes to holiness those who believe in Christ, detaching them from worldly vice and all the murk of sin. On this night Christ burst the bonds of death and rose victorious from the grave.

. . . What good would life have been to us without redemption? How wonderful the pity and care thou has shown us; how far beyond all reckoning thy loving-kindness! To ransom thy slave, thou gavest up thy Son! O truly necessary sin of Adam, that Christ's death blotted out; and happy fault, that merited so great a Redeemer! Blessed indeed is this, the sole night counted worthy to mark the season and the hour in which Christ rose again from the grave. It is this night of which the Scripture says: 'And the night shall be bright as day'. 'Such is my joy that night itself is light!' So holy, this night, it banishes all crimes, washes guilt away, restores lost innocence, brings mourners joy; it drives forth hate, fosters harmony, and humbles the pride of earthly rule.

Pascal Proclamation

The Exultet [III]

On this gracious night, then, holy Father, accept the evening sacrifice of this flame, which Holy Church, by the hands of her ministers, renders to thee in the solemn offering of wax the bees have made. Who now can doubt the message that this candle brings? A brilliant fire burns here to the glory of God, which though it be divided into parts, yet suffers no loss of light, being fed from the ever-melting wax that the parent bee brought forth to form the substance of this precious torch.

Blessed indeed is the night, which despoiled the Egyptians and enriched the Hebrews! The night on which heaven is wedded to earth, the Godhead to humanity!

We, therefore, pray thee, Lord, that this candle hallowed in honour of thy name, may continue bravely burning to dispel the darkness of this night. Welcome it as a sweet fragrance, mingling with the lights of heaven. May the morning-star find its flame alight, that Morning-Star which knows no setting, which came back from the grave and shed its clear light upon humankind.

Pascal Proclamation

Descent into Hell [I]

What is happening? Today there is a great silence over the earth, a great silence, and stillness, a great silence because the King sleeps; the earth was in terror and was still, because God slept in the flesh and raised up those who were sleeping from the ages. God has died in the flesh, and the underworld has trembled.

Truly he goes to seek out our first parent like a lost sheep; he wishes to visit those who sit in darkness and in the shadow of death. He goes to free the prisoner Adam and his fellow-prisoner Eve from their pains, he who is God, and Adam's son.

The Lord goes in to them holding his victorious weapon, his cross. When Adam, the first created man, sees him, he strikes his breast in terror and calls out to all: 'My Lord be with you all.' And Christ in reply says to Adam: 'And with your spirit.' And grasping his hand he raises him up, saying: 'Awake, O sleeper, and arise from the dead, and Christ shall give you light.'

An Ancient Homily for Holy Saturday

Descent into Hell [II]

'I am your God, who for your sake became your son, who for you and your descendants now speak and command with authority those in prison: Come forth, and those in darkness: Have light, and those who sleep: Rise.

'I command you: Awake, sleeper, I have not made you to be held a prisoner in the underworld. Arise from the dead; I am the life of the dead. Arise, O man, work of my hands, arise, you who were fashioned in my image. Rise, let us go hence; for you in me and I in you, together we are one undivided *person*.

'For you, I your God became your son; for you, I the Master took on your form, that of slave; for you, I who am above the heavens came on earth and under the earth; for you, man, I became as a man without help, free among the dead; for you, who left a garden, I was handed over to Jews from a garden and crucified in a garden.

'Look at the spittle on my face, which I received because of you, in order to restore you to that first divine inbreathing at creation. See the blows on my cheeks, which I accepted in order to refashion your distorted form to my own image.'

An Ancient Homily for Holy Saturday

Descent into Hell [III]

'See the scourging of my back, which I accepted in order to disperse the load of your sins which was laid upon your back. See my hands nailed to the tree for a good purpose, for you, who stretched out your hand to the tree for an evil one.

'I slept on the cross and a sword pierced my side, for you, who slept in paradise and brought forth Eve from your side. My side healed the pain of your side; my sleep will release you from your sleep in Hades; my sword has checked the sword which was turned against you.

'But arise, let us go hence. The enemy brought you out of the land of paradise; I will reinstate you, no longer in paradise, but on the throne of heaven. I denied you the tree of life, which was a figure, but now I myself am united to you, I who am life. I posted the cherubim to guard you as they would slaves; now I make the cherubim worship you as they would God.

'The cherubim throne has been prepared, the bearers are ready and waiting, the bridal chamber is in order, the food is provided, the everlasting houses and rooms are in readiness, the treasures of good things have been opened; the kingdom of heaven has been prepared before the ages.'

An Ancient Homily for Holy Saturday

The Lamb Slain [I]

The prophets announced many wonderful things about the Passover mystery which is Christ. To him be glory forever. Amen.

He descended from heaven to earth for the sake of suffering mankind, clothed himself with a human nature through the Virgin Mary, and appearing in our midst as a man with a body capable of suffering, took upon himself the suffering of those who suffered. By his Spirit which could not die, he slew death, the slayer of men. Led forth like a lamb, slain like a sheep, he ransomed us from the servitude of the world, just as he ransomed Israel from the land of Egypt. He freed us from the slavery of the devil, just as he had freed Israel from the hand of Pharaoh; and he has marked our souls with the signs of his own blood. He has clothed death with dishonour and he has grieved the devil, just as Moses dishonoured and grieved Pharaoh. He has punished wickedness and taken away the children of injustice, just as Moses punished Egypt and unchilded it. He has brought us from slavery to freedom, from darkness to light, from death to life, from tyranny to an eternal kingdom.

St Melito of Sardis (d. c. 190)

The Lamb Slain [II]

He is the Passover of our salvation. He was present in many so as to endure many things. In Abel he was slain; in Isaac bound; in Jacob a stranger; in Joseph sold; in Moses exposed; in David persecuted; in the prophets dishonoured. He became incarnate of the Virgin. Not a bone of his was broken on the tree. He was buried in the earth, but he rose from the dead, and was lifted up to the heights of heaven. He is the silent lamb, the slain lamb, who was born of Mary the fair ewe. He was seized from the flock and dragged away to slaughter. Towards evening he was sacrificed, and at night he was buried. But he who had no bone broken upon the cross, was not corrupted in the earth, for he rose from the dead and raised up man from the depths of the grave.

St Melito of Sardis (d. c. 190)

The New Vine

Since death could not devour him without a body and the world of the dead could not swallow him up without flesh, he came to the Virgin, so that he might receive from her a chariot on which to ride to the underworld. In the body he had assumed he entered death's domain, broke open its strong-room and scattered the treasure.

And so he came to Eve, the mother of all the living. She is the vineyard whose hedge death opened by Eve's own hands so that she might taste death's fruit. Thus Eve, the mother of all the living, became the source of death for all the living.

But Mary blossomed, the new vine compared with the old vine, Eve. Christ, the new life, lived in her, so that when death, brazen as ever, approached her in search of his prey, life, the bane of death, was hidden within her mortal fruit. And so when death, suspecting nothing, swallowed him up, death set life free, and with life a multitude of men.

This glorious son of the carpenter, who set up his cross above the all-consuming world of the dead, led the human race into the abode of life. Because through the tree the human race had fallen into the regions below, he crossed over on the tree of the cross into the abode of life. The bitter shoot had been grafted on to the tree, and now the sweet shoot was grafted on to it so that we might recognize the one whom no creature can resist.

St Ephrem the Syrian (c. 306–73)

The Glory of the Cross [I]

If there had been no cross, Christ would not have been crucified. If there had been no cross, Life would not have been nailed to the tree. If he had not been nailed, the streams of everlasting life would not have welled from his side, blood and water, the cleansing of the world; the record of our sins would not have been cancelled, we would not have gained freedom, we would not have enjoyed the tree of life, paradise would not have been opened. If there had been no cross, death would not have been trodden under foot, the underworld would not have yielded up its spoils.

How great the cross, through which we have received a multitude of blessings, because, against all reckoning, the miracles and sufferings of Christ have been victorious! How precious, the means of God's suffering, and his trophy of victory! On it of his own will he suffered unto death. On it he won his victory, wounding the devil, and conquering death, and shattering the bars of the underworld. The cross has become the common salvation of the whole world.

St Andrew of Crete (c. 660–740)

The Glory of the Cross [II]

The cross is called the glory of Christ, and his exaltation; it is the chalice for which he longed, the consummation of his sufferings on our behalf. It is the glory of Christ – listen to his words: 'Now is the Son of man glorified, and God is glorified in him, and God will glorify him at once.' And again: 'Glorify me, Father, with the glory which I had with you before the world was made.' And again: 'Father, glorify your name. So there came a voice from the heavens: I have glorified it, and I will glorify it again.' By this he means the glory which Christ received on the cross.

The cross is also Christ's exaltation – listen again to his own words: 'When I am lifted up, I will draw all men to myself.' You see then that the cross is the glory and the exaltation of Christ.

St Andrew of Crete (c. 660–740)

The Dream of the Rood [I]

Hearken, the rarest of dreams I purpose to tell
Which I dreamed one midnight
When men with their voices were at rest.
It seemed to me that I saw a most wondrous tree
Rising in the sky and encircled with light,
Brightest of beams. The whole of the beacon
Was decked in gold. Gems gleamed
Fair at the earth's four corners, and five there were
High up on the cross-beam. Hosts of angels beheld it,
Timeless in their beauty. It was no felon's gibbet,
Rather, it held the gaze of holy souls,
Of men on the earth and the whole glorious creation.
Wondrous, this triumphant tree, and I stained with vice,
Sore wounded with sins. I gazed on the tree of glory,
Royally decked as it was, gleaming brightly,
Attired in gold: gems had covered
Befittingly the tree of a Ruler.
Yet beneath that gold I could make out agony
Once suffered at the hands of wretched men.
Soon it ran sweat on its right side . . .

Old English

The Dream of the Rood [II]

So lay I there for a long time,
Gazing sad at heart on a healer's tree
Till I heard it give voice,
Uttering words, this most precious wood:
'It was long since — yet I well remember —
That I was hewn down at wood-edge,
Struck off from my stem.
Men bore me on their shoulders, setting me on a hill
Where foes aplenty fastened me. Then I saw Man's Lord
Hasten with great courage, intent on climbing me.
Durst I not then oppose the word of the Lord
And bend or break, though I saw tremble
The surface of earth. All those foes
I could have felled, yet I stood firm.
Then the young warrior — it was God Almighty —
Stalwart, resolute, stripped himself; climbed the high gallows
Gallantly before the throng, resolved to loose Man's bonds.
Trembled I when this warrior embraced me
Yet durst I neither bow nor fall. I must needs stand fast.
As a rood I was raised up, bearing a noble king,
The heavens' lord; waver I durst not.
With dark nails they pierced me, leaving scars yet visible,
Open strokes of malice. Yet harm them I might not.
Each of us two they reviled at once. I stood drenched with
   blood
Poured forth from his side when he yielded up his spirit . . .
      All creation wept,
Lamenting a king's fall. It was Christ who hung there on a
   cross.'

Old English

O Gentle Gatekeeper

O gentle gatekeeper!
O humble Lamb!
You are the gardener,
and once you have opened the gate of the heavenly garden,
paradise,
you offer us the flowers
and the fruits
of the eternal Godhead.
And now I know for certain
that you spoke the truth
when you appeared to your two disciples
on the road
as a traveller.
You said that Christ had to suffer so,
and by the way of the cross
enter into his glory.
And you showed them
that it had been foretold thus
by Moses,
Elijah,
Isaiah,
David,
and the others who had prophesied about you.
You explained the Scriptures to them,
but they failed to understand
because their minds were darkened.
But you understood yourself.
What then was your glory,
O gentle loving Word?
You yourself –
and you had to suffer
in order to enter into your very self!
Amen.

St Catherine of Siena (c. 1347–80)

Night

Every man has the right to bury his son. Every man on earth who has had the great misfortune not to have died before his son. I alone, I, God – my hands tied by this affair – I alone, father at the end of a long line of fathers, I alone could not bury my son. It was then, O Night, that you came and with an enormous shroud you enveloped the centurion with his Romans, the Virgin and the holy women, this mountain, that valley, over which the dark descended: over my people Israel, and over sinners and, with them all, the dying man, the man who was dying for them, and over the servants of Joseph of Arimathea, already approaching with a white shroud.

O night, so dear to the heart for what you have done! What you did for my son made man in your great love, you do for all his brothers. You enwrap them in silence and shadow and in life-giving forgetfulness of the day's deadly unrest. What you did once for my son made man, what you did one evening above all evenings, you do again every evening for the least of men – so true is it, so real is it that he was become one of them, tied to their mortal condition without limit or measure. For before this perpetual, this imperfect, this perpetually imperfect imitation of Christ men speak of endlessly, there was Christ's perfect imitation of man, the relentless imitation by Christ Jesus of the mortal wretchedness and condition of man.

Charles Péguy (1873–1914)

Veneration of the Cross [I]

Many pass by the unveiled cross.

Many remain. Because they belong there. Because here they have found everything. They stay. They kneel down. . . . Sinners kiss the wounds that they themselves have caused. The murderers flee from their guilt to the murdered One, the executioners to their own victim. And so I go to him. And sinners, who themselves are crucified with him on the cross of their own guilt, speak: 'Lord, think of me when you come into your kingdom.'

The dying lie at his feet. For they suffer *his* destiny. They die because he died. True, everyone must die because of sin. But God has allowed this deadly guilt in his kingdom of this world for a reason. He held this world embraced in his love for his incarnate Son, in whose death he was so able to overcome sin through greater grace that the world could not escape his mercy. And therefore death, which we ourselves caused and which we suffer as the wages of sin, is first, last, and always only the death that causes the death of sin.

Those who suffer weep before his cross. What night of need was not his night? What fears are not sanctified by his? To be raised up in hope, what grief needs to know more than that it has been borne by the Son of Man, who is the Son of God?

Karl Rahner (1904–84)

Veneration of the Cross [II]

Before him the children kneel. For he has loved them, and although he knew what is in each person, he relied on them and threatened with his woe whoever scandalized one of these little ones.

Before him kneel the old people, who – let us be honest – have nothing more in sight and can count on nothing but to die. They kneel before their dying God. And they know that the greatest grace and hardest act of their lives are still to come. Only the man who dies in him and with him receives this grace rightly and carries out the act perfectly.

Before him kneel the homeless, and they gaze upon him who willed to die abandoned by his own people, outside the city near the highway, after living a hard life, not knowing where he would lay his head, poorer than the foxes, who have their dens.

The lonely kneel silently before him. For, as he was dying, the loneliest man of all, he knew them in the solitude of death and of abandonment by God. And he allowed all their bitter loneliness into his own heart, until everything else was driven out, except love for the abandoned.

Karl Rahner (1904–84)

Veneration of the Cross [III]

Widows and mothers who have lost their sons kneel before him, weeping. For his eyes still look lovingly and with concern through the dark shadows of death that surround him, upon the mother whom he must leave lonely.

Lovers prostrate themselves before the crucified. For with him is all the strength of love and all the strength that turns the disillusion of love into that love which is stronger than death, into that unique love of Christ that can feed on its own fire and stay alive.

Before the cross the scholars and wise men of this world kneel. They learn thereby that all wisdom that does not burn in the blessed foolishness of love is vain; they learn thereby that the logic of the cross, which to the Greeks is folly and to the Jews a scandal, is God's wisdom and God's strength for those who are saved by it. And they learn that it has pleased God to save the world through the folly of the cross, before which every mouth is dumb and all the wisdom of the world humbles itself – before the folly of divine love.

God's priests kneel before the cross, because they have to preach the cross and they are always drinking from the chalice of his failure. They kneel there because, with their sins and weakness, they are always putting themselves between God's light and men, because more than all others they need his mercy.

Karl Rahner (1904–84)

THE SPIRIT, SAINTS
AND ANGELS

The Coming of the Spirit

When Pentecost day came round, they had all met together, when suddenly there came from heaven a sound as of a violent wind which filled the entire house in which they were sitting; and there appeared to them tongues as of fire; these separated and came to rest on the head of each of them. They were all filled with the Holy Spirit and began to speak different languages as the Spirit gave them power to express themselves.

Now there were devout men living in Jerusalem from every nation under heaven, and at this sound they all assembled, and each one was bewildered to hear these men speaking his own language. They were amazed and astonished. 'Surely,' they said, 'all these men speaking are Galileans? How does it happen that each of us hears them in his own native language? Parthians, Medes and Elamites; people from Mesopotamia, Judaea and Cappadocia, Pontus and Asia, Phrygia and Pamphylia, Egypt and the parts of Libya round Cyrene; residents of Rome – Jews and proselytes alike – Cretans and Arabs; we hear them preaching in our own language about the marvels of God.' Everyone was amazed and perplexed; they asked one another what it all meant. Some, however, laughed it off. 'They have been drinking too much new wine,' they said.

Acts 2:1–13

Invoking the Spirit

Father, you are holy indeed,
and all creation rightly gives you praise.
All life, all holiness comes from you
through your Son, Jesus Christ our Lord,
by the working of the Holy Spirit.

From age to age you gather a people to yourself,
so that from east to west
a perfect offering may be made
to the glory of your name.

And so, Father, we bring you these gifts.
We ask you to make them holy by the power of your Spirit,
that they may become the body and blood
of your Son, our Lord Jesus Christ,
at whose command we celebrate this eucharist.

Third Eucharistic Prayer

The Indwelling Spirit

A person is deemed worthy of constant prayer once he has become a dwelling-place of the Spirit. For unless someone has received the gift of the Comforter, in all certainty he will not be able to accomplish this constant prayer in quiet.

But once the Spirit dwells in someone, as the Apostle says, the Spirit never ceases but prays continuously: then whether he sleeps or wakes, prayer is never absent from that person's soul. If he eats or drinks, goes to sleep or is active; yes, even if he is sunk in deep sleep, the sweet fragrance of prayer effortlessly breathes in his heart. Then he is in the possession of prayer that knows no limit. For at all times, even when he is outwardly still, prayer constantly ministers within him secretly.

The silence of the serene is prayer, as one of those clothed in Christ says, for their thoughts are divine stirrings. The stirring of a pure mind constitutes still utterances, by means of which such people sing in a hidden way to the hidden God.

Isaac of Nineveh (d. c. 700)

Calming the Waters

Those who are engaged in spiritual warfare must always keep their hearts tranquil. Only then can the mind sift the impulses it receives and store in the treasure house of the memory those that are good and come from God, while rejecting altogether those that are perverse and devilish.

When the sea is calm, the fishermen's eyes can see the movements of the fish deep down, so that hardly any of them can escape. But when the sea is ruffled by the wind, the turmoil of the waves hides from sight the creatures that would easily have been seen if the sea wore the smile of calm. The skill of the fisherman is of little use in rough weather.

Something of the same sort happens with the soul, especially when it is stirred to the depths by anger.

At the beginning of a storm, oil is poured on the waters to calm them, and in fact the oil defeats their commotion. In this way, when the soul receives the anointing of the gift of the Holy Spirit, it gladly gives in to this inexpressible and untroubled sweetness. And even if it is continually attacked by temptation it maintains its peace and joy.

Diadochus of Photike (mid 5th century)

Come Down, O Love Divine

Come down, O love divine,
Seek thou this soul of mine,
And visit it with thine own ardour glowing;
O Comforter draw near,
Within my heart appear,
And kindle it, thy holy flame bestowing.

O let it freely burn,
Till earthly passions turn
To dust and ashes in its heat consuming;
And let thy glorious light
Shine ever on my sight,
And clothe me round, the while my path illuming.

Let holy charity
Mine outward vesture be,
And lowliness become mine inner clothing.
True lowliness of heart,
Which takes the humbler part,
And o'er its own shortcomings weeps with loathing.

And so the yearning strong,
With which the soul will long,
Shall far outpass the power of human telling;
For none can guess its grace,
Till he become the place
Wherein the Holy Spirit makes his dwelling.

Bianco da Siena (d. 1412)

Come, Holy Spirit

You do not remain, Holy Spirit, in the unmoved Father, nor in the Word, and yet you are always in the Father and in the Word and in yourself, and in all blessed spirits and creatures. All creatures need you, since the only-begotten Word, by shedding his blood, in his burning love placed all creatures in need of him. You repose in creatures who dispose themselves so that, by receiving your gifts, they may in purity receive your own image in themselves. You repose in those who receive in themselves the effect of the blood of the Word, and make themselves worthy dwelling-places for you.

Come, Holy Spirit. May the union of the Father and the will of the Son come to us. You, Spirit of truth, are the reward of the saints, the refreshment of souls, light in darkness, the riches of the poor, the treasury of lovers, the satisfaction of the hungry, the consolation of the pilgrim Church; you are he in whom all treasures are contained.

Come, you who, descending into Mary, caused the Word to take flesh: effect in us by grace what you accomplished in her by grace and nature.

Come, you who are the nourishment of all chaste thoughts, the fountain of all clemency, the summit of all purity.

Come, and take away from us all that hinders us from being absorbed in you.

St Mary Magdalene de'Pazzi (1566–1607)

God's Grandeur

The world is charged with the grandeur of God.
   It will flame out, like shining from shook foil;
   It gathers to a greatness, like the ooze of oil
Crushed. Why do men then now not reck his rod?
Generations have trod, have trod, have trod;
   And all is seared with trade; bleared, smeared with toil;
   And wears man's smudge and shares man's smell: the soil
Is bare now, nor can foot feel, being shod.

And for all this, nature is never spent;
   There lives the dearest freshness deep down things;
And though the last lights off the black West went
   Oh, morning, at the brown brink eastward, springs –
Because the Holy Ghost over the bent
   World broods with warm breast and with ah! bright wings.

Gerard Manley Hopkins (1844–89)

The Satin Slipper

When the wind blows, the windmills go wheeling round all together.

But there is another Wind, I mean the Spirit, which is sweeping nations with a broom.

When you have it unchained, it sets all the human landscape a-moving.

Ideas from one end of the world to the other are catching fire like stubble!

From Thames to Tiber is heard a great clatter of arms and of hammers in the shipyards.

The sea is at one stroke all covered with white poppies, the night is plastered all over with Greek letters and algebraic signs.

There's dark America yonder like a whale bubbling out of the Ocean! Hark! howling Asia feels a new god leaping in her womb!

And look at that fiery lover, what does he say? I think he has found the right word at last, look at that proud lady whose head droops and who crumbles piecemeal like a wall!

In all those things there is not any logical sequence, but please climb to the top of a tree with me, ladies and gentlemen.

Then you will understand all things, simply by seeing them together, they are all parts of one wide panorama.

All is contrived somehow by that fierce wind blowing without intermission, and the meaning of all –

To find it you need only to look up at that rude horseplay in the clouds, that dishevelled cavalry in the singing sky with that untiring trumpet!

It could not last any longer! it is the same mouth everywhere clamouring for air, it is the same deep heart which says: Open here!

Paul Claudel (1868–1955)

Our Lady

My soul proclaims the greatness of the Lord
and my spirit rejoices in God my Saviour;
because he has looked upon the humiliation of his servant.
Yes, from now onwards all generations will call me blessed,
for the Almighty has done great things for me.
Holy is his name,
and his faithful love extends age after age to those who fear him.
He has used the power of his arm,
he has routed the arrogant of heart.
He has pulled down princes from their thrones and raised high the lowly.
He has filled the starving with good things, sent the rich away empty.
He has come to the help of Israel his servant, mindful of his faithful love
  – according to the promise he made to our ancestors –
of his mercy to Abraham and to his descendants for ever.

Luke 1:46–55

The Annunciation

In the sixth month the angel Gabriel was sent by God to a town in Galilee called Nazareth, to a virgin betrothed to a man named Joseph, of the House of David; and the virgin's name was Mary. He went in and said to her, 'Rejoice, you who enjoy God's favour! The Lord is with you.' She was deeply disturbed by these words and asked herself what this greeting could mean, but the angel said to her, 'Mary, do not be afraid; you have won God's favour. Look! You are to conceive in your womb and bear a son, and you must name him Jesus. He will be great and will be called Son of the Most High. The Lord God will give him the throne of his ancestor David; he will rule over the House of Jacob for ever and his reign will have no end.' Mary said to the angel, 'But how can this come about, since I have no knowledge of man?' The angel answered, 'The Holy Spirit will come upon you, and the power of the Most High will cover you with its shadow. And so the child will be holy and will be called Son of God. And I tell you this too: your cousin Elizabeth also, in her old age, has conceived a son, and she whom people called barren is now in her sixth month, for nothing is impossible to God.' Mary said, 'You see before you the Lord's servant, let it happen to me as you have said.' And the angel left her.

Luke 1:26–38

Son of Mary

Scripture says that the Word of God was made flesh, that is, that he was united to flesh which had a rational soul. The Word of God took to himself descent from Abraham and shared in flesh and blood, forming for himself a body from a woman, so that he should not only be God but should become man too and be regarded as one of our race because of his union with us.

Emmanuel therefore is made up of two realities, divinity and humanity, as we must acknowledge. But the Lord Jesus Christ is *one*, the one true Son, who is both God and man. He is not deified as we are by grace, but rather is true God made manifest in human form for us. Saint Paul confirms this with his words: 'When the fulness of time came, God sent forth his Son, born of a woman, born under the law; to redeem those who were under the law, so that we might receive adoption as sons.'

St Cyril of Alexandria (d. 444)

The Immaculate Conception

Lo, thou the glory of the great earth,
purest of women over all the world
of all who have been since time began
how right it is that all voices,
all heroes on earth, hail thee, and say
with blithe mood that thou art the bride
of the Noblest One, he sky's King.
So too the highest in the heavens,
Christ's thanes, cry out and sing
that thou art Lady by thy holy might
of the glorious armies, of the race of men
living under the heavens, and of all hell-dwellers.
For thou alone of all mankind
thought gloriously in thy strong mind
that thou wouldst bring to thy Maker thy maidenhood,
give it, sinless.

       Not again
will such another come of men
a maiden ring-adorned who will thus send
heaven-homeward with ever pure heart
her bright treasure. So the Lord of triumphs
bade His high messengerfly hither
from his strong glory, and say to thee
that His might should speed thee, and thou shouldst bear
the Lord's Son, coming soon
in mercy to men, and thou, Maria,
for ever and ever be held unstained.

Cynewulf (9th century)

The Sun Rides Forth

Sing the Dawn, holy Church,
The Immaculate Daybreak
In which Eternity, Creator, was himself created.
Sing the Dawn: Innocence, the skies are shaken
And the Sun rides forth, the Sun of all joys,
The Sun who made you, dazzling whiteness, empurpled
By redemptive flames which protected you
From the night which covered the heavens
When you were born, who now possess him within you.
The sun will leap and the world tremble
And the earth give birth
For you have given it fruitfulness,
Light whence falls the dew
Of the Mystery which enkindles you as you lean towards us
To bring him; smiling majesty and greatness of the Word
Which fills you, Flower full of sweetness.
Drawn by your fragrance the Bee flies down to you
From the splendour of the Father,
Your calyx closes round him
And shuts him in.

St Hildegard of Bingen (1098–1179)

Mary Our Mother [I]

Let us come to his bride, let us come to his mother, let us come to the best of his handmaidens. All of these descriptions fit Blessed Mary.

But what are we to do for her? What sort of gifts shall we offer her? O that we might at least repay to her the debt we owe her! We owe her honour, we owe her devotion, we owe her love, we owe her praise. We owe her honour because she is the Mother of our Lord. He who does not honour the mother, will without doubt dishonour the son. Besides, scripture says: 'Honour your father and your mother.'

What then shall we say, brethren? Is she not our mother? Certainly, brethren, she is in truth our mother. Through her we are born, not to the world but to God.

We all, as you believe and know, were in death, in the infirmity of old age, in darkness, in misery. In death because we had lost the Lord; in the infirmity of old age, because we were in corruption; in darkness because we had lost the light of wisdom, and so we had altogether perished.

St Aelred of Rievaulx (1109–67)

Mary, Our Mother [II]

But through Blessed Mary we all underwent a much better birth than through Eve, inasmuch as Christ was born of Mary. Instead of the infirmity of age we have regained youth, instead of corruption incorruption, instead of darkness light.

She is our mother, mother of our life, of our incorruption, of our light. The Apostle says of our Lord, 'Whom God made our wisdom, our righteousness, our sanctification and redemption.'

She therefore who is the mother of Christ is the mother of our wisdom, mother of our righteousness, mother of our sanctification, mother of our redemption. Therefore she is more our mother than the mother of our flesh. Better therefore is our birth which we derive from Mary, for from her is our holiness, our wisdom, our righteousness, our sanctification, our redemption.

Scripture says, 'Praise the Lord in his saints'. If our Lord is to be praised in those saints through whom he performs mighty works and miracles, how much more should he be praised in her in whom he fashioned himself, he who is wonderful beyond all wonder.

St Aelred of Rievaulx (1109–67)

Maiden, yet a Mother

Maiden, yet a Mother,
Daughter of thy Son,
High beyond all other —
Lowlier is none;
Thou the consummation
Planned by God's decree,
When our lost creation
Nobler rose in thee!

Thus his place prepared,
He who all things made
'Mid his creatures tarried,
In thy bosom laid;
There his love he nourished, —
Warmth that gave increase
To the Root whence flourished
Our eternal peace.

Nor alone thou hearest
When thy name we hail;
Often thou art nearest
When our voices fail;
Mirrored in thy fashion
All creation's good,
Mercy, might, compassion
Grace thy womanhood.

Lady, lest our vision
Striving heavenward, fail,
Still let thy petition
With thy Son prevail,
Unto whom all merit,
Power and majesty,
With the Holy Spirit
And the Father be.

Dante Alighieri (1265–1321)

The Perfect Mediator

God wills to love.
God wills to be loved.
God wills to have co-lovers of himself.

The perfect mediator
has to effect a perfect mediation
in respect of the person in whose favour he mediates
and in the perfection of his function as mediator.
Mary was the one above all
for whom he became mediator
therefore Christ achieved
the most perfect mediation and redemption
in his own function as mediator and redeemer
in regard to Mary.
  Christ was able to redeem others.
  He has indeed redeemed us through the Cross
  so as to attract us to his love
  and because he willed
  that men and women should be more worthy
  of the love of God.

Blessed John Duns Scotus (c. 1265–1308)

Our Gracious Mother

Our natural mother, our gracious mother – for he willed wholly to become our mother in all things – humbly and gently found the place to begin his work in the maiden's womb. And he showed this in the first Showing, where he brought that gentle maid into my mind's eye, at the tender age she was when she first conceived. That is to say, it was in this humble place that our high God, who is the sovereign wisdom of all, set himself to grow, and clothed himself in our poor flesh so that he himself could undertake the work and care of motherhood in all things.

A mother's care is the closest, nearest and surest – for it is the truest. This care never might, nor could, nor should, be fully done except by him alone. We know our own mother bore us into pain and dying. But our true Mother Jesus, who is all love, bears us into joy and endless living. Blessed may he be!

And so he nourished us within himself for love, and he laboured until the full term, because he willed to suffer the sharpest pangs and deepest pains that ever were or ever shall be. And at the end he died. And when he had done this – and so borne us into bliss – yet even all this could not assuage his marvellous love. And he showed this in those high, wonderful words of love: 'If I could have suffered more, I would have suffered more.'

Julian of Norwich (c. 1342–after 1416)

By Grace and Glory

God, the Incomprehensible, allowed himself to be perfectly comprehended and contained by the humble Virgin Mary without losing anything of his immensity. So we must let ourselves be perfectly contained and led by the humble Virgin without any reserve on our part.

God, the Inaccessible, drew near to us and united himself closely, perfectly and even personally to our humanity through Mary without losing anything of his majesty. So it is also through Mary that we must draw near to God and unite ourselves to him perfectly, intimately and without fear of being rejected.

Lastly, He Who Is deigned to come down to us who are not and turned our nothingness into God, or He Who Is. He did this perfectly by giving and submitting himself entirely to the young Virgin Mary, without ceasing to be in time He Who Is from all eternity. Likewise it is through Mary that we, who are nothing, may become like God by grace and glory. We accomplish this by giving ourselves to her so perfectly and so completely as to remain nothing, as far as self is concerned, and to be everything in her, without any fear of illusion.

St Louis Marie de Montfort (1673–1716)

The Lady Spoke to Me [I]

One day, when I had gone with the two girls to collect wood by the bank of the river Gave, I heard a sound. I turned toward the meadow and saw that the trees were not moving at all. I looked up and saw a grotto. And I saw a Lady wearing a white dress with a blue sash. On each foot she had a yellow rose; her rosary was the same colour.

When I saw her, I rubbed my eyes, I thought I must be mistaken. I put my hands in my pocket, where I kept my rosary. I wanted to make the sign of the cross, but I could not lift my hand to my forehead; it fell back. Then the Lady crossed herself. I again tried, and although my hand was trembling, I was eventually able to make the sign of the cross. I began to say my rosary. The Lady slipped the beads of her rosary through her fingers, but she did not move her lips. When I finished the rosary, she immediately disappeared.

I asked the two girls if they had seen anything. They said, 'No', and asked what I had to tell them. I told them that I had seen a Lady wearing a white dress but that I did not know who she was. But I warned them to keep silent about it. Then they urged me not to go back there, but I refused. I went back on Sunday, feeling drawn by an inner force.

St Bernadette Soubirous (1844–79)

The Lady Spoke to Me [II]

The Lady spoke to me a third time and asked me if I was willing to come to her over a period of a fortnight. I replied that I was. She added that I must tell the priests to have a chapel built there. Then she told me to drink at the spring. Not seeing any spring I was going to drink from the Gave. She told me that she did not mean that, and pointed with her finger to the spring. When I went there I saw only a little dirty water. I put my hand in it, but I could not get hold of any. I scratched, and at last a little water came for drinking. Three times I threw it away; the fourth time I was able to drink it. Then the vision disappeared, and I went away.

I went back there for fifteen days, and each day the Lady appeared to me, with the exception of a Monday and a Friday. She reminded me again to tell the priests to build the chapel, asked me to wash in the spring, and to pray for the conversion of sinners. I asked her several times who she was, but she gently smiled at me. Finally, she held her arms outstretched and raised her eyes to heaven and told me that she was the Immaculate Conception.

During that fortnight she also revealed three secrets to me, and forbade me to disclose them to anyone. I have kept them faithfully to this day.

St Bernadette Soubirous (1844–79)

True Inner Peace

Many of us, who want to offer consolation, experience deep inner desolation. Many of us, who want to offer healing and affection to others, experience a seemingly inexhaustible hunger for intimacy. Many of us, who speak to others about the beauty of family life, friendship, and community, come home at night to a place that feels more like an empty cave than a true home. Many of us who let water flow on the heads of those who search for a new family, give bread to those who search for a new community, and touch with oil those who search for healing, find ourselves with dry, hungry, and sick hearts, restless during the day and anxious during the night. Yes, indeed, many of us have lost touch with our identity as children of God.

But it is precisely this childhood that Mary wants us to claim. She, who offered an immaculate space for God to take on human flesh, wants to offer us also a space where we can be reborn as Jesus was born. With the same heart that she loved Jesus, she wants to love us. It is a heart that will not make us wonder anxiously whether we are truly loved. It is a heart that has not been marked by the infidelities of the human race and so will never bring wounds to those who seek peace there. Jesus has given her to us so that she could guide us in our search for a second childhood, assist us as we try to shake off our sadness, and open the way to true inner peace.

Henri J.M. Nouwen (1932–96)

Saints and Angels

I saw that there was a huge number, impossible for anyone to count, of people from every nation, race, tribe and language; they were standing in front of the throne and in front of the Lamb, dressed in white robes and holding palms in their hands. They shouted in a loud voice, 'Salvation to our God, who sits on the throne, and to the Lamb!' And all the angels who were standing in a circle round the throne, surrounding the elders and the four living creatures, prostrated themselves before the throne, and touched the ground with their foreheads, worshipping God with these words:

> Amen. Praise and glory and wisdom,
> thanksgiving and honour and power and strength
> to our God for ever and ever. Amen.

Revelation 7:9–12

At God's Beck and Call

So far as we are concerned, angels must be incorporeal or very near it. You see how we become dizzy with the theme and can get no further than the stage of being aware of angels and archangels, thrones, dominions, princedoms, powers, of glowing lights, ascents, intellectual powers or minds, beings of nature pure and unalloyed. Fixed, almost incapable of changing for the worse, they encircle God, the first cause, in their dance. What words can one use to hymn them? He makes them shine with purest brilliance or each with a different brilliance to match his nature's rank. So strongly do they bear the shape and imprint of God's beauty, that they become in their turn lights, able to give light to others by transmitting the stream which flows from the primal light of God.

As ministers of the divine will, powerful with inborn and acquired strength, they range over the universe. They are quickly at hand to all in any place, so eager are they to serve, so agile is their being. Each has under him a different part of the Earth or the universe, which God alone, who defined their ranks, knows. They unify the whole, making all things obey the beck and call of him alone who fashioned them. They hymn God's majesty in everlasting contemplation of everlasting glory, meaning, not to make God glorious – God, whose fullness supplies all else with excellence, cannot be added to – but to leave beings supreme after God with no kindness unshown them.

St Gregory of Nazianzus (c. 329–c. 390)

Martin Shares his Cloak

Martin happened to meet at the gate of the city of Amiens a poor man destitute of clothing. He was entreating those that passed to have compassion on him. . . .

Martin had nothing except the cloak in which he was clad, for he had already parted with the rest of his garments for similar purposes. Taking, therefore, his sword, with which he was girt, he divided his cloak into two equal parts, and gave one part to the poor man, while he again clothed himself with the remainder. Upon this, some of the by-standers laughed, because he was now an unsightly object and stood out as but poorly dressed. Many, however, who were of sounder understanding, groaned deeply because they themselves had done nothing similar . . .

In the following night when Martin had resigned himself to sleep, he had a vision of Christ arrayed in that part of his cloak with which he had clothed the poor man.

He contemplated the Lord with the greatest attention and was told to own as his own the robe which he had given. Ere long, he heard Jesus saying with a clear voice to the multitude of angels standing round – 'Martin, who is still a catechumen, clothed me with this robe.'

St Martin of Tours (d. 397)

Preaching the Good News [I]

I give thanks to my God tirelessly who kept me faithful in the day of trial, so that today I offer sacrifice to him confidently, the living sacrifice of my life to Christ, my Lord, who preserved me in all my troubles. I can say therefore: Who am I, Lord, and what is my calling that you should co-operate with me with such divine power? Today, among heathen peoples, I praise and proclaim your name in all places, not only when things go well but also in times of stress. Whether I receive good or ill, I return thanks equally to God, who taught me always to trust him unreservedly. His answer to my prayer inspired me in these latter days to undertake this holy and wonderful work in spite of my ignorance, and to imitate in some way those who, as the Lord foretold, would preach his Good News as a witness to all nations before the end of the world.

How did I come by this wisdom which was not my own, I who neither knew what was in store for me, nor what it was to relish God? What was the source of the gift I got later, the great and beneficial gift of knowing and loving God, even if it meant leaving my homeland and my relatives?

St Patrick (5th century)

Preaching the Good News [II]

I came to the Irish heathens to preach the Good News and to put up with insults from unbelievers. I heard my mission abused, I endured many persecutions even to the extent of chains; I gave up my free-born status for the good of others. Should I be worthy I am ready to give even my life, promptly and gladly, for his name; and it is there that I wish to spend it until I die, if the Lord should graciously allow me.

I am very much in debt to God, who gave me so much grace that through me many people were born again in God and afterwards confirmed, and that clergy were ordained for them everywhere. All this was for a people newly come to belief whom the Lord took from the very ends of the earth as he promised long ago, through his prophets: 'To you the nations will come from the ends of the earth and will say, "How false are the idols our fathers made for themselves, how useless they are." ' And again: 'I have made you a light for the nations so that you may be a means of salvation to the ends of the earth.'

I wish to wait there for the promise of one who never breaks his word, as he promises in the gospel: 'They will come from the east and the west to take their places with Abraham and Isaac and Jacob,' just as we believe the faithful will come from every part of the world.

St Patrick (5th century)

Light of Light

In their goodness [the angels] raise their inferiors to become, so far as possible, their rivals. They ungrudgingly impart to them the glorious ray which has visited them so that their inferiors may pass this on to those yet farther below them. Hence, on each level, predecessor hands on to successor whatever of the divine light he has received and this, in providential proportion, is spread out to every being.

Of course God himself is really the source of illumination for those who are illuminated, for he is truly and really Light itself. He is the Cause of being and of seeing. But, in imitation of God, it has been established that each being is somehow superior to the one to whom he passes on the divine light. And so all the other angelic beings follow the first rank of intelligent beings in heaven as the source, after God, of all sacred knowledge of God and of all imitation of God, for it is this latter order which mediates the divine enlightenment to all other beings, including ourselves . . .

Angels of the first rank possess, more than the others, the power of fire and a share of the divine wisdom which has been poured out to them, a knowledge of the ultimate in divine enlightenment, and that capacity which is summed up in the word 'thrones'.

Dionysius the Pseudo-Areopagite (c. 500)

Columba of Iona

In the forty-second year of his age Colum Cille sailed away from Ireland to Britain, wishing to be a pilgrim for Christ. During his life of thirty-four years as a soldier of Christ on the island of Iona, he could not let even one hour pass that was not given to prayer or reading or writing or some other good work. Night and day he so unwearyingly gave himself to fasts and vigils that the burden of each single work seemed beyond the strength of man. Yet through all he was loving to everyone, his holy face was always cheerful, and in his inmost heart he was happy with the joy of the Holy Spirit.

When the end of his years was at hand, he gave his last commands to his brothers, saying: 'I commend to you, my children, these last words of mine, that you keep among you unfeigned love with peace.' Then when the bell was rung for the midnight office he arose quickly and went to the church, where he went in alone before the others and knelt down in prayer before the altar. Diormuit his attendant followed, and the whole community of monks ran in with lights; when they saw that their father was dying they began to lament. Then Diormuit raised the saint's holy right hand, to bless the monastic company. At the same time the venerable father himself moved his hand, as well as he was able, and immediately after he had so expressed his holy blessing he breathed his last.

St Columba (c. 521–97)

Angels and Archangels [I]

It must be realized that the word 'angel' is the name of an office, and not of a nature. For these holy spirits of our homeland in heaven are always spirits, but in no way can they always be called 'angels' or 'messengers' since they are angels only when something is announced through them. Those who make minor announcements are called angels, those who make important ones are called archangels.

Hence it is that not just any angel was sent to the Virgin Mary but that Gabriel the archangel was sent: it was right that the proper one for this role should be of the highest rank of angels since he was to announce the greatest news of all.

Angels are known by proper names as well, to indicate their powers and their work. In that holy city where perfect knowledge is derived from the vision of Almighty God, if proper names are assigned to them, it is not that their persons could not be identified without names. But when angels come to minister to us, even the names by which we know them are taken from their ministry – Michael means 'Who is like God', Gabriel 'Strength of God', Raphael 'Healing of God'.

St Gregory the Great (c. 540–604)

Angels and Archangels [II]

Whenever a mighty deed is in question, Michael is assigned, so that by his actions and name it may be made known that no one can do what God can do. So in the case of our ancient enemy, who in his pride wanted to be like God when he said: 'I will ascend to heaven; above the stars of God I will set my throne on high; I will make myself like the Most High': when he is shown to be condemned to eternal punishment at the end of the world, he is described as about to do battle with Michael, as Saint John says: 'War broke out with Michael the archangel.'

Gabriel was sent to Mary, for Gabriel means 'Strength of God'. He came to announce him who deigned to be lowly so as to wage war on the spiritual powers of the air. He who came as God of power and as one strong in battle was to be announced by Gabriel, the strength of God.

Finally Raphael is interpreted, as we have said, as 'Healing of God', since he wiped away the shadows of blindness from Tobias when he touched his eyes to cure him. The one who is sent to cure, was indeed worthy of the name 'Healing of God'.

St Gregory the Great (c. 540–604)

The Angelic Host

In God's love the angels live in concord and happiness. Each of them loves all the others, and all of them love each; they all want the same things and all of them are averse to the same things; what pleases one is displeasing to none, and what one wants, they all want. There is one purpose and one will for all; all feel the same thing, and all sense the same thing. . . .

There is nothing disordered, nothing undisciplined, nothing contrary to order or obedience, nothing secretly put away with the intention of keeping it for oneself. Everything is open and above board, everything is plain, and things which are proper to each individual are common to all through the sharing of love and the love of sharing. They are all assembled in one temple and raise their shouts of joy to God in common; all at the same time read and meditate and contemplate in the book of life; and they all refresh themselves communally at one and the same table. They take their rest together in the place of eternal repose, and there is no one who does anything on his own which can disturb or damage their common peace, obedience or order.

Such is the fellowship – the happiest and most joyous of fellowships – of the citizens of the realms above who live the common life, and we who are still on earth should follow their way of life by living the common life after their example.

Baldwin of Canterbury (d. 1190)

Herald of the Gospel [I]

So noble in character, so ardently on fire with divine love was Dominic that there can be no doubt that he was a chosen vessel of grace. Except when he was moved to pity and compassion he always displayed great firmness of mind. A joyous heart is reflected in the countenance, and Dominic revealed his tranquillity of soul by the joyful kindliness of his look.

Everywhere, in word and in deed, he showed himself to be a herald of the gospel. By day no one was more affable, more friendly than he with his brethren and companions, no one more fervent than he in vigils and prayer at night. His conversation was always either with God or about God; rarely did he speak on other matters, and this practice he commended to his disciples.

Dominic's frequent and special prayer for himself was to beg from God true and efficacious charity for the salvation of men, for he was convinced that just as our Saviour, the Lord Jesus, gave himself totally for our salvation, only when he, Dominic, had devoted himself to the winning of souls would he be truly a member of Christ. When he had pondered the matter long and deeply he founded the Order of Friars Preachers for this very purpose.

St Dominic (c. 1172–1221)

Herald of the Gospel [II]

Dominic often exhorted the friars, both in his writings and by his words, to study constantly the sacred scriptures, in the old and new testaments. He always carried a copy of the gospel according to Saint Matthew and the epistles of Saint Paul; these he had studied to such an extent that he almost knew them off by heart.

Several times Dominic was chosen as bishop, but he always refused the office, preferring to live in poverty with his brethren, than to possess any bishopric. All his life long he preserved his purity intact. He longed ardently to be beaten, to be cut in little pieces, to die for his faith. Gregory IX declared: 'I knew him as a wholehearted follower of the apostolic way of life, and there is no doubt that he shares in heaven the glory of the apostles themselves.'

St Dominic (c. 1172–1221)

Martin the Charitable

Saint Martin, in his total openness to Christ's teachings, loved his brethren with a love that sprang from humility and an unclouded faith. He loved men because he saw them as God's children and his own brothers. He loved them indeed more than himself, and in his humility believed everyone to be better and holier than he was.

He never failed to find excuses for the faults of others; he ignored even bitter slights and insults done to himself since he was quite convinced that his sins deserved far greater punishments. He made every effort to bring sinners to repentance: he nursed the sick devotedly, procuring food, clothes and medicine for those too poor to buy them. Peons, negroes and half-castes, who were treated as all but slaves, these he worked for to the limits of his abilities, offering them every help and tenderness until he truly deserved his popular title, 'Martin the Charitable'.

St Martin de Porres (1579–1639)

Guardian Angels

There is no creature, no matter how mean, vile or abject, faithful or unfaithful, who has not his angel to guard him and to urge him continually to do right.

These blessed spirits offer our prayers to the divine Goodness; they kindle in our hearts the love of virtue; they strengthen us and obtain for us the courage and vigour to practise it – if we are sad and in adversity, they are ever near, to cheer us and exhort us to patience. They never cease to inspire us with good thoughts, to help us to make progress in divine love; until at last we reach the heavenly country, to dwell for ever in their company.

This is what they desire, knowing that for this end we were created. They are so jealous of our happiness that they rejoice when they see that we are faithful to God and that we are corresponding with his love; and when we do not, if they could grieve they would. It is to our guardian angels that we owe all our good inspirations, suitable to our vocation and circumstances.

St Francis de Sales (1567–1622)

Saint of Auschwitz

One of the prisoners on the parade ground at Auschwitz cried 'My poor wife and children!' It sounded strange and hopeless. Suddenly a slight figure stepped out of line, took off his cap and moved with halting gait to stand at attention before the SS.

'What does this Polish pig want? Who are you?'

'I am a Catholic priest, I want to die for that man; I am old; he has a wife and children.'

The deputy commandant signalled to the man with the family to return to his place in the line and the numbers on the list were changed.

While the sun set in beauty over Auschwitz the condemned men were driven into the bunker, naked, humiliated and afraid. But they were shepherded by a priest who went with them to die and to help them to die. Father Kolbe took charge of his suffering flock and filled their last days with prayer and psalms.

There were only four alive after two weeks and of these men only Kolbe was fully conscious. The authorities became impatient and ordered the head of the hospital barracks to inject phenol into the priest's veins. Father Kolbe was alone at the moment of his death: 12.50 p.m. on 14 August 1941, the Vigil of the Assumption. He was forty-seven years old.

St Maksymilian Kolbe (1894–1941)

SACRAMENTS AND
PRAYER

Church and Sacraments

He is the image of the unseen God,
the first-born of all creation,
for in him were created all things
in heaven and on earth:
everything visible and everything invisible,
thrones, ruling forces, sovereignties, powers –
all things were created through him and for him.
He exists before all things
and in him all things hold together,
and he is the Head of the Body,
that is, the Church.

He is the Beginning,
the first-born from the dead,
so that he should be supreme in every way;
because God wanted all fullness to be found in him
and through him to reconcile all things to him,
everything in heaven and everything on earth,
by making peace through his death on the cross.

Colossians 1:15–20

Newly Baptized at Jerusalem [I]

You were conducted by the hand to the holy pool of sacred baptism, just as Christ was conveyed from the cross to the sepulchre close at hand.

Each person was asked if he believed in the name of the Father and of the Son and of the Holy Spirit. You made the confession that brings salvation, and submerged yourselves three times in the water and emerged: by this symbolic action you were secretly re-enacting the burial of Christ three days in the tomb.

Just as our Saviour spent three days and nights in the womb of the earth, so you upon first emerging were representing Christ's first day in the earth, and by your immersion his first night. For at night one can no longer see but during the day one has light; so you saw nothing when immersed as if it were night, but you emerged as if to the light of day. In one and the same action you died and were born: that water of salvation became both tomb and mother for you.

What Solomon said in another context is apposite to you: 'There is a time to be born, and a time to die', but the opposite is true in your case — there is a time to die and a time to be born. A single moment achieves both ends, and your begetting was simultaneous with your death.

Ancient Instructions

Newly Baptized at Jerusalem [II]

What a strange and astonishing situation! We did not really die, we were not really buried, we did not really hang from a cross and rise again. Our imitation was symbolic, but our salvation a reality.

Christ truly hung from a cross, was truly buried, and truly rose again. All this he did gratuitously for us, so that we might share his sufferings by imitating them, and gain salvation in actuality.

What boundless love! The innocent hands and feet of Christ were pierced by the nails: he suffered the pain. I suffer neither pain nor anguish: yet by letting me participate in his pain he gives me the free gift of salvation.

No one should think, then, that his baptism is merely for the remission of sins and for adoption as sons in the way that John's baptism brought only remission of sins. We know well that not merely does it cleanse sins and bestow on us the gift of the Holy Spirit – it is also the counterpart of Christ's suffering. This is why, as we heard just now, Paul cried out: 'Do you not know that all of us who have been baptized into Christ Jesus were baptized into his death? We were buried therefore with him by baptism into death.'

Ancient Instructions

Christians in the World [I]

The difference between Christians and the rest of mankind is not a matter of nationality, or language, or customs. Christians do not live apart in separate cities of their own, speak any special dialect, nor practise any eccentric way of life. The doctrine they profess is not the invention of busy human minds and brains, nor are they, like some, adherents of this or that school of human thought.

They pass their lives in whatever township – Greek or foreign – each man's lot has determined; and conform to ordinary local usage in their clothing, diet, and other habits. Nevertheless, the organization of their community does exhibit some features that are remarkable, and even surprising. For instance, though they are residents at home in their own countries, their behaviour there is more like that of transients; they take their full part as citizens, but they also submit to anything and everything as if they were aliens. For them, any foreign country is a motherland, and any motherland is a foreign country. Like other men, they marry and beget children, though they do not expose their infants. Any Christian is free to share his neighbour's table, but never his marriage-bed.

Letter to Diognetus (c. 2nd/3rd century)

Christians in the World [II]

Though destiny has placed them here in the flesh, they do not live after the flesh; their days are passed on the earth, but their citizenship is above in the heavens. They obey the prescribed laws, but in their own private lives they transcend the laws. They show love to all men – and all men persecute them. They are misunderstood and condemned; yet by suffering death they are quickened into life. They are poor, yet making many rich; lacking all things, yet having all things in abundance. They are dishonoured, yet made glorious in their very dishonour; slandered, yet vindicated. They repay calumny with blessings, and abuse with courtesy. For the good they do, they suffer stripes as evildoers; and under the strokes they rejoice like men given new life. Jews assail them as heretics, and Greeks harass them with persecutions; and yet of all their ill-wishers there is not one who can produce good grounds for his hostility.

Letter to Diognetus (c. 2nd/3rd century)

Christians in the World [III]

To put it briefly, the relation of Christians to the world is that of a soul to the body. As the soul is diffused through every part of the body, so are Christians through all the cities of the world. The soul, too, inhabits the body, while at the same time forming no part of it; and Christians inhabit the world, but they are not part of the world. The soul, invisible herself, is immured within a visible body; so Christians can be recognized in the world, but their Christianity itself remains hidden from the eye. The flesh hates the soul, and wars against her without any provocation, because she is an obstacle to its own self-indulgence; and the world similarly hates the Christians without provocation, because they are opposed to its pleasures.

All the same, the soul loves the flesh and all its members, despite their hatred for her; and Christians, too, love those who hate them. The soul, shut up inside the body, nevertheless holds the body together; and though they are confined within the world as in a dungeon, it is Christians who hold the world together. The soul, which is immortal, must dwell in a mortal tabernacle; the Christians, as they sojourn for a while in the midst of corruptibility here, look for incorruptibility in the heavens. Finally, just as to be stinted of food and drink makes for the soul's improvement, so when Christians are every day subjected to ill-treatment, they increase the more in numbers. Such is the high post of duty in which God has placed them, and it is their moral duty not to shrink from it.

Letter to Diognetus (c. 2nd/3rd century)

The Ship of the Church

The Church is like a great ship sailing the sea of the world and tossed by the waves of temptation in this life. But it is not to be abandoned – it must be brought under control.

As an example of this we have the Fathers of the past, Clement and Cornelius and many others in the city of Rome, Cyprian in Carthage and Athanasius in Alexandria. Living under pagan emperors, they steered the ship of Christ, that is the Church, his beloved spouse. And they did this by teaching, defending, working and suffering even to the shedding of their blood.

When I considered the example of these men and of men like them, I was filled with fear. Dread came upon me and trembling, and the darkness of my sins almost overwhelmed me. I should have been only too glad to give up the government of the Church which I had accepted, if only I could have found some support for this course of action in the example of the Fathers or in sacred scripture.

St Boniface (c. 675–754)

The Eucharistic Banquet

The only-begotten Son of God, wishing to enable us to share in his divinity, assumed our nature, so that by becoming man he might make men gods.

Moreover, he turned the whole of our nature, which he assumed, to our salvation. For he offered his body to God the Father on the altar of the cross as a sacrifice for our reconciliation; and he shed his blood for our ransom and our cleansing, so that we might be redeemed from wretched captivity and cleansed from all sins.

Now in order that we might always keep the memory of this great act of love, he left his body as food and his blood as drink, to be received by the faithful under the appearances of bread and wine.

How precious and wonderful is this banquet, which brings us salvation and is full of all delight! What could be more precious? It is not the meat of calves or kids that is offered, as happened under the Old Law; at this meal Christ, the true God, is set before us for us to eat. What could be more wonderful than this sacrament?

No sacrament contributes more to our salvation than this; for it purges away our sins, increases our virtues, and nourishes our minds with an abundance of all the spiritual gifts.

St Thomas Aquinas (c. 1225–74)

The Divine Mysteries

Suppose that this most holy Sacrament were celebrated in one place only; suppose there were only one priest in the whole world to say the words of consecration. How men would long to go to that place, to visit that one priest of God and see the divine mysteries celebrated! But now there are many priests, and in many places Christ is offered, so that the further afield Holy Communion is spread throughout the world, the greater proof it may yield of God's grace and love for men. Thank you, O good Jesus, eternal shepherd, for deigning to refresh us poor outcasts with your precious body and blood; for inviting us with your own lips to partake of this mystery, when you say: *Come to me, all you that labour and are burdened; I will give you rest. . . .*

O Jesus, sweetest, kindest, what great worship and thanksgiving we ought to shew you, what never-ending praise, in return for the gift of your holy body! There is not a man to be found able to unfold in words its wonderful power.

Thomas à Kempis (c. 1380–1471)

On the Eucharist

I have not yet said anything about the most sacred of all devotions – the holy and sacred sacrifice and sacrament of the Eucharist, the heart of the Christian religion. It is an ineffable mystery which embraces the untold depths of divine love, and in which God, giving himself to us, bestows freely upon us all his blessings and graces.

Prayer united to this divine sacrifice has unutterable power. Endeavour if possible to be present each day at holy Mass, so that together with the priest you may offer the sacrifice of your Redeemer to God his Father on your own behalf and that of the whole Church. What a privilege it is to be united in so blessed and mighty an action!

If you are unavoidably prevented from being present at the celebration of this great sacrifice by real and bodily presence, do not fail to join in it by a spiritual communion. So that, if you cannot go to church, at least go there in spirit, unite your intention with all your brethren and offer the same spiritual service that you would offer if you were able to be present in person.

If you wish to make your daily meditation at this time, turn your mind to offering this sacrifice through your prayer and meditation.

St Francis de Sales (1567–1622)

The Author of Life

Love of the 'Blackrobes' is general among the Indians everywhere, even among the Sioux, a most savage tribe. A priest who has been among them and who often comes here tells me that they would supply all his needs were he willing to accept it, but that he does not want to be indebted to them for fear they ask him for fire-water, that is, brandy. One Indian was strikingly converted. As he lay on his death-bed he spoke of a previous illness during which he had thought he was dying, and he said aloud: 'I then saw the Author of Life and He said to me, "Go back, your hour is not yet!" But I know that this time I *shall* go to the Author of Life.' Francis, a Christian Iroquois present, said to him: 'The Author of Life probably sent you back so that you might have water poured on your head.' The dying Sioux made answer: 'Indeed, I think it was precisely for that I was told to return to life.' Francis replied: 'Do you want me to go and get a Blackrobe to pour water upon you?' The Sioux answered: 'Go quickly. There is need of haste.' The priest who came at once was quite satisfied with the dying man's answers and baptized him; a few moments later he died. He was solemnly buried by the priest, who also baptized the dead Sioux' son who was very ill. The priest was Father Acquaroni, a Lazarist from Rome, and one of our most zealous friends.

St Philippine Duchesne (1769–1852)

Mass on the World

Since once again, Lord – though this time not in the forests of the Aisne but in the steppes of Asia – I have neither bread, nor wine, nor altar, I will raise myself beyond these symbols, up to the pure majesty of the real itself; I, your priest, will make the whole earth my altar and on it will offer you all the labours and sufferings of the world.

Over there, on the horizon, the sun has just touched with light the outermost fringe of the eastern sky. Once again, beneath this moving sheet of fire, the living surface of the earth wakes and trembles, and once again begins its fearful travail. I will place on my paten, O God, the harvest to be won by this renewal of labour. Into my chalice I shall pour all the sap which is to be pressed out this day from the earth's fruits.

My paten and my chalice are the depths of a soul laid widely open to all the forces which in a moment will rise up from every corner of the earth and converge upon the Spirit. Grant me the remembrance and the mystic presence of all those whom the light is now awakening to the new day.

Pierre Teilhard de Chardin (1881–1955)

To Preach Christ Jesus [I]

'Woe to me if I do not preach the gospel!' I am sent by Christ himself to do this. I am an apostle, I am a witness. The more distant the goal, the more difficult my mission, the more pressing is the love that urges me to it. I must bear witness to his name: Jesus is the Christ, the Son of the living God. He reveals the invisible God, he is the first-born of all creation, the foundation of everything created. He is the teacher of mankind, and its redeemer. He was born, he died and he rose again for us.

He is the centre of history and of the world; he is the one, who knows us and who loves us; he is the companion and friend of our life. He is the man of sorrows and of hope. It is he who will come and who one day will be our judge and – we hope – the everlasting fullness of our existence, our happiness.

I could never finish speaking about him: he is the light and the truth; indeed, he is the way, the truth and the life. He is the bread and the spring of living water to satisfy our hunger and our thirst. He is our shepherd, our guide, our model, our comfort, our brother.

Pope Paul VI (1897–1978)

To Preach Christ Jesus [II]

Like us, and more than us, he has been made little, poor, humiliated; he has been a worker; he has known misfortune and been patient. For our sake he spoke, worked miracles and founded a new kingdom where the poor are happy, where peace is the principle for living together, where the pure of heart and those who mourn are raised up and comforted, where those who hunger and thirst after justice have their fill, where sinners can be forgiven, where all are brothers.

Jesus Christ: you have heard him spoken of; indeed the greater part of you are already his: you are Christians. So, to you Christians I repeat his name, to everyone I proclaim him: Jesus Christ is the beginning and the end, the Alpha and the Omega; he is the king of the new world; he is the secret of history; he is the key to our destiny. He is the mediator, the bridge, between heaven and earth. He is more perfectly than anyone else the Son of Man, because he is the Son of God, eternal and infinite. He is the son of Mary, blessed among all women, his mother according to the flesh, and our mother through the sharing in the Spirit of his mystical body.

Jesus Christ is our constant preaching; it is his name that we proclaim to the ends of the earth and throughout all ages.

Pope Paul VI (1897–1978)

Pathways in Prayer

'In your prayers do not babble as the gentiles do, for they think that by using many words they will make themselves heard. Do not be like them; your Father knows what you need before you ask him. So you should pray like this:

Our Father in heaven,
may your name be held holy,
your kingdom come,
your will be done,
on earth as in heaven.
Give us today our daily bread.
And forgive us our debts,
as we have forgiven those who are in debt to us.
And do not put us to the test,
but save us from the Evil One.

'Yes, if you forgive others their failings, your heavenly Father will forgive you yours; but if you do not forgive others, your Father will not forgive your failings either.'

Matthew 6:7–15

Inexhaustible Fountain

The word of God is a tree of life that from all its parts offers you fruits that are blessed. It is like that rock opened in the desert that from all its parts gave forth a spiritual drink. As the Apostle says, 'All ate the same supernatural food and all drank the same supernatural drink'.

He who comes into contact with some share of its treasure should not think that the only thing contained in the word is what he himself has found. He should realize that he has only been able to find that one thing from among many others. Nor, because only that one part has become his, should he say that the word is void and empty and look down on it; but because he could not exhaust it he should give thanks for its riches. Be glad that you were overcome and do not be sad that it overcame you. The thirsty man rejoices when he drinks and he is not downcast because he cannot empty the fountain. Rather let the fountain quench your thirst than have your thirst quench the fountain. Because if your thirst is quenched and the fountain is not exhausted you can drink from it again whenever you are thirsty.

St Ephrem the Syrian (c. 306–73)

The Soul Plaint

O Jesu! to-night,
Thou Shepherd of the poor,
Thou sinless person
Who didst suffer full sore,
By ban of the wicked,
And wast crucified.

Save me from evil,
Save me from harm,
Save Thou my body,
Sanctify me to-night,
O Jesu! to-night,
Nor leave me.

Endow me with strength,
Thou Herdsman of might,
Guide me aright,
Guide me in Thy strength,
O Jesu! in Thy strength
Preserve me.

Celtic tradition (c. 500–c. 800)

Life Is in His Will

The first step in contemplation, dearly beloved, is to consider steadily what God wants, what is pleasing to him, what is acceptable in his sight. And since we all make many mistakes and the boldness of our will revolts against the rightness of his, and since the two cannot be brought into agreement and made to fit together, let us humble ourselves under the mighty hand of the most high God. In the sight of his mercy, let us take pains to show how in all things we stand in need of his mercy, saying: 'Heal me, O Lord, and I shall be healed; save me and I shall be saved', and, 'O Lord, be gracious to me, heal me, for I have sinned against you.'

Once the eye of our heart has been cleansed by dwelling on thoughts of this kind we are no longer left in bitterness in our own spirit, but we have great joy in the Spirit of God. We do not now consider what is God's will for us, but what God's will is, in itself.

'Life is in his will.' Hence we may be sure that what is in harmony with his will is both useful and beneficial for us. It follows that we must take as much care never to deviate from that will as we do to preserve the life of our soul.

St Bernard of Clairvaux (1090–1153)

The Dart of Longing Love

But now you put me a question and say: 'How might I think of him in himself, and what is he?' And to this I can only answer thus: 'I have no idea.' For with your question you have brought me into that same darkness, into that same cloud of unknowing where I would you were yourself. For a man may, by grace, have the fullness of knowledge of all other creatures and their works, yes, and of the works of God's own self, and he is well able to reflect on them. But no man can think of God himself. Therefore, it is my wish to leave everything that I can think of and choose for my love the thing that I cannot think. Because he can certainly be loved, but not thought. He can be taken and held by love but not by thought. Therefore, though it is good at times to think of the kindness and worthiness of God in particular, and though this is a light and a part of contemplation, nevertheless, in this exercise, it must be cast down and covered over with a cloud of forgetting. You are to step above it stalwartly but lovingly, and with a devout, pleasing, impulsive love strive to pierce that darkness above you. You are to smite upon that thick cloud of unknowing with a sharp dart of longing love. Do not leave that work for anything that may happen.

Author of The Cloud of Unknowing *(14th century)*

The Name of Jesus

If you wish to be on good terms with God, and have his grace direct your life, and come to the joy of love, then fix this name 'Jesus' so firmly in your heart that it never leaves your thought. And when you speake to him using your customary name 'Jesu', in your ear it will be joy, in your mouth honey, and in your heart melody, because it will seem joy to you to hear that name being pronounced, sweetness to speak it, cheer and singing to think it.

Richard Rolle (c. 1300–49)

Blessed be Jesus who is always near in times of stress. Even when we cannot feel his presence he is close.

Jesus said within my heart, 'I will never leave you either in happiness or distress. I will always be there to help you and watch over you. Nothing in heaven or earth can part you from me.'

'When you are quiet and still I can speak to your heart.'

Margery Kempe (c. 1373–after 1438)

Prayer of the Heart

We make our recollection in God because we long for him, and we long for him so that we may be recollected – so the one helps the other, and both arise from holy thoughts. You should therefore seek after God by short but ardent efforts of your heart.

Wonder at his beauty, invoke his aid, cast yourself in spirit at the foot of the cross, adore his goodness, speak frequently to him about your salvation; hold out your hand to him as a child to his father, that he may guide you. In every way excite your heart to the love of God.

This prayer is not difficult to practise. It can be interwoven with all our business and occupations without hindering them in the slightest degree. Indeed, our external pursuits are helped rather than hindered by our recollection and short ejaculations from the heart.

There are many useful collections of short vocal prayers, but I advise you not to confine yourself to any formal words. It is better to use those which are prompted by the feelings of your heart, as you need them. They will never fail you. But some surpass others, like the various invocations of the name of Jesus.

St Francis de Sales (1567–1622)

No Grace Without Suffering

The Lord, our Saviour, raised his voice and spoke with incomparable majesty. 'Let all know', he said, 'that after sorrow grace follows; let them understand that without the burden of affliction one cannot arrive at the height of glory; that the measure of heavenly gifts is increased in proportion to the labours undertaken. Let them be on their guard against error or deception; this is the only ladder by which paradise is reached; without the cross there is no road to heaven.'

When I heard these words I felt a great impulse to rush out into the street and shout at the top of my voice to everybody, no matter what their age, sex or condition; 'Listen, all you people; listen, all you nations. By Christ's command, using the very words which he uttered, I tell you most solemnly: no grace without suffering. Labour must be heaped upon labour to plumb the depths of the divine nature, the glory of the sons of God and the perfect happiness of the soul.' . . .

No one would complain about the cross or about hardships coming seemingly by chance upon him, if he realized in what balance they are weighed before being distributed to men.

St Rose of Lima (1586–1617)

Peace of Heart

Do you find that you are making no progress in prayer? Let it be enough for you to offer to God the prayer which our Saviour makes for us in the most holy sacrament of the altar, using his fervent offering to make reparation for your own lukewarmness. And whenever you do anything, pray in this way: 'My God, I am going to do this or endure that in the sacred heart of your divine Son and according to his holy intentions which I offer you to make reparation for whatever evil or imperfection there may be in my own deeds.' Continue in this way in all the circumstances of life. And whenever anything happens to you that is painful, hard to hear or mortifying, tell yourself this: 'Accept what the Sacred Heart of Jesus sends you in order to unite you to himself.'

But above all things maintain peace of heart which surpasses every treasure. For maintaining this peace nothing is more effective than to renounce one's own will and to set in its place the will of the Sacred Heart, so that he may do for us whatever redounds to his glory and that we may joyfully submit to him and place in him our full confidence.

St Margaret Mary Alacoque (1647–90)

In the Presence of God

As you are less busy than others, employ more of your time in reading good books, and in order to make this more efficacious, set about it in this way:

Begin by placing yourself in the presence of God and by begging his help.

Read quietly, slowly, word for word, to enter into the subject more with the heart than with the mind.

At the end of each paragraph that contains a complete meaning, stop for the time it would take you to recite an 'Our Father', or even a little longer, to assimilate what you have read, or to rest and remain peacefully before God.

Should this peace and rest last for a longer time, it will be all the better; but when you feel that your mind wanders, resume your reading, and continue thus, frequently renewing these same pauses.

Nothing need prevent you from continuing the same method, if you find it useful to your soul, during the time you have fixed for meditation.

Jean-Pierre de Caussade (1675–1751)

Foretaste of Heaven

My children, your hearts are small, but prayer enlarges them and renders them capable of loving God. Prayer is a foretaste of heaven, an overflowing of heaven. It never leaves us without sweetness; it is like honey, it descends into the soul and sweetens everything. In a prayer well made, troubles vanish like snow under the rays of the sun.

Prayer makes time seem to pass quickly, and so pleasantly that one fails to notice how long it is. When I was parish priest of Bresse, once almost all my colleagues were ill, and as I made long journeys I used to pray to God, and, I assure you, the time did not seem long to me. There are those who lose themselves in prayer, like a fish in water, because they are absorbed in God. There is no division in their hearts. How I love those noble souls. Saint Francis of Assisi and Saint Colette saw our Lord and spoke to him as we speak to one another.

As for ourselves, how often do we come to church without thinking what we are going to do or for what we are going to ask.

And yet, when we go to call upon someone, we have no difficulty in remembering why it was we came. Some appear as if they were about to say to God: 'I am just going to say a couple of words, so I can get away quickly.' I often think that when we come to adore our Lord we should get all we ask if we asked for it with a lively faith and a pure heart.

St Jean Vianney, The Curé d'Ars (1786–1859)

How to Pray

The power of prayer is indeed wonderful. It is like a queen, who, having free access always to the king, can obtain whatever she asks. To secure a hearing there is no need to recite set prayers composed for the occasion – were this the case, I should indeed deserve to be pitied!

Apart from the Office [the daily prayer of the Church] which is a daily joy, I do not have the courage to search through books for beautiful prayers. They are so numerous that it would only make my head ache. Unable either to say them all or to choose between them, I do as a child would who cannot read – I just say what I want to say to God, quite simply, and he never fails to understand.

For me, prayer is an uplifting of the heart, a glance towards heaven, a cry of gratitude and love in times of sorrow as well as joy. It is something noble, something supernatural, which expands the soul and unites it to God.

When my state of spiritual aridity is such that not a single good thought will come, I repeat very slowly the Our Father and the Hail Mary, which are enough to console me, and provide food for my soul.

St Thérèse of Lisieux (1873–97)

No Other Creature

'Lord, my God, you have asked everything of your servant; take and receive everything, then. This day I belong to you without any reservations, forever. O Beloved of my soul! It is you only whom I want, and for your love I renounce *all*.

'O God of Love! Take my memory and all its memories, take my intelligence so that it will act only for your greatest glory; take my will entirely, so that it will forever be drowned in your own; never again what I want, O most sweet Jesus, but always what you want; receive me, guide me, sanctify me, direct me; to you I abandon myself.

'O God of all goodness, take my body and all its senses, my spirit and all its faculties, my heart and all its affections; O adorable Saviour, you are the sole owner of my soul and of all my being; receive the immolation, that every day and every hour, I offer you in silence; deign to accept it and change it into graces and blessings for all those I love, for the conversion of sinners, and for the sanctification of souls.

'O Jesus! Take all of my heart; it begs and sighs to belong to you alone; hold it always in your powerful hands so that it will surrender and pour itself out on no other creature.

'Lord, take and sanctify all my words, my actions, my desires. Be for my soul its good and its all. To you I give and abandon it.'

Marthe Robin (1902–81)

Maranatha (Come, Lord Jesus)

Reciting the mantra brings us to stillness and to peace. We recite it for as long as we need to before we are caught up into the prayer of Jesus. The general rule is that we must first learn to say it for the entire period of our meditation each morning and each evening, and then to allow it to do its work of calming over a period of years.

A day will come when the mantra ceases to sound and we become lost in the eternal silence of God. The rule when this happens is not to possess this silence or to use it for one's own satisfaction.

As soon as we consciously realize that we are in this profound silence and then begin to reflect about it we must gently and quietly return to our mantra.

Gradually the silences become longer and we are simply absorbed in the mystery of God. The important thing is to have the courage and generosity to return to the mantra as soon as we become self-conscious of the silence.

Each of us is summoned to the heights of Christian prayer, to the fullness of life. What we need, however, is the humility to tread the way very faithfully over a period of years so that the prayer of Christ may indeed be the grounding experience of life.

John Main (1926–82)

Mystical Prayer

My love lifts up his voice,
he says to me,
'Come then, my beloved,
my lovely one, come.
For see, winter is past,
the rains are over and gone.

'Flowers are appearing on the earth.
The season of glad songs has come,
the cooing of the turtledove is heard in our land.
The fig tree is forming its first figs
and the blossoming vines give out their fragrance.
Come then, my beloved,
my lovely one, come.'

Song of Songs 2:10–13

Enlighten Our Eyes [I]

Come now, insignificant man, fly for a moment from your affairs, escape for a little while from the tumult of your thoughts. Put aside now your weighty cares and leave your wearisome toils. Abandon yourself for a little to God and rest for a little in him.

Enter into the inner chamber of your soul, shut out everything save God and what can be of help in your quest for him and having locked the door seek him out. Speak now, my whole heart, speak now to God: 'I seek your countenance, O Lord, your countenance I seek.'

Come then, Lord my God, teach my heart where and how to seek you, where and how to find you.

Lord, if you are not present here, where, since you are absent, shall I look for you? On the other hand, if you are everywhere why then, since you are present, do I not see you? But surely you dwell in light inaccessible. And where is this inaccessible light, or how can I approach the inaccessible light? Or who shall lead me and take me into it that I may see you in it? Again, by what signs, under what aspect, shall I seek you? Never have I seen you, Lord my God, I do not know your face.

St Anselm of Canterbury (c. 1033–1109)

Enlighten Our Eyes [II]

What shall he do, most high Lord, what shall this exile do, far away from you as he is? What shall your servant do, tormented by love of you and yet cast off far from your face? He yearns to see you and your countenance is too far away from him. He desires to come close to you, and your dwelling place is inaccessible; he longs to find you and does not know where you are; he is eager to seek you out and he does not know your countenance.

Lord, you are my God and my Lord, and never have I seen you. You have created me and re-created me and you have given me all the good things I possess, and still I do not know you. In fine, I was made in order to see you, and I have not yet accomplished what I was made for.

And you, O Lord, how long? How long, Lord, will you be unmindful of us? How long will you turn your countenance from us? When will you look upon us and hear us? When will you enlighten our eyes and show your countenance to us? When will you give yourself again to us?

Look upon us, Lord; hear us, enlighten us, show yourself to us. Give yourself to us that it may be well with us, for without you it goes so ill for us. Have pity upon our efforts and our strivings towards you, for we can avail nothing without you.

Teach me to seek you, and reveal yourself to me as I seek, because I can neither seek you if you do not teach me how, nor find you unless you reveal yourself. Let me seek you in desiring you; let me desire you in seeking you; let me find you in loving you; let me love you in finding you.

St Anselm of Canterbury (c. 1033–1109)

Love Is Its Own Reward [I]

Love is self-sufficient; it is pleasing to itself and on its own account. Love is its own payment, its own reward. Love needs no extrinsic cause or result. Love is the result of love, it is intrinsically valuable. I love because I love; I love in order to love. Love is a valuable thing only if it returns to its beginning, consults its origin and flows back to its source. It must always draw from that endless stream. Love is the only one of the soul's motions, senses and affections by which the creature in his inadequate fashion may respond to his Creator and pay him back in kind. When God loves, he wishes only to be loved in return; assuredly he loves for no other purpose than to be loved. He knows that those who love him are happy in their love.

The Bridegroom's love, that Bridegroom who is himself love, seeks only reciprocal love and loyalty. She who is loved may well love in return! How can the bride not love, the very bride of Love? Why should Love itself not be loved?

St Bernard of Clairvaux (1090–1153)

Love Is Its Own Reward [II]

The bride, duly renouncing all other affections, submits with all her being to love alone; she can respond to love by giving love in return. When she has poured forth her whole being in love, how does her effort compare with the unending flow from the very source of love? Love itself of course is more abundant than a lover, the Word than a created soul, the Bridegroom than the bride, the Creator than the creature. As well compare a thirsty man with the fountain which satisfies his thirst!

Can it be that all will perish and come to nought, the promised love of the bride, the longing of the creature here below, the passion of the lover, the confidence of the believer, simply because it is futile to race against a giant, or to contend with honey in sweetness, with the lamb in gentleness, with the lily in whiteness, with the sun in splendour, with Love in love? Not at all. Even though the creature loves less than the Creator, for that is his nature, nevertheless if he loves with all his being, he lacks nothing. One who so loves, therefore, has indeed become a bride; for she cannot so offer love and not be loved in return: in the agreement of the partners lies the wholeness and the perfection of marriage. Who can doubt that the Word's love for the soul is prior to, and greater than, the soul's love for him?

St Bernard of Clairvaux (1090–1153)

Make Room for Christ

Many are his visits to the man of inward life. With such a one he holds delightful converse, granting him sweet comfort, much peace, and an intimacy astonishing beyond measure.

Come then, faithful soul, prepare your heart for this your Spouse, so that he may vouchsafe to come to you and dwell within you.

For so he says: 'If any man love me, he will keep my word; and we will come to him and make our dwelling with him.'

Make room therefore for Christ, and refuse entrance to all others.

When you have Christ, you are rich and have need of nought else.

He will provide for you, and be in all things your faithful procurator; you shall not need to look to men.

Put your whole trust in God; let him be your fear and your love.

Thomas à Kempis (c. 1380–1471)

Angelic Dart

'It pleased the Lord that I should sometimes see the following vision. I would see beside me, on my left hand, an angel in bodily form – a type of vision which I am not in the habit of seeing, except very rarely. Though I often see representations of angels, my visions of them are of the type which I first mentioned. It pleased the Lord that I should see this angel in the following way. He was not tall, but short, and very beautiful, his face so aflame that he appeared to be one of the highest types of angel who seem to be all afire. They must be those who are called cherubim: they do not tell me their names but I am well aware that there is a great difference between certain angels and others, and between these and others still, of a kind that I could not possibly explain. In his hands I saw a long golden spear and at the end of the iron tip I seemed to see a point of fire. With this he seemed to pierce my heart several times so that it penetrated to my entrails. When he drew it out, I thought he was drawing them out with it, and he left me completely afire with a great love of God. The pain was so sharp that it made me utter several moans; and so excessive was the sweetness caused me by this intense pain that one can never wish to lose it, nor will one's soul be content with anything less than God. It is not bodily pain, but spiritual, though the body has a share in it – indeed a great share. So sweet are the colloquies of love which pass between the soul and God that if anyone thinks I am lying I beseech God, in His Goodness, to give him the same experience.'

St Teresa of Avila (1515–82)

The Dark Night [I]

So dark the night! At rest
and hushed my house, I went with no one knowing
upon a lover's quest
    – Ah the sheer grace! – so blest,
my eager heart with love aflame and glowing.

    In darkness, hid from sight
    I went by secret ladder safe and sure
    – Ah grace of sheer delight! –
    so softly veiled by night,
    hushed now my house, in darkness and secure.

Hidden in that glad night,
regarding nothing as I stole away,
no one to see my flight,
no other guide or light
save one that in my heart burned bright as day.

    Surer than noonday sun,
    guiding me from the start this radiant light
    led me to that dear One
    waiting for me, well-known,
    somewhere apart where no one came in sight.

St John of the Cross (1542–91)

The Dark Night [II]

Dark of the night, my guide,
fairer by far than dawn when stars grow dim!
Night that has unified
the Lover and the Bride,
transforming the Beloved into him.

There on my flowered breast
that none but he might ever own or keep,
he stayed, sinking to rest,
and softly I caressed
my Love while cedars gently fanned his sleep.

Breeze from the turret blew
ruffling his hair. Then with his tranquil hand
wounding my neck, I knew
nothing: my senses flew
at touch of peace too deep to understand.

Forgetting all, my quest
ended, I stayed lost to myself at last.
All ceased: my face was pressed
upon my Love, at rest,
with all my cares among the lilies cast.

St John of the Cross (1542–91)

Her Unique Spouse

Kateri Tekakwitha was half Iroquoian, the daughter of a Mohawk warrior and an Algonkian captive, born in a palisaded longhouse of the Turtle clan near present-day Fonda, New York. She received baptism on Easter Day, 1676. For months thereafter she endured the contempt and derision of her village for nonconformity to tribal ways, such as refusing to work on Sunday or to marry. In 1677 she was able, through the help of Christian visitors, to escape her past and flee to an Indian mission near the Lachine rapids (Sault St. Louis) in Upper Canada.

※ 丞 ※

It was on the day of the Annunciation, the twenty-fifth of March, 1679, at eight o'clock in the morning, that Kateri Tekakwitha a moment after Jesus Christ had been given to her in Holy Communion, gave herself also entirely to Him, and renouncing marriage forever, promised to Him her perpetual virginity, and finally with a heart on fire with love called on Him to deign to be her unique spouse, and to take herself as His spouse in return. She prayed Our Lady that Our Lady might with tender devotion present her to her Divine Son; then wishing to make a double sacrifice in a single act, she at the same time as she gave herself devout to Jesus Christ, consecrated herself wholly to Mary begging her to be from then on her mother, and to take her as her daughter.

Blessed Kateri Tekakwitha (c. 1656–80)

Interior Priesthood

. . . As I was plunged in the most profound recollection, uniting myself to the Divine Victim for the glory of his Father, I felt myself in the inmost depths of my soul, penetrated by the presence of Jesus within me. He let me hear words (in a language other than ours), which ravished me with love and bliss. He promised me an ever increasing intimate union with his immolation – a continuous participation, if I so wished, in the adorable Sacrifice continually offered.

He made me understand that there is an intimate and universal priesthood, absolutely and necessarily united to his, which should be the portion of all souls, but which is so of only very few. This priesthood is wholly interior, and is only granted to a soul who consents to it, who has desired it, and who to obtain it wills to immolate itself at all times with Jesus; that even so, in reality it is not the soul who immolates itself but Jesus who immolates it with himself. But as the soul wills to be immolated and abandons itself for that purpose, Jesus makes it participate in his state of victim and priesthood at one and the same time. He consecrates it and ordains it to an interior priesthood which conforms it to his Eucharistic life more than any other gift it has received. This priesthood communicates to the soul a far more perfect grace of union in view of being immolated to the glory of God, thereby rendering infinite honour to God the Father, since it is no longer separated from the Divine Lamb.

Marie-Adele Garnier (1838–1924)

Descent to Simplicity [I]

Imagine a man of forty. His Mother is still alive; he loves and respects her and each day faithfully he visits her and spends half an hour in her company. He does this in spite of a busy and increasingly demanding professional and family life. They talk of this and that and when the half-hour is over, he leaves – to return the next day. What more could a Mother ask?

This represents the beginning of a life of prayer. Each day a set time is spent on meditation and a method is faithfully followed point by point. This is a beginning, it is something . . . but one might sometimes think, from what they say, that those who set time aside in this way for prayer are doing wonders!

But if this soul is faithful in prayer and God draws him closer, he will become surprisingly younger! No longer the man of forty spending the dutiful half-hour with his Mother but a young man of twenty who lives away from home, has his own friends and interests. But he comes back often and spends long hours with his family. And the soul grows younger still: a youngster of fifteen is still living at home and feels the security of his parent's house. Our heavenly Father grants to the soul the request of the psalmist to 'live in the house of the Lord all the days of his life'. The house of the Lord is the house of prayer. It is not a matter of continually speaking to God or of God, but rather that the eyes of the soul are continually on God, all action is initiated by God, God seems to envelop the soul. What extraordinary progress this is: not to be able to leave God.

Thomas Dehau (1870–1956)

Descent to Simplicity [II]

As the soul moves along the path of prayer he can be compared to a child of ten whose conversation is not yet that of an adult, and his Mother loves his sayings just because of this. If we continue to move 'forward' we find a child of two years old or so. An age at which Mother and child can each fill the world of the other. The child's babbling is incomprehensible to any but his Mother who knows and understands. His Mother becomes small for his sake, to babble with him.

We should indeed be surprised if we heard a recording of the prayer of the saints. We would be surprised by their simplicity, their childlikeness, their stammerings of love. This extreme simplicity is necessary to them as a means of holding fast to God in the midst of their work, their suffering and difficulties. God suffices – and here is a strange thing – the saints suffice for God . . . When a Mother is listening to her young child, does she notice what goes on around her? And so it is with God. All the iniquities of men, all the blasphemies are no longer heard. God does not punish; he is with his saints and hears only their childlike words and it is these words which bring us mercy.

Thomas Dehau (1870–1956)

Descent to Simplicity [III]

But we must carry the comparison further. A baby does not talk, or walk but depends entirely on his Mother, he is moved in her arms. This age is that of great saints. They are lost in God and no longer able to talk, a sacred silence, more telling than the babbling of childhood. These great saints can live only on God, they depend on him utterly, as a young infant depends on his Mother. The great saints cannot leave God.

Is that as far as we can go? Surely the greatest union between Mother and child is before birth? He is one with her. We do not see him; he lives in her.

Thus, the greatest saints, the closest to God. One no longer sees them for they seem lost, melted into God, having no other life than the life they share with him. They seem dead and yet they live a mysterious, intimate life with God. This is the life of which St. Paul spoke when he said 'We are dead and our life is hidden in God.'

Thomas Dehau (1870–1956)

Dryness in Prayer

You may think that I am exaggerating the night of my soul. If one judged by the poems I have composed this year, it might seem that I have been inundated with consolation, that I am a child for whom the veil of faith is almost rent asunder . . . But it is not a veil . . . it is a wall which reaches to the very heavens, shutting out the starry sky.

When I sing in my verses of the happiness of heaven and of the eternal possession of God, I feel no joy. I sing out of what I wish to believe. Sometimes, I confess a feeble ray of sunshine penetrates my dark night and brings me a moment's relief, but after it has gone, the remembrance of it, instead of consoling me, makes the blackness seem denser still.

And yet I have never experienced more fully the sweetness and mercy of the Lord. He did not send this heavy cross when it would, I believe, have discouraged me, but chose a time when I was able to bear it. Now it does no more than deprive me of all natural satisfaction in my longing for heaven.

St Thérèse of Lisieux (1873–97)

A Mystical Heart

Many mystics tell us that, in addition to the mind and heart with which we ordinarily communicate with God we are, all of us, endowed with a mystical mind and mystical heart, a faculty which makes it possible for us to know God directly, to grasp and *intuit* him in his very being, though in a dark manner, apart from all thoughts and concepts and images.

Ordinarily all our contact with God is indirect – through images and concepts that necessarily distort his reality. To be able to grasp him beyond these thoughts and images is the privilege of this faculty which, in the course of this explanation, I shall call the Heart (a word dear to the author of *The Cloud of Unknowing*) though it has nothing to do with our physical heart or our affectivity.

In most of us this Heart lies dormant and undeveloped. If it were to be awakened it would be constantly straining towards God and, given a chance, would impel the whole of our being towards him. But for this, it needs to be developed, it needs to have the dross that surrounds it removed so that it can be attracted towards the Eternal Magnet.

Anthony de Mello (1931–87)

THE JOURNEY
TO GOD

Conversion and Call

As he was walking by the Lake of Galilee he saw two brothers, Simon, who was called Peter, and his brother Andrew; they were making a cast into the lake with their net, for they were fishermen. And he said to them, 'Come after me and I will make you fishers of people.' And at once they left their nets and followed him.

Going on from there he saw another pair of brothers, James son of Zebedee and his brother John; they were in their boat with their father Zebedee, mending their nets, and he called them. And at once, leaving the boat and their father, they followed him.

Matthew 4:18–22

The Calling of Antony [I]

After the death of his parents, Antony was left alone with an only sister who was very young. He was about eighteen or twenty years old, and undertook the care of the household and his sister.

Less than six months had passed after the death of his parents, and he was going to the church, as was his custom, turning over in his mind the way that the apostles had left everything to follow the Saviour, and also how those people in the Acts of the Apostles had sold their possessions and had laid the proceeds at the feet of the apostles for distribution among the needy. He was also thinking of the great hope stored up in heaven for these people. With these things in his mind, he went into the church. It happened that the gospel was then being read, and he heard what the Lord had said to the rich man 'If you would be perfect, go, sell what you possess and give to the poor, and you will have treasure in heaven; and come, follow me.'

As though this reminder of the saints had been sent to him by God, and as though that passage had been read specially for his sake, Antony went out immediately, and gave to the villagers the possessions he had inherited from his ancestors – they consisted of some three hundred very pleasant and fertile acres – so that they would not be an encumbrance to him and to his sister. He sold all his possessions and gave the considerable sum he raised to the poor, keeping back only a little of it for his sister.

St Antony of Egypt (c. 251–356)

The Calling of Antony [II]

Again when he went into church, he heard what the Lord said in the gospel, 'Do not be anxious about tomorrow.' He could not wait any longer, but went out and gave away even what he had kept back to the poor. He left his sister in the care of some well-known, trustworthy virgins, putting her in a convent to be brought up, and he devoted himself to the ascetic life not far from his home, living in recollection and practising self-denial.

He laboured with his own hands, for he had heard that 'If anyone will not work, let him not eat.' And of what he earned, part he spent on food, and part he gave to the poor.

He prayed frequently, for he had learned that one ought to pray in secret, and pray without ceasing. He was so careful in his reading of scripture that nothing escaped him, but he retained it all; so that afterwards his memory served him in place of books.

And so all the people of the village, and the good men with whom he associated saw what kind of man he was, and they called him 'The friend of God.' Some loved him as a son, and others as though he were a brother.

St Antony of Egypt (c. 251–356)

Reluctant Bishop

Anselm, with some misgiving, came over to visit a sick friend in England at a time when the archbishopric of Canterbury had long been left vacant, so that King William Rufus and his creatures might enjoy the sequestrated revenues of the See. At Christmas 1092, the clergy were allowed to pray for a remedy for the misfortunes of the Church. Early in 1093 King William fell sick and was evidently at the point of death; fortunately for himself, the Norman king was more prompt in seeing the point of the situation. He promised amendment and restitution of every possible kind, and sent for Anselm at once as the obvious person to be elected archbishop.

And then began a scene which has been enacted with various results a thousand times in the history of sanctity, but seldom with so much publicity or so much dramatic interest as in St Anselm's case. When you try to make a saint accept a bishopric, it is like trying to make a child take medicine; the result is a perfect fury of dissent. In this case not merely the ordinary considerations but the whole welfare of a long-widowed Church and, as seemed probable, the life of a notorious sinner were depending upon St Anselm's acceptance, and he simply refused. It was only by the use of physical force that they dragged the saint to the King's bedside: and there, pressing the crozier against the knuckles that would not open so as to hold it, they elected the Archbishop of Canterbury.

St Anselm of Canterbury (c. 1033–1109)

Test the Spirits [I]

Ignatius was very addicted to reading aimless and exaggerated books about the illustrious deeds of the famous, and when he felt well again he asked for some to pass the time. But there were no books of that type in the house and he was given a book called *The Life of Christ* and another *The Flower of the Saints*, both in his native language.

By reading these regularly he developed a certain sympathy with what was written in them. Sometimes he took his mind off them and turned his thoughts to the type of story he used to read earlier on; sometimes, according as it occurred to him, he thought about those idle inclinations, and things of that nature, such as he used to think about formerly.

But divine mercy was at hand and, in place of these thoughts, it used to substitute others from what he had recently read. For when he had read the lives of Christ our Lord and the saints he would think to himself and ponder: 'What, if I were to do what blessed Francis did or what blessed Dominic did?' And he used to meditate a good deal in this manner. This way of thinking lasted for some time, but then other things intervened, and he resumed his idle and worldly thoughts, and these persisted for a long time. He was involved in that succession of changes of mind for a considerable time.

St Ignatius of Loyola (c. 1491–1556)

Test the Spirits [II]

But there was a difference in his two types of subject for thought. When he was intent on his worldly interests he got great pleasure at the time, but whenever he wearied of them and gave them up, he felt dejected and empty. On the other hand, when he thought about the austerities which he found that holy men practised, not only did he find joy in the account of them, but when he stopped thinking of them his joy remained unabated. However, he never noticed the difference or thought about it, until one day it dawned on him, and he began to wonder at it. He understood from experience that the one subject of thought left him dejection, while the other left him joy. This was the first conclusion which he reached concerning things of a supernatural nature. Afterwards, however, when he had undertaken spiritual exercises, this experience was the starting point for teaching his followers the discernment of spirits.

St Ignatius of Loyola (c. 1491–1556)

Thy Will in Me

O Parent of parents and Friend of all friends,
Thy intent in thus disposing was different from this;
For here without entreaty thou tookest me into thy care,
And by degrees led me from all else
That at length I might see and settle my love in thee.
What had I ever done to please thee?
Or what was there in me wherewith to serve thee?
Much less could I ever deserve to be chosen by thee.
O happy begun freedom the beginning of all my good,
And more worth to me at that time than the whole world besides.
Had I never since hindered thy will and working in me
What degrees of grace should I now have had!
It is more than nineteen years since and where as yet am I?
    My Jesus, forgive me,
    Remember what thou hast done for me
    And whither thou hast brought me,
    And for this excess of goodness and love
    Let me no more hinder thy will in me.

Mary Ward (1585–1645)

Created for Service

God has created me to do Him some definite service;
He has committed some work to me which He has not committed to another.
I have my mission – I may never know it in this life,
but I shall be told it in the next.
I am a link in a chain, a bond of connection between persons.
He has not created me for nothing. I shall do good. I shall do His work.
I shall be an angel of peace, a preacher of truth in my own place,
if I do but keep His commandments.
Therefore, I will trust Him.
Whatever, wherever I am. I can never be thrown away.
If I am in sickness, my sickness may serve Him.
In perplexity, my perplexity may serve Him;
if I am in sorrow, my sorrow may serve Him.
He does nothing in vain. He knows what he is about.
He may take away my friends, throw me among strangers.
He may make me feel desolate, make my spirits sink, hide my future from
   me,
still He knows what He is about.

Venerable John Henry Newman (1801–90)

The Hound of Heaven [I]

I fled Him, down the nights and down the days;
  I fled Him, down the arches of the years;
I fled Him, down the labyrinthine ways
  Of my own mind; and in the mist of tears
I hid from Him, and under running laughter.
      Up vistaed hopes I sped;
      And shot, precipitated,
Adown Titanic glooms of chasmèd fears,
  From those strong Feet that followed, followed after.

      But with unhurrying chase,
      And unperturbèd pace,
    Deliberate speed, majestic instancy,
      They beat — and a Voice beat
      More instant than the Feet —
  'All things betray thee, who betrayest Me. . . .'

Francis Thompson (1859–1907)

The Hound of Heaven [II]

Now of that long pursuit
Comes on at hand the bruit;
That Voice is round me like a bursting sea:
'And is thy earth so marred,
Shattered in shard on shard?
Lo, all things fly thee, for thou fliest Me!
Strange, piteous, futile thing!
Wherefore should any set thee love apart?
Seeing none but I makes much of naught?' (He said),
'And human love needs human meriting:
How hast thou merited –
Of all man's clotted clay the dingiest clot?
Alack, thou knowest not
How little worthy of any love thou art!
Whom wilt thou find to love ignoble thee,
Save Me, save only Me?
All which I took from thee I did but take,
Not for thy harms,
But just that thou might'st seek it in My arms.
All which thy child's mistake
Fancies as lost, I have stored for thee at home:
Rise, clasp My hand, and come!'

Halts by me that footfall:
Is my gloom, after all,
Shade of His hand, outstretched caressingly?
'Ah, fondest, blindest, weakest,
I am He Whom thou seekest!
Thou dravest love from thee, who dravest Me.'

Francis Thompson (1859–1907)

My Vocation Is Love

All the gifts of heaven, even the most perfect of them, without love, are absolutely nothing; charity is the best way of all, because it leads straight to God. . . . When Saint Paul was talking about the different members of the mystical body I couldn't recognize myself in any of them; or rather I could recognize myself in all of them. But charity – that was the key to my vocation. If the Church was a body composed of different members, it couldn't lack the noblest of all; it must have a heart, and a heart burning with love. And I realized that this love was the true motive force which enabled the other members of the Church to act; if it ceased to function the apostles would forget to preach the gospel, the martyrs would refuse to shed their blood. Love, in fact, is the vocation which includes all others; it's a universe of its own, comprising all time and space – it's eternal. Beside myself with joy, I cried out: 'Jesus, my love! I've found my vocation, and my vocation is love.' I had discovered where it is that I belong in the Church, the niche God has appointed for me. To be nothing else than love, deep down in the heart of Mother Church; that's to be everything at once – my dream wasn't a dream after all.

St Thérèse of Lisieux (1873–97)

Beauty and Joy

Mrs Barrett gave me my first impulse towards Catholicism. It was around ten o'clock in the morning that I went up to Kathryn's to call for her to come out and play. There was no one on the porch or in the kitchen. The breakfast dishes had all been washed. They were long railroad apartments, those flats, and thinking the children must be in the front room, I burst in and ran through the bedrooms.

In the front room Mrs Barrett was on her knees, saying her prayers. She turned to tell me that Kathryn and the children had all gone to the store and went on with her praying. And I felt a warm burst of love towards Mrs Barrett that I have never forgotten, a feeling of gratitude and happiness that still warms my heart when I remember her. She had God, and there was beauty and joy in her life.

All through my life what she was doing remained with me. And though I became oppressed with the problem of poverty and injustice, though I groaned at the hideous sordidness of man's lot, though there were years when I clung to the philosophy of economic determination as an explanation of man's fate, still there were moments when in the midst of misery and class strife, life was shot through with glory. Mrs Barrett in her sordid little tenement flat finished her breakfast dishes at ten o'clock in the morning and got down on her knees and prayed to God.

Dorothy Day (1897–1980)

Man of Hope

The monk leaves the world, retires to the wilderness, the forest, the mountains, the lonely shores of the sea: and there, descending by his prayer into the empty spaces of his own spirit, he waits for the fulfilment of the divine promises: 'The land that was desolate and impassable shall be glad, and the wilderness shall rejoice and shall flourish like the lily' (Isaiah 35:1).

The monk is a man of sorrow, a man discontented with every illusion, aware of his own poverty, impatient of evasion, who seeks the naked realities that only the desert can reveal. But the monk is also a man of joy, a man at peace with the emptiness of the wilderness, glad of his limitations, loving reality as he finds it, and therefore secure in his humility. He is a man of joy and a man of sorrow both together because he is a man of desires. And because he lives by pure hope, he has entered into the secret which Christ has taught His chosen ones.

Thomas Merton (1915–68)

States of Life

Try to discover what the Lord wants of you, take no part in the futile works of darkness but, on the contrary, show them up for what they are. The things which are done in secret are shameful even to speak of; but anything shown up by the light will be illuminated and anything illuminated is itself a light. That is why it is said:

Wake up, sleeper,
rise from the dead,
and Christ will shine on you.

So be very careful about the sort of lives you lead, like intelligent and not like senseless people. Make the best of the present time, for it is a wicked age. This is why you must not be thoughtless but must recognise what is the will of the Lord.

Ephesians 5:10–17

A Bishop's Prayer

Christ my God, you humbled yourself in order to lift me, a straying sheep, on to your shoulders. You fed me in green pastures and nourished me with the waters of true doctrine by the hands of your shepherds. They, whom you yourself fed, afterwards fed your elect and chosen flock.

Now you have called me, Lord, by the hands of your bishop to minister to your disciples. Why, indeed, in your providence you acted so, I do not know. You alone know that.

Lord, lighten the heavy burden of my sins by which I have seriously offended you. Cleanse my mind and my heart. Like a bright lamp, guide me along the right path.

Put the right word on my lips. Grant me a clear and ready tongue by the tongues of fire of your Holy Spirit that your presence may ever protect me.

Feed me, Lord, and feed with me, that my heart may not deviate either to right or left. Let your good Spirit guide me in the right way and may my works be in accordance with your will. Let it be so, right to the end.

St John of Damascus (c. 655–c. 750)

Continual Prayer

The monk, who continues faithfully in his cell and lets himself be moulded by it, will gradually find that his whole life tends to become one continual prayer. But he cannot attain to this repose except at the cost of stern battle; both by living austerely in fidelity to the law of the Cross, and willingly accepting the tribulations by which God will try him as gold in the furnace. In this way, having been cleansed in the night of patience, and having been consoled and sustained by assiduous meditation of the Scriptures, and having been led by the Holy Spirit into the depths of his own soul, he is now ready, not only to serve God, but even to cleave to him in love.

St Bruno (c. 1032–1101)

The Bishop-elect

It was a gallant and bravely equipped escort that awaited the bishop-elect; knights and canons, with chaplains, squires and servants to do honour to the king's friend, the bishop-elect of the great see of Lincoln. Only one person in the procession was but poorly arrayed and that was the bishop-elect himself. The shabbily dressed monk who rode in the midst of the canons was still a Carthusian, would be indeed a Carthusian till his death; he was not yet a bishop and therefore it did not behove him to put off his habit.

They were put to shame, canons and knights, chaplains and esquires and servants, the latter in especial, by the mean attire of the principal member of the cavalcade. And to make it worse the bishop-elect insisted on carrying a wretched bundle of sheepskins, tied to the saddle-bow, which he said was his bedding. Of course while they were journeying through the country it did not matter so much how the bishop-elect was dressed, there was nobody to see him, and no one to comment on the horrible bundle. But it was too embarrassing when they came to towns and remarks were passed by irreverent burgesses. So just before the procession entered the city of Winchester, where royalty and nobles, it was said, would greet the bishop-elect, a certain chaplain managed to cut the strap which held the odious sheepskins to the saddle-bow, and the offensive bundle fell to the ground. Hugh did not notice the loss; wrapped in meditation he was aware neither of the embarrassment he caused nor of the dexterous removal of his bedding.

St Hugh of Lincoln (c. 1140–1200)

The Flower of Holiness

Elizabeth's holiness began to come to its full flower. All her life she had been the comfort of the poor: now she became the helper of the starving. Outside one of her castles she built a hospice and gathered in it sick, diseased and crippled men and women. Besides, anyone who came asking for alms received unstinted gifts from her charity. She did the same wherever her husband's jurisdiction ran, pouring out all the resources she had in all parts of his territories, until in the end she sold even her jewels and her sumptuous dresses.

She went twice a day to see the sick, in the early morning and at nightfall, and it was those with the foulest diseases she made her personal care. She fed them herself, made and cleaned their pallets, carried them in her arms and nursed them in whatever way they needed. Her husband, of happy memory, gave a completely ungrudging consent to all she did. When he died she felt she should now attempt the heights of perfection. She came to me and begged me with tears to let her beg her way from door to door.

On the Good Friday of that year, after the altars had been stripped, she knelt in front of the altar of the chapel she had given to the Friars Minor and laid her hands on it. Then in their presence she renounced her own will, her earthly estate and all that our Saviour counsels us in the gospel to put aside.

St Elizabeth of Hungary (1207–31)

The Inferno

Midway this way of life we're bound upon,
I woke to find myself in a dark wood,
Where the right road was wholly lost and gone.

Ay me! how hard to speak of it — that rude
And rough and stubborn forest! the mere breath
Of memory stirs the old fear in the blood;

It is so bitter, it goes nigh to death;
Yet there I gained such good, that, to convey
The tale, I'll write what else I found therewith.

How I got into it I cannot say,
Because I was so heavy and full of sleep
When first I stumbled from the narrow way;

But when at last I stood beneath a steep
Hill's side, which closed that valley's wandering maze
Whose dread had pierced me to the heart-root deep,

Then I looked up, and saw the morning rays
Mantle its shoulder from that planet bright
Which guides men's feet aright on all their ways.

Dante Alighieri (1265–1321)

On Being a Martha

His Majesty does not lead all souls by the same way. St Martha was holy, though we are never told she was a contemplative; would you not be content with resembling this blessed woman who deserved to receive Christ our Lord so often into her home, where she fed and served him, and where he ate at her table?

Imagine that this little community is the house of St Martha where there must be different kinds of people. Remember that someone must cook the meals and count yourselves happy in being able to serve like Martha.

Reflect that true humility consists in being willing and ready to do what our Lord asks of us. It always makes us consider ourselves unworthy to be reckoned among his servants.

Then if contemplation, mental and vocal prayer, nursing the sick, the work of the house and the most menial labour, all serve this Guest, why should we choose to minister to him in one way rather than in another?

St Teresa of Avila (1515–82)

The Presence of God

[Brother Lawrence said]:

That he was then happily employed in the cobbler's workshop; but that he was as ready to quit that post as the former, since he was always finding pleasure in every condition by doing little things for the love of God.

With him the *set* times of prayers were not different from other times.

He retired to pray, according to the direction of his Superior, but he did not want such retirement or ask for it, because his greatest business did not divert him from God.

As he knew his obligation to love God in all things, and as he endeavoured so to do, he had no need of a director to advise him, but he needed much a confessor to absolve him.

He was very sensible of his faults, but not discouraged by them.

He confessed them to God, but did not plead against him to excuse them.

When he had done so, he peaceably resumed his usual practice of love and adoration.

Brother Lawrence (c. 1614–91)

Seventeenth-century Nun's Prayer

Lord, Thou knowest better than I know myself that I am growing older and will some day be old. Keep me from the fatal habit of thinking I must say something on every subject and on every occasion. Release me from craving to straighten out everybody's affairs. Make me thoughtful but not moody: helpful but not bossy. With my vast store of wisdom, it seems a pity not to use it all, but Thou knowest Lord that I want a few friends at the end.

Keep my mind free from the recital of endless details; give me wings to get to the point. Seal my lips on my aches and pains. They are increasing, and love of rehearsing them is becoming sweeter as the years go by. I dare not ask for grace enough to enjoy the tales of others' pains, but help me to endure them with patience.

I dare not ask for improved memory, but for a growing humility and lessening cocksureness when my memory seems to clash with the memories of others. Teach me the glorious lesson that occasionally I may be mistaken. Keep me reasonably sweet; I do not want to be a Saint – some of them are so hard to live with – but a sour old person is one of the crowning works of the devil. Give me the ability to see good things in unexpected places, and talents in unexpected people. And, give me, O Lord, the grace to tell them so.

Source Unknown

All-encompassing Mystery

When asked whether a Christian could live among atheists and keep the faith, Madeleine usually responded that to keep the faith as if guarding a fortress had nothing to do with real faith. She maintained that a person could become a better Christian living beside unbelievers because they provided the stimulus for a healthier and more authentic faith. Atheists tended to unmask the complacency of believers which, in other contexts, remains forever masked. They made her aware that the silence of Christians often indicated apathy or ignorance. Therefore Christians were not hurt but helped when awakened from their dreamy indifference or shaken out of their stupor . . .

Rather than well recited words or a simple call for help, her prayer was a wordless cry for God that rose from the depths of her being. Madeleine later wrote that during days of intensive prayer she had felt not so much that she had found God but that God had found her. Through this prayer she also sensed that God had to remain her ultimate question and not her fixed answer, her all-encompassing mystery and not her limited possession. She was now willing to accept God as greater and more profound than her former abyss.

Madeleine Delbrêl (1904–64)

Joseph, Your Brother

The good shepherd is one who lays down his life for his people. Some live this calling literally, shedding their blood as martyrs. Others live it in the unstinting giving of their time, their energy, their very selves to those they have been called to serve. Whatever the future holds for me, I pledge this day to live as a good shepherd who willingly lays down his life for you.

❧❧

As our lives and ministries are mingled together through the breaking of the Bread and the blessing of the Cup, I hope that long before my name falls from the eucharistic prayer in the silence of death you will know well who I am. You will know because we will work and play together, fast and pray together, mourn and rejoice together, despair and hope together, dispute and be reconciled together. You will know me as a friend, fellow priest, and bishop. You will know also that I love you. For I am Joseph, your brother!

Joseph Bernardin (1928–96)

Marriage

On the third day there was a wedding at Cana in Galilee. The mother of Jesus was there, and Jesus and his disciples had also been invited. And they ran out of wine, since the wine provided for the feast had all been used, and the mother of Jesus said to him, 'They have no wine.' Jesus said, 'Woman, what do you want from me? My hour has not come yet.' His mother said to the servants, 'Do whatever he tells you.' There were six stone water jars standing there, meant for the ablutions that are customary among the Jews: each could hold twenty or thirty gallons. Jesus said to the servants, 'Fill the jars with water,' and they filled them to the brim. Then he said to them, 'Draw some out now and take it to the president of the feast.' They did this; the president tasted the water, and it had turned into wine. Having no idea where it came from – though the servants who had drawn the water knew – the president of the feast called the bridegroom and said, 'Everyone serves good wine first and the worse wine when the guests are well wined; but you have kept the best wine till now.'

John 2:1–10

Nuptial Blessing

May almighty God bless you by the word of His mouth, and unite your hearts in the enduring bond of pure love.

May you be blessed in your children and may the love that you lavish on them be returned a hundred fold.

May the peace of Christ dwell always in your hearts and in your home; may you have true friends to stand by you, both in joy and in sorrow. May you be ready with help and consolation for all those who come to you in need; and may the blessings promised to the compassionate descend in abundance on your house.

May you be blessed in your work and enjoy its fruits. May cares never cause you distress, nor the desire for earthly possessions lead you astray; but may your hearts' concern be always for the treasures laid up for you in the life of heaven.

May the Lord grant you fullness of years, so that you may reap the harvest of a good life, and, after you have served Him with loyalty in His kingdom on earth, may He take you up into His eternal dominions in Heaven.

Source Unknown

One in Spirit

How beautiful . . . the marriage of two Christians, two who are one in hope, one in desire, one in the way of life they follow, one in the religion they practise. They are as brother and sister, both servants of the same Master. Nothing divides them, either in flesh or in spirit. They are, in very truth, two in one flesh; and where there is but one flesh there is also but one spirit. They pray together, they worship together, they fast together; instructing one another, encouraging one another, strengthening one another. Side by side they visit God's church and partake of God's Banquet; side by side they face difficulties and persecution, share their consolations. They have no secrets from one another; they never shun each other's company; they never bring sorrow to each other's hearts. Unembarrassed they visit the sick and assist the needy. They give alms without anxiety; they attend the Sacrifice without difficulty; they perform their daily exercises of piety without hindrance. They need not be furtive about making the Sign of the Cross, nor timorous in greeting the brethren, nor silent in asking a blessing of God. Psalms and hymns they sing to one another, striving to see which one of them will chant more beautifully the praises of their Lord. Hearing and seeing this, Christ rejoices. To such as these He gives His peace. Where there are two together, there also He is present; and where He is, there evil is not.

Tertullian (c. 160–c. 225)

Lifelong Union

Marriage is rightly recommended to the faithful for its fruits, the gift of children, and for the conjugal modesty of which the mutual fidelity of the spouses is the guarantee and bond.

But there is another reason too. In this union there is also a mystery which makes it sacred and causes the Apostle to say: 'Husbands, love your wives as Christ has loved the Church.'

The effect of such a marriage is that man and woman once they are committed and bound to one another remain irrevocably united for their whole lives without being permitted to separate, except for the reason of adultery.

Is it not perhaps the same as with the union of Christ and his Church? They are alive together eternally; no divorce can ever separate them.

St Augustine of Hippo (354–430)

Wayward Son

I am sorry your son has behaved badly towards you. I deplore as much the conduct of the son as the wrongs of his mother. Yet, after all, such conduct is excusable in a young son. Youth is ever prone to such faults and is itself an excuse for them. Do you not realize that 'all the thoughts and imaginations of a man's heart are bent towards evil from youth'? You may be sure that the merits and alms of his father will bring about a change for the better in him. You must offer more and more vows and prayers to God for him, because, even though at the moment his conduct towards you is not what it should be, yet nevertheless a mother ought not and cannot lose her maternal affection for her children. 'Can a mother ever forget the son she bore in her womb?' asks the Prophet, and he adds: 'even if she were to forget, I will not be forgetful of thee.' This young man has so many excellent qualities that we must offer prayers and tears to the Lord, that God may enable him (as I am sure he will) to emulate the goodness of his father. He must be treated with gentleness and kindly forbearance, because by such treatment he will be more encouraged to do good than if he were exasperated by nagging and scolding. I am sure that by these means we will soon be able to rejoice over a happy change in him.

St Bernard of Clairvaux (1090–1153)

Spiritual Union

'Marriage is a great sacrament: I speak in Christ and in the Church' (Ephesians 5:32). It is honourable to all, in all, and in everything, that is, in all its parts. The unmarried should esteem it in humility. It is as holy to the poor as to the rich. Its institution, its end, its purpose, its form and its matter are all holy.

It greatly concerns the public welfare that the sanctity of marriage, which is the source of all its well-being, should be preserved inviolate.

I exhort married persons to have that mutual love which is so earnestly enjoined by the Holy Spirit in Scripture.

The first result of such love is the indissoluble union of your hearts. This spiritual union of the heart, with its affections and love, is stronger than that of mere bodily union.

The second result of this love is absolute faithfulness.

The third end of marriage is the birth and bringing-up of children.

Love and faithfulness always breed confidence.

St Francis de Sales (1567–1622)

Two Stubborn Pieces of Iron

Very few people ever state properly the strong argument in favour of marrying for love or against marrying for money. The argument is not that all lovers are heroes and heroines, nor is it that all dukes are profligates or all millionaires cads. The argument is this, that the differences between a man and a woman are at the best so obstinate and exasperating that they practically cannot be got over unless there is an atmosphere of exaggerated tenderness and mutual interest. To put the matter in one metaphor, the sexes are two stubborn pieces of iron; if they are to be welded together, it must be while they are red-hot. Every woman has to find out that her husband is a selfish beast, because every man is a selfish beast by the standard of a woman. But let her find out the beast while they are both still in the story of 'Beauty and the Beast'. Every man has to find out that his wife is cross – that is to say, sensitive to the point of madness: for every woman is mad by the masculine standard. But let him find out that she is mad while her madness is more worth considering than anyone else's sanity.

G.K. Chesterton (1874–1936)

Total Surrender

Priests undergo long years of preparation in seminaries. So do all religious, male and female. But who gets preparation for marriage and where is its novitiate? Frankly, it should begin at the fathers' or mothers' knee . . ., by seeing the parents' example . . .

The boy and girl about to marry are 'in love'. But do they love? Do they understand that theirs is the vocation to love – and to love so well that their children will learn love by just being their children and going into the school of their love?

Do they comprehend that love is total surrender? Do they comprehend that it is surrender to one another, for the love of God and each other? Do they understand that love never uses the pronoun 'I' and is neither selfish nor self-centred? On the answer to these questions depends so much. Who can truthfully say, when they are entering marriage, that they know the answers? . . .

The two become one. The man and the woman leave parents and home and cleave to one another, becoming one flesh. This means a surrender, a giving of oneself until, in truth, two are one flesh, one mind, one heart, one soul. For those who understand this – and alas, how few they are – the veil of faith becomes gossamer thin, especially at Communion, when husband and wife become one in the heart of Christ. That is where this oneness is felt most by those who believe, and believing, see.

Catherine de Hueck Doherty (1896–1985)

Water into Wine

There can hardly have been a commentator who has not connected the running out of the wine with the arrival of Our Lord, who may have been expected, and his five disciples, who can hardly have been. Given that practically the whole town had probably been invited to the wedding, one cannot feel that an extra half-dozen would have made all that difference. But this particular half-dozen would have made a difference to the celebrations as a whole. Within a few minutes Peter would have been holding the floor; it was his nature to. John may have attracted less notice; what matters to us is that he was meeting the woman who would be given to him as his mother on Calvary . . .

The changing of water into wine – 'this beginning of miracles' as St John calls it – must have been known all over the area by nightfall. Half the grown-ups of Cana would have been at the wedding feast; heaven knows what the hundred and fifty gallons had swollen to as they told their families.

Nazareth was only four miles off, and the fury of finding one of their own townsmen working miracles somewhere else must already have begun; if he *must* work miracles, what was wrong with Nazareth?

Frank Sheed (1897–1981)

The Daily Cherishing

I believe deeply that God is at work in all marriages, in the peak experiences, in the daily cherishing, in the continual reconciliation. Who can set limits to God's activity? Christians have the privilege of reflecting on this presence, of recognizing God in their marriage and pointing God out to each other, naming God by name. And over a lifetime I believe this naming changes the quality of a marriage, in an indefinable way enriching it.

At most weddings there is wine: wife and husband bring joy to each other and are glad. But Christians believe that the best wine for a wedding, the greatest gladness, comes through the transforming power of Jesus Christ. Not every couple recognizes this source of their joy, just as the steward at Cana did not know the source of the improved wine. Yet the steward had no doubt about its quality. To those who know Jesus Christ, to his disciples, he lets his glory be seen, and two-by-two they recognize him in their married love. And they believe in him.

Margaret Grimer (1933–95)

Holy Chaos

The primeval chaos that results when I am working on a book does have its negative side beyond the lack of matching socks for six children and one husband. When this happens, it usually coincides with an influx of clothes for Poland or Mother Teresa, and Don is greeted at the door with a pile of black plastic bags which prevents him from coming into the house. Then, too, the kitchen overflows with bottles, tins and newspapers waiting to be recycled.

When it gets to the point that the cat food tins are all still waiting to be washed before joining the recycling pile then tension in the house begins to rise. Then I have to stop and think again about the breadth of my vocation and find new ways of reconciling the different elements. I am reminded at such times of the advice of a Russian Orthodox Archbishop to one of his married priests who was having difficulties reconciling the demands of family life with his responsibilities as a priest. 'Remember always', said the Archbishop, 'that God gave you your wife before he gave you the priesthood.'

Barbara Wood (1946–)

Letter to Maria [I]

You ask if mysticism is possible for a married woman. You say that you feel called to deep prayer but do not quite see your path, and you ask what I think.

Your question is both simple and complicated. Of course it is possible for a married person to attain to the very pinnacle of mysticism. And knowing you as I do, your deep faith, your sense of God's presence, your love for your family, your concern for the poor, I feel quite sure that you are called. You have the further advantage that David is a deeply prayerful person. It matters not that his spiritual path is a bit different from yours. Walk together. Two mystics. So, Maria, surrender to God and go on your way with confidence and joy.

Yet I do see the difficulties. The first is that most of the literature on mysticism has been written by celibates for celibates — as though mysticism was the preserve of monks and nuns. Alas, the Catholic tradition is not free from élitism. *The Cloud of Unknowing*, for example, written in fourteenth-century England, distinguishes between those called to salvation and those called to perfection. Those called to salvation are the masses of people, the laity — and for these the author will write no mystical treatise. Those called to perfection are the monks and nuns (and perhaps priests and bishops are thrown in).

The distinction between those called to salvation and those called to perfection was hit on the head by the Second Vatican Council which declared that every Christian is called to perfection.

William Johnston (1925–)

Letter to Maria [II]

By reason of baptism every Christian is called to holiness and at times even to martyrdom; for all are called to love God with their whole heart and soul and mind and strength. The Council also spoke enthusiastically about holiness in the family, hinting at a mysticism of interpersonal relations and saying that in marriage 'authentic human love is caught up into divine love'.

. . . Is it by prayer in common? Or is it by uncompromising fidelity to another person? . . . You and David, together with thousands of modern people are pioneers in the search for mysticism in family life and for a mysticism of sexuality.

One thing is clear. You will experience God as a wife and mother, just as David will experience God as a husband and father – and you both have your work. You are called to experience God in all things. . . .

Since in the mystical life one is purified by both action and suffering, remember that a great purification will take place through the struggles of married life. . . . This suffering can constitute a dark night that is no less purifying than St John of the Cross's dark night of the soul. And it leads to an intimacy and a union and a spiritual marriage that is consummated beyond the grave.

William Johnston (1925–)

Holy Living

Blessed are the poor in spirit:
the kingdom of heaven is theirs.
Blessed are the gentle:
they shall have the earth as inheritance.
Blessed are those who mourn:
they shall be comforted.
Blessed are those who hunger and thirst for uprightness:
they shall have their fill.
Blessed are the merciful:
they shall have mercy shown them.
Blessed are the pure in heart:
they shall see God.
Blessed are the peacemakers:
they shall be recognised as children of God.
Blessed are those who are persecuted in the cause of uprightness:
the kingdom of Heaven is theirs.
How blessed are the poor in spirit:
the kingdom of Heaven is theirs.

Matthew 5:3–10

Sing Alleluia

How happy will be our shout of Alleluia, how carefree, how secure from any adversary, where there is no enemy, where no friend perishes. There praise is offered to God, and here, too, but here it is by men who are anxious, there by men who are free from care, here by men who must die, there by men who will live for ever. Here praise is offered in hope, there by men who enjoy the reality, here by men who are pilgrims on the way, there by men who have reached their own country.

So, brethren, now let us sing Alleluia, not in the enjoyment of heavenly rest, but to sweeten our toil. Sing as travellers sing along the road: but keep on walking. Solace your toil by singing – do not yield to idleness. Sing but keep on walking. What do I mean by 'walking'? I mean, press on from good to better. The apostle says there are some who go from bad to worse. But if you press on, you keep on walking. Go forward then in virtue, in true faith and right conduct. Sing up – and keep on walking.

St Augustine of Hippo (354–430)

Prayer of St Francis

Lord, make me an instrument of your peace.
Where there is hatred, let me sow love.
Where there is injury, pardon.
Where there is doubt, faith.
Where there is despair, hope.
Where there is darkness, light.
Where there is sadness, joy.
O Divine Master, grant that I may not
   so much seek
to be consoled, as to console;
to be understood, as to understand;
to be loved, as to love;
for it is in giving that we receive,
it is in pardoning that we are pardoned.
It is in dying that we are born to eternal life.

St Francis of Assisi (c. 1181–1226)

True and Perfect Joy [I]

Blessed Francis called Brother Leo and said: 'Brother Leo, write.' He responded: 'Look, I'm ready!' 'Write,' he said, 'what true joy is.'

'A messenger arrives and says that all the Masters of Paris have entered the Order. Write: this isn't true joy! Or, that all the prelates, archbishops and bishops beyond the mountains, as well as the King of France and the King of England [have entered the Order]. Write: this isn't true joy! Again, that my brothers have gone to the non-believers and converted all of them to the faith; again, that I have so much grace from God that I heal the sick and perform many miracles. I tell you true joy doesn't consist in any of these things.'

St Francis of Assisi (1181–1226)

True and Perfect Joy [II]

'Then what is true joy?'

'I return from Perugia and arrive here in the dead of night. It's winter time, muddy and so cold that icicles have formed on the edges of my habit and keep striking my legs and blood flows from such wounds. Freezing, covered with mud and ice, I come to the gate and, after I've knocked and called for some time, a brother comes and asks: 'Who are you?' 'Brother Francis,' I answer. 'Go away!' he says. 'This is not a decent hour to be wandering about! You may not come in!' When I insist, he replies: 'Go away! You are simple and stupid! Don't come back to us again! There are many of us here like you – we don't need you!' I stand again at the door and say: 'For the love of God, take me in tonight!' And he replies: 'I will not! Go to the Crosiers's place and ask there!'

'I tell you this: If I had patience and did not become upset, true joy, as well as true virtue and the salvation of my soul, would consist in this.'

St Francis of Assisi (1181–1226)

His Faithful Keeping

In life and in death keep close to Jesus and give yourself into his faithful keeping; he alone can help you when all others fail you. He is of such a kind, this beloved friend of yours, that he will not share your love with another; he wishes to have your heart for himself alone, to reign there like a king seated on his rightful throne. If only you knew the way to empty your heart of all things created! If you did, how gladly would Jesus come and make his home with you! When you put your trust in men, excluding Jesus, you will find that it is nearly all a complete loss. Have no faith in a reed that shakes in the wind, don't try leaning upon it; mortal things are but grass, remember, the glory of them is but grass in flower and will fall. Look only at a man's outward guise and you will quickly be led astray; look to others to console you and bring you benefit, and as often as not you will find you have suffered loss. If you look for Jesus in everything, you will certainly find him; but if it's yourself you're looking for, it's yourself you're going to find, and that to your own hurt, because a man is a greater bane to himself, if he doesn't look for Jesus, than the whole world is, or the whole host of his enemies.

Thomas à Kempis (c. 1380–1471)

Lead, Kindly Light

Lead, kindly Light, amid the encircling gloom,
Lead thou me on;
The night is dark, and I am far from home,
Lead thou me on.
Keep thou my feet; I do not ask to see
The distant scene; one step enough for me.

I was not ever thus, nor prayed that thou
Shouldst lead me on;
I loved to choose and see my path; but now
Lead thou me on.
I loved the garish day, and, spite of fears,
Pride ruled my will: remember not past years.

So long thy power hath blest me, sure it still
Will lead me on
O'er moor and fen, o'er crag and torrent, till
The night is gone,
And with the morn those Angel faces smile,
Which I have loved long since, and lost awhile.

Venerable John Henry Newman (1801–90)

Helping Hand

Mrs Chisholm is a lady who is not rich, or related to any great people; but she has been engaged nearly all her life in helping labouring and poor people, by teaching them how to help themselves; and she has succeeded so well, that there are thousands who look upon her with feelings of as much affection as if she were their mother. . . .

She has a husband, who has gone out to Australia lately to help her good work, and six children; from morning until late at night any man or woman, or young girl, no matter how humble, how poorly dressed, is welcome to come and consult her, and tell her their griefs. At breakfast, dinner, tea and supper, she is at the command of the unhappy and distressed; and when she is not talking, she is writing letters. For besides all those in England who consult her, hundreds and hundreds of people in Australia send to her to get their relations out to join them. Mrs Chisholm never asks what country or what religion anyone is who comes to her; but she just sets about to see the way of helping them to get out of their difficulties.

Caroline Chisholm (1808–77)

Hard to Love

We are not expecting utopia here on this earth. But God meant things to be much easier than we have made them. A man has a natural right to food, clothing and shelter. A certain amount of goods is necessary to lead a good life. A family needs work as well as bread. Property is proper to man. We must keep repeating these things. Eternal life begins now. 'All the way to heaven is heaven, because He said, "I am the Way."' The Cross is there of course, but 'in the Cross is joy of spirit.' And love makes all things easy. If we are putting off the old man and putting on Christ, then we are walking in love, and love is all that we want. But it is hard to love, from the human standpoint and from the divine standpoint, in a two-room apartment.

Dorothy Day (1897–1980)

Scottish Saints

'My frequent visits to Margaret Sinclair always impressed and uplifted me. She was very spiritual but she had a keen sense of humour, and up to the last she thoroughly enjoyed a good joke.'

[Hospital Chaplain]

Margaret's sense of humour never left her, even when facing death. One is reminded of her fellow-countryman, St John Ogilvie, Jesuit and martyr. When he was on his way to the scaffold in Glasgow in 1615 a Presbyterian minister, shocked at the apparent levity with which he was laughing with those around him, asked if he were not afraid to be so merry when he was so near his death. 'We have a proverb in Scotland,' replied the priest: 'It's past joking when the head's off!'

'One day,' says one of the Sisters, 'when Margaret was still able to be up for a little while with the other invalids, a new nun, by name Sister Clare, was brought in. Margaret glanced at her. "She is the only lady among you," she said calmly to the others. They were slightly astonished. "You are all Sister Bernard, or Sister John or Sister Columba," she explained, laughing.'

Venerable Margaret Sinclair (1900–25)

True Happiness

Do you want to know the secret of true happiness? Of deep and genuine peace? Do you want to solve at a blow all your difficulties in relations with your neighbour, bring all polemic to an end, avoid all dissension?

Well, decide here and now to love things and men as Jesus loved them, that is, to the point of self-sacrifice. Do not bother with the book-keeping of love; love without keeping accounts.

If you know someone who is decent and likeable, love him, but if someone else is very *un*likeable, love him just the same. If someone greets you and smiles, greet him and smile back, but if someone else treads on your feet, smile just the same. If someone does you a good turn, thank the Lord for it, but if someone else slanders you, persecutes you, curses you, strikes you, thank him and carry on.

Do not say: 'I'm right, he's wrong'. Say: 'I must love him as myself'. This is the kind of love Jesus taught: a love which transforms, vivifies, enriches, brings peace.

Carlo Carretto (1910–88)

Call Within a Call

At the beginning, between twelve and eighteen, I didn't want to become a nun. We were a very happy family. But when I was eighteen, I decided to leave my home and become a nun. I wanted to be a missionary, I wanted to go out and give the life of Christ to the people in the missionary countries. At that time some missionaries had gone to India from Yugoslavia. They told me the Loreto nuns were doing work in Calcutta and other places. I offered myself to go out to the Bengal Mission, and they sent me to India in 1929.

I took the first vows in Loreto in 1931. Then in 1937 I took final vows in Loreto. At Loreto I was in charge of a school in the Bengali department. At that time many of the girls that are now with me were girls in school. I was teaching them.

In 1946 I was going to Darjeeling, to make my retreat. It was in that train, I heard the call to give up all and follow Jesus into the slums to serve Him among the poorest of the poor. I knew it was His will, and that I had to follow Him. There was no doubt that it was going to be His work.

Mother Teresa of Calcutta (1910–97)

GROWING AND
SERVING

Ministry

'All authority in heaven and on earth has been given to me. Go, therefore, make disciples of all nations; baptise them in the name of the Father and of the Son and of the Holy Spirit, and teach them to observe all the commands I gave you. And look, I am with you always; yes, to the end of time.'

Matthew 28:18–20

Send the Remedy

O Godhead,
my love,
I have one thing to ask of you.
When the world was lying sick
you sent your only-begotten Son as doctor,
and I know you did it for love.
But now I see the world lying completely dead –
so dead that my soul faints at the sight.
What way can there be now
to revive this dead one once more?
For you, God, cannot suffer,
and you are not about to come again
to redeem the world but to judge it.
How then
shall this dead one be brought back to life?
I do not believe, O infinite goodness,
that you have no remedy.
Indeed, I proclaim it:
your love is not wanting,
nor is your power weakened,
nor is your wisdom lessened.
So you want to, you can,
and you know how to
send the remedy that is needed.
I beg you then,
let it please your goodness
to show me the remedy,
and let my soul be roused to pick it up courageously.

St Catherine of Siena (c. 1347–80)

Spiritual Mothers

Mothers of families, even if they had a thousand sons and daughters, would still find room for every single one in their hearts, because that is how true love works. It even seems that the more children a mother has, the greater is her love and care for each one individually. With still more reason spiritual mothers can and should so act, since spiritual love is beyond comparison more powerful than human love.

Therefore, dearest Mothers, if you love these dear children of yours with true and selfless charity, it will be impossible for you not to have them all clearly present in your memory and in your heart.

I ask you, please, do try to bring them up with love, with a gentle and kindly hand, not overbearingly nor harshly. Try to be kind always. Notice what Jesus Christ says, 'Learn of me for I am gentle and humble of heart.' And of God we read, 'He orders all things graciously.' That is, he arranges and governs all things gently. And again Jesus Christ says, 'My yoke, my service, is light and sweet.'

That is how you yourselves must try to act, using all possible gentleness. And above all, be careful not to use force, because God has given free will to everybody and wants to force nobody, but only points out, invites and counsels. I do not mean, however, that at times one must not make use of some restraint, even of severity in some cases, depending on the importance of the circumstances and the need of the individuals. But even then, we must be moved solely by charity and zeal for souls.

St Angela Merici (c. 1474–1540)

From Village to Village

We went through the villages of the new converts who received baptism a few years ago. No Portuguese lives in these parts [of India], which are utterly barren and poverty-stricken. The native Christians are without any priest. The only thing they know about Christianity is that they are Christians. There is no one to offer Mass for them; no one to teach them the Creed, the Our Father, the Hail Mary, the commandments.

So, since I came here, I have had no rest. I have been going from village to village and every child not yet baptized I have baptized. So I have brought redemption to a very great number of children who, as the saying goes, cannot tell their right hand from their left. But the children would not let me say my office or eat or rest till I had taught them some prayer. It was then that I really began to feel that of such is the kingdom of heaven.

I could not reject so religious a request without myself being irreligious. I made a start with the sign of the cross, and taught them the Apostles' Creed, the Our Father and the Hail Mary. I saw immediately that they were very intelligent. If only there were someone to train them in the principles of Christianity, I am sure that they would be extremely good Christians.

St Francis Xavier (1506–52)

More Learning Than Love

Very many out here fail to become Christians simply because there is nobody available to make them Christian. I have very often had the notion to go round the universities of Europe, and especially Paris, and to shout aloud everywhere like a madman, and to bludgeon those people who have more learning than love, with these words, 'Alas, what an immense number of souls are excluded from heaven through your fault and thrust down to hell!'

If only those people devoted themselves to this care in the way they do to literature. Then they would be able to render God an account of their doctrine and of the talents entrusted to them!

Many of them, moved by this thought, and helped by meditation on the things of God, would take pains to hear what the Lord is speaking in them and, putting aside their own selfish desires and worldly matters, would put themselves fully at God's beck and call. They would indeed cry from their soul: 'Lord, here I am. What would you have me do? Send me wherever you wish, even as far as India.'

St Francis Xavier (1506–52)

Freedom to Captives [I]

Yesterday, 30 May 1627, the feast of the Most Holy Trinity, a great number of black people who had been seized from along the African rivers were put ashore [in Colombia] from one very large vessel. We hurried out with two baskets full of oranges, lemons, sweet biscuits and all sorts of other things. When we reached their huts it was like entering another Guinea. We had to force our way through the crowds till we reached the sick. There was a great number of them, lying on the damp earth, or rather in mud; but someone had formed the idea of making a heap of tiles and broken bricks in case the damp should be too much for them. This was all they had for a bed, all the more uncomfortable because they were naked without any covering at all.

We took off our cloaks, went to a store, brought from there all the wood that was available and put it together to make a platform; then, forcing a way through the guards, we eventually managed to carry all the sick on to it. Then we separated them into two groups; one of them my companion addressed with the aid of an interpreter, the other I spoke to myself.

Two of the black slaves were more dead than alive; they were already cold, and we could hardly feel any pulse in their veins. We got together some glowing embers on a tile, placed the dying men near them, and then threw aromatic spices on the fire. We had two bags of these spices, and used them all. Then with the help of our cloaks – for the slaves have none of their own, and it would have been a waste of time to ask their masters – we got them to inhale the vapours, which seemed to restore their warmth and vitality. You should have seen the expression of gratitude in their eyes!

St Peter Claver (1581–1654)

Freedom to Captives [II]

In this way we spoke to them, not with words but with deeds; and for people in their situation who were convinced that they had been brought there to be eaten, any other form of address would have been pointless. Then we sat or knelt beside them and washed their faces and bodies with wine; by such acts of kindness we tried to cheer them up, and performed for them all the natural services which are calculated to raise the spirits of the sick.

Then we began to instruct them for baptism. We first explained to them the wonderful effects of the sacrament on both body and soul, and when they showed by their answers to our questions that they understood us sufficiently well, we began to teach them at greater length concerning the one God who rewards and punishes each according to his deserts, and so on. We urged them to repent and give some indication of sorrow for their sins. Finally, when they seemed to be sufficiently prepared, we explained to them the mysteries of the Trinity, Incarnation and Passion. We showed them a representation of Christ crucified above a baptismal font, into which the blood flowed from his wounds. Then we taught them to repeat after us the act of contrition in their own language.

St Peter Claver (1581–1654)

Children Evangelise Children

Nano Nagle of Cork was well aware of the status God gave to the poor. What was done to the least of them was done to Him. Each one of them was made in the image of God and made out of love. Personal dignity, personal worth depended on that love. This was the essence of religion and the essence of Nano's educational system. Her pupils were not only well instructed in the Faith but were so brought up to love instructing others. Herein was the secret of her success; her pupils were convinced that they had good news to tell.

'All my children are brought up to be fond of instructing, as I think it lies in the power of the poor to be of more service that way than the rich.'

A notable point about Nano was that she addressed herself to those who could not read at all. For an illiterate people, the spoken word was very important.

She elicited a promise from those emigrating from Ireland to the West Indies that they 'would take great pains with the little blacks to instruct them'. Pictures were at once visual aids and little gifts for the native West Indians, miniatures of the Good News and ready access to the Gospel story. The Irish victims of injustice brought the good news of Jesus Christ to those more abject still. Children evangelised children.

Nano Nagle (1718–84)

Constant Prayer

St Jean Vianney was sure that 'a good priest must be devoted to constant prayer. . . .

'The thing that keeps us priests from gaining sanctity is thoughtlessness. It annoys us to turn our minds away from external affairs; we do not know what we really ought to do. What we need is deep reflection, together with prayer and an intimate union with God.

'We are beggars who must ask God for everything . . . How many people we can call back to God by our prayers.' And he used to say over and over again: 'Ardent prayer addressed to God: this is our greatest happiness on earth.'

And he enjoyed this happiness abundantly when his mind rose with the help of heavenly light to contemplate the things of heaven, and his pure and simple soul rose with all its deepest love from the mystery of the incarnation to the Heights of the Holy Trinity. The crowds of pilgrims who surrounded him in the church could feel something coming forth from the depths of the inner life of this humble priest when words like these burst forth from his inflamed breast, as they often did: 'To be loved by God, to be joined to God, to walk before God, to live for God, O blessed life, O blessed death.'

St Jean Vianney, the Curé d'Ars (1786–1859)

A True Father [I]

If we want to be thought of as men who have the real happiness of our pupils at heart and who help each to fulfil his role in life, you must never forget that you are taking the place of parents who love their children. I have always worked, studied, and exercised my priesthood out of love for them. And not I alone, but the whole Salesian Order.

My sons, how often in my long career has this great truth come home to me! It is so much easier to get angry than to be patient, to threaten a boy rather than persuade him. I would even say that usually it is so much more convenient for our own impatience and pride to punish them than to correct them patiently with firmness and gentleness.

I recommend to you the love Saint Paul had for his new converts. When he found them inattentive and unresponsive to his love, that same love led him to tears and prayers.

Be careful not to give anyone reason to think that you act under the impulse of anger. It is difficult to keep calm when administering punishment. But it is very necessary if you are not to give the impression that you are simply asserting your authority or giving vent to your anger.

St John Bosco (1815–88)

A True Father [II]

Let us look on those over whom we have a certain authority, as sons. Let us be determined to be at their service, even as Jesus came to obey, and not to command. We should be ashamed to give the least impression of domineering. We should only exercise authority in order the better to serve the boys.

That was how Jesus treated his apostles. He put up with their ignorance and dullness and their lack of faith. His attitude towards sinners was full of kindness and loving friendship. This astonished some and scandalized others, but to others it gave enough hope to ask forgiveness from God.

Because the boys are our sons, we must put aside all anger when we correct their faults, or at least restrain it so much that it is almost completely suppressed. There must be no angry outburst, no look of contempt, no hurtful words. Instead, like true fathers, really intent on their correction and improvement, show them compassion at the present moment and hold out hope for the future.

In serious matters it is better to ask God's help in humble prayer, than to make a long speech that wounds those who hear it and does no good at all to the guilty ones.

St John Bosco (1815–88)

St Anthony's Pigs

Here [New Orleans] I have invented a way to collect a little more money to enlarge the orphanage. I took the money-box shaped like a little pig, which they call Saint Anthony's pigs here, and the people compete to see who is able to fatten it, that is fill it up with nickles. In three days the sisters gave out 150 and I want them to give out a thousand. There are various sizes, the smallest, which we give to the more trustworthy schoolchildren, can hold $5, others $10, others $20. Can you imagine what a fine collection? You should do the same thing right away, and if you don't find the pig, take another form, but do it immediately for the month of Saint Anthony. For the close of the month the money-boxes will all be full at the altar of the saint. . . . Set your wits to work!

St Frances Cabrini (1850–1917)

The Legion of Mary

Confer, O Lord, on us,
Who serve beneath the standard of Mary,
That fullness of faith in you and trust in her,
To which it is given to conquer the world.
Grant us a lively faith, animated by charity,
Which will enable us to perform all our actions
From the motive of pure love of you,
And ever to see you and serve you in our neighbour;
A faith, firm and immovable as a rock,
Through which we shall rest tranquil and steadfast
Amid the crosses, toils and disappointments of life;
A courageous faith which will inspire us
To undertake and carry out without hesitation
Great things for your glory and for the salvation of souls;
A faith which will be our Legion's Pillar of Fire –
To lead us forth united –
To kindle everywhere the fires of divine love –
To enlighten those who are in darkness and in the shadow
    of death –
To inflame those who are lukewarm –
To bring back life to those who are dead in sin;
And which will guide our own feet in the way
    of peace;
So that – the battle of life over –
Our Legion may reassemble,
Without the loss of any one,
In the kingdom of your love and glory.

Frank Duff (1889–1980)

Unworthy Poor

God is on the side even of the unworthy poor, as we know from the story Jesus told of His Father and the prodigal son. Readers may object that the prodigal son returned penitent to his father's house. But who knows, he might have gone out and squandered money on the next Saturday night; he might have refused to help with the farm work, and asked to be sent to finish his education instead, thereby further incurring his brother's righteous wrath, and the war between the worker and the intellectual, or the conservative and the radical, would be on. Jesus has another answer to that one: to forgive one's brother seventy times seven. There are always answers, although they are not always calculated to soothe.

Dorothy Day (1897–1980)

The Face of Jesus

Today I baptized thirty adults and children. And not only from here; for the Christians make their way through the mountains from Miyahara, Kuzushima and Haratsuka. I then heard more than fifty confessions. After Sunday Mass for the first time I intoned and recited the prayers in Japanese with the people. The peasants stare at me, their eyes alive with curiosity. And as I speak there often arises in my mind the face of one who preached the Sermon on the Mount; and I imagine the people who sat or knelt fascinated by his words. As for me, perhaps I am so fascinated by his face because the Scriptures make no mention of it. Precisely because it is not mentioned, all its details are left to my imagination. From childhood I have clasped that face to my breast just like the person who romantically idealizes the countenance of one he loves. While I was still a student, studying in the seminary, if ever I had a sleepless night, his beautiful face would rise up in my heart.

Shusako Endo (1923–96)

Spiritual Guidance

Peter turned and saw the disciple whom Jesus loved following them – the one who had leant back close to his chest at the supper and had said to him, 'Lord, who is it that will betray you?' Seeing him, Peter said to Jesus, 'What about him, Lord?' Jesus answered, 'If I want him to stay behind till I come, what does it matter to you? You are to follow me.'

John 21:20–2

Old and New

First drink from the Old Testament, so that you may drink from the New as well. You cannot drink from the second without drinking from the first. Drink from the Old Testament to slake your thirst, and from the New to quench it completely. Compunction is found in the Old Testament, joy in the New.

Drink Christ because he is the vine; drink Christ because he is the rock that poured out water. Drink Christ because he is the fountain of life; drink Christ because he is the river whose running waters give joy to the city of God, and because he is peace, and because out of his heart will flow rivers of living water. Drink Christ to drink the blood which redeemed you; drink Christ to drink his words: The Old Testament is his word; the New Testament is his word. Holy scripture is drunk and swallowed when the power of the eternal Word penetrates the depths of the mind and the virtue of the soul. In short, we do not live by bread alone, but by every word of God. Drink this word, but according to its own order. Drink it first in the Old Testament; then hasten to drink it also in the New.

St Ambrose of Milan (c. 339–97)

Of Calling the Brethren to Council

As often as any important business has to be done in the monastery, let the abbot call together the whole community and himself set forth the matter. And, having heard the advice of the brethren, let him take counsel with himself and then do what he shall judge to be most expedient. Now the reason why we have said that all should be called to council, is that God often reveals what is better to the younger. Let the brethren give their advice with all deference and humility, nor venture to defend their opinions obstinately; but let the decision depend rather on the abbot's judgement, so that when he has decided what is the better course, all may obey. However, just as it is proper for disciples to obey their master, so is it becoming that he on his part should dispose all things with prudence and justice.

St Benedict of Nursia (c. 480–c. 550)

Loved not Feared

Let [the abbot] study rather to be loved than feared. Let him not be turbulent or anxious, overbearing or obstinate, jealous or too suspicious, for otherwise he will never be at rest. Let him be prudent and considerate in all his commands; and whether the work which he enjoins concern God or the world, let him always be discreet and moderate, bearing in mind the discretion of holy Jacob, who said: If I cause my flocks to be overdriven, they will all perish in one day. So, imitating these and other examples of discretion, the mother of the virtues, let him so temper all things that the strong may still have something to long after, and the weak may not draw back in alarm. And, especially, let him keep this present Rule in all things; so that having ministered faithfully he may hear from the Lord what the good servant heard who gave his fellow-servants wheat in due season: Amen, I say unto you, he will set him over all his goods.

St Benedict of Nursia (c. 480–c. 550)

Love the Lord

Be compassionate towards the poor, the destitute and the afflicted; and, as far as lies in your power, help and console them. Give thanks to God for all the gifts he has bestowed upon you, so that you will become worthy of still greater gifts. Towards your subjects, act with such justice that you may steer a middle course, swerving neither to the right nor to the left, but lean more to the side of the poor man than of the rich until such time as you are certain about the truth. Do your utmost to ensure peace and justice for all your subjects but especially for clergy and religious.

Devotedly obey our mother, the Roman Church, and revere the Supreme Pontiff as your spiritual father. Endeavour to banish all sin, especially blasphemy and heresy, from your kingdom.

Finally, my dear son, I impart to you every blessing that a loving father can bestow on his son; may the Father, Son and Holy Spirit, and all the saints, guard you from all evil. May the Lord grant you the grace to do his will so that he may be served and honoured by you, and that, together, after this life we may come to see him, love him and praise him for ever.

St Louis of France (1214–70)

The Hidden God

If you want to be without sin and perfect, don't chatter about God. Nor should you (seek to) understand anything about God, for God is above all understanding. One master says: 'If I had a God I could understand, I would no longer consider him God'. So, if you understand anything of Him, that is not He, and by understanding anything of Him you fall into misunderstanding, and from this misunderstanding you fall into brutishness, for whatever in creatures is uncomprehending is brutish. So, if you don't want to become brutish, understand nothing of God the unutterable.

꒰꒱

Indeed, if a man thinks he will get more of God by meditation, by devotion, by ecstasies or by special infusion of grace than by the fireside or in the stable that is nothing but taking God, wrapping a cloak around His head and shoving Him under a bench. For whoever seeks God in a special way gets the way and misses God, who lies hidden in it. But whoever seeks God without any special way gets Him as He is in Himself, and that man lives with the Son, and he is life itself.

Meister Eckhart (c. 1260–c. 1328)

True Guidance

'Those who guide souls should realise that the principal agent and guide and motive force in this matter is not them, but *the Holy Spirit, who never fails in his care* for people; they are only instruments to guide people to perfection by faith and the law of God, according to the spirit *that God is giving* to the individual person.'

⁂

There are three tests to ascertain whether dryness in prayer is the result of God's purgation or of our own sins.

The first is when we find no comfort either in the things of God or in created things. For when God brings the soul into the dark night in order to wean it from sweetness and to purify its sensual desires, he does not allow it to find sweetness or comfort anywhere.

The second is that the memory is ordinarily centred on God with painful anxiety and carefulness. The spirit becomes strong, more vigilant and more careful lest there be any negligence in serving God.

The third sign is inability to meditate or make reflections, and to excite the imagination as before, despite all the efforts we may make. For God now begins to communicate himself, no longer through the channels of sense as formerly, but in pure spirit.

St John of the Cross (1542–91)

Daily Duty

Let not a day pass without employing at least one quarter of an hour in reading some spiritual book; and a more considerable time on Sundays and holidays; advise with your director what books may be most proper, and endeavour to procure them for yourself and your family. . . . As you are praying, you are speaking to God, so when you are reading or hearing his word, he is speaking to you. As then you desire he should hear you when you speak to him; so take you care to hearken faithfully to him when he speaks to you.

Richard Challoner (1691–1781)

❈

All goes well when God is, so to speak, both the author and the object of our faith, the one complementing and augmenting the other. It is like the right side of a beautiful tapestry being worked stitch by stitch on the reverse side. Neither the stitches nor the needle are visible, but, one by one, those stitches make a magnificent pattern that only becomes apparent when the work is completed and the right side exposed to the light of day; although while it is in progress there is no sign of its beauty and wonder.

The same applies to self-surrendered souls who see only God and their duty. The accomplishment of that duty is at each moment one imperceptible stitch added to the tapestry. And yet it is with these stitches that God performs wonders of which one occasionally has a presentiment at the time, but which will not be fully known until the great day of judgement.

Jean-Pierre de Caussade (1675–1751)

Pray As You Can

... Prayer, in the sense of union with God, is the most crucifying thing there is. One must do it for God's sake; but one will not get any satisfaction out of it, in the sense of feeling 'I am good at prayer', 'I have an infallible method'. That would be disastrous, since what we want to learn is precisely our own weakness, powerlessness, unworthiness. Nor ought one to expect 'a sense of the reality of the supernatural' of which you speak. And one should wish for no prayer, except precisely the prayer that God gives us – probably very distracted and unsatisfactory in every way!

On the other hand, the only way to pray is to pray; and the way to pray well is to pray much. If one has no time for this, then one must at least pray regularly. But the less one prays, the worse it goes. And if circumstances do not permit even regularity, then one must put up with the fact that when one does try to pray, one can't pray – and our prayer will probably consist of telling this to God.

✶✶

The rule is simply: – *Pray as you can, and do not try to pray as you can't.*
Take yourself as you find yourself, and start from that.

John Chapman (1865–1933)

Trust in God

When the soul grieves and is afraid of offending God, it does not offend Him and is very far from committing sin. Divine grace is with you continually and you are very dear to the Lord. Shadows and fears and convictions to the contrary are diabolical stratagems which you should despise in the name of Jesus. Do not listen to these temptations. The spirit of evil is busily engaged in trying to make you believe that your past life has been all strewn with sins.

Listen, rather, to me when I tell you, just as we are told by the Spouse of our souls, that your present state is an effect of your love for God and a proof of his incomparable love for you. Cast away those fears, dispel those shadows which the devil is increasing in your soul in order to torment you and drive you away, if possible, even from daily Communion. . . .

Never fall back on yourself alone, but place all your trust in God and don't be too eager to be set free from your present state. Let the Holy Spirit act within you. Give yourself up to all his transports and have no fear. He is so wise and gentle and discreet that He never brings about anything but good. How good this Holy Spirit, this Comforter, is to all, but how supremely good He is to those who seek Him!

Blessed Padre Pio (1887–1968)

Into Thy Hands

Lately I learnt something which made me understand as never before the beauty of the habit of prayer. A Jew was telling me that he so wished in these days [during the 1939–45 war] that he had faith; he was building a sandbag wall and foolishly I had dropped my crucifix into it; he insisted on undoing his wall and getting it for me. He was a stranger, and I did not know him; he was standing holding my crucifix, looking at it with a puzzled wistfulness. 'Of course,' he said, 'I'm a Jew, my mother was a good Jewess, I never learnt nothing about Christ, we don't bother to, but I did learn to say my prayers day and night, and I wish I 'ad kept it up.'

'What did you say?' I asked.

'Well, the morning ones was long, but the night was short; all us little Jew kids said it as we fell asleep.'

'What was it?'

'Well, Miss, it went like this: "Father, into Thy hands I commend my spirit." It's what mothers teached little Jewish boys ever since the world began, they do say. They tells 'em to say it just before they falls asleep.'

Caryll Houselander (1901–54)

God Gives Us Everything

Prayer is the most difficult thing in the world for human beings. To pray is to remain face to face with the Invisible. Prayer is said to be the lifting of the soul to God. That is very hard for us because we need sensible and visible objects; hence we are always on the lookout for pretexts to diminish the place of prayer in our life.

❧❧

The subject matter of prayer is of little importance; what matters above all is the degree of our love. We must realize that if, in terms of love, God gives us everything, he often gives us little in terms of light. The domain of knowledge here below is always limited; only in heaven, in the beatific vision, will knowledge be complete.

❧❧

We must always let the Holy Spirit do as he pleases with us. Nevertheless, seeing how important Mary is, we have the right to ask our Lord – if we have understood these things – to give us a deeper understanding of this mystery, to lead us into that intimacy with Mary which he himself had, and to let us experience a little of the trust he had in her.

Thomas Philippe (1905–93)

A Burden to Others

In order to face suffering in peace: suffer without imposing on others a theory of suffering . . . without proclaiming yourself a martyr, without counting out the price of your courage, without disdaining sympathy and without seeking too much of it.

We must be sincere in our sufferings as in anything else. We must recognize at once our weakness and our pain, but we do not need to advertise them. We must face the fact that it is much harder to stand the long monotony of slight suffering than a passing onslaught of intense pain.

In either case, what is hard is our own poverty, and the spectacle of our own selves reduced more and more to nothing, wasting away in our own estimation and in that of our friends. We must be willing to accept also the bitter truth that, in the end, we may have to become a burden to those who love us.

But it is necessary that we face this also. It takes heroic charity and humility to let others sustain us when we are absolutely incapable of sustaining ourselves.

We cannot suffer well unless we see Christ everywhere – both in suffering and in the charity of those who come to the aid of our affliction.

Thomas Merton (1915–68)

Spiritual Friendship

No one can have greater love
than to lay down his life for his friends.
You are my friends,
if you do what I command you.
I shall no longer call you servants,
because a servant does not know
his master's business;
I call you friends,
because I have made known to you
everything I have learnt from my Father.
You did not choose me,
no, I chose you;
and I commissioned you
to go out and to bear fruit,
fruit that will last;
so that the Father will give you
anything you ask him in my name.

John 15:13–16

My Friend Basil

Not only did I myself hold my friend, the great Basil, in high regard for his seriousness of character and the maturity and prudence of his discourse, but I also persuaded other young men who did not know him to share my sentiments. For he was already respected by many of them since his renown had preceded him. . . .

We seemed to have a single soul animating two bodies. And, while those who claim that all things are in all things are not readily to be believed, we, at least, had to believe that we were in and with each other.

The sole ambition of both of us was virtue and a life so led in view of future hopes, as to sever our attachment to this life before we had to depart it.

With this in view we directed our life and actions, following the guidance of the divine precept, and at the same time spurring each other to virtue. And, if it is not too much to say it, we were for each other a rule and a scales for the discernment of good and evil.

Different men have different names, derived from their ancestors or their own pursuits and deeds. Our great concern, our great name, was to be Christians and be called Christians.

St Gregory of Nazianzus (c. 329–c. 390)

Scholastica and Benedict [I]

Saint Benedict's sister, Scholastica, who had been consecrated to almighty God in early childhood, used to visit her brother once a year. On these occasions he would go down to meet her in a house belonging to the monastery, a short distance from the entrance.

For this particular visit he joined her there with a few of his disciples and they spent the whole day singing God's praises and conversing about the spiritual life. When darkness was setting in, they took their meal together and continued their conversation at table until it was quite late. Then the holy nun said to him, 'Please do not leave me tonight; let us keep on talking about the joys of heaven till morning.'

'What are you saying, sister?' he replied. 'You know I cannot stay away from the monastery.'

At her brother's refusal, Scholastica folded her hands on the table and rested her head upon them in earnest prayer. When she looked up again, there was a sudden burst of lightning and thunder, accompanied by such a downpour that Benedict and his companions were unable to set foot outside the door.

St Scholastica (c. 480–c. 543)

Scholastica and Benedict [II]

Realizing that he could not return to the monastery in this terrible storm, Benedict complained bitterly. 'God forgive you, sister', he said. 'What have you done?'

Scholastica simply answered, 'When I appealed to you, you would not listen to me. So I turned to my God and he heard my prayer. Leave now if you can. Leave me here and go back to your monastery.'

This, of course, he could not do. He had no choice now but to stay, in spite of his unwillingness. They spent the entire night together and both of them derived great profit from the holy converse they had about the interior life.

We need not be surprised that in this instance the woman proved mightier than her brother. Do we not read in Saint John that God is love? Surely it is no more than right that her influence was greater than his, since hers was the greater love.

Three days later as he stood in his room looking up toward the sky, the man of God beheld his sister's soul leaving her body and entering the court of heaven in the form of a dove.

Overjoyed at her eternal glory, he gave thanks to almighty God in hymns of praise. Then, he sent some of his brethren to bring her body to the monastery and bury it in the tomb he had prepared for himself. The bodies of these two were now to share a common resting place just as in life their souls had always been one in God.

St Scholastica (c. 480–c. 543)

To Dom Gondulph

Whenever I make up my mind to write to you, soul most beloved of my soul, whenever I make up my mind to write, I feel puzzled to know how best to begin. My feeling towards you is indeed sweetness and song to my heart, and I wish you the greatest blessings my mind can devise. From the moment I laid eyes on you, you know how deeply I loved you; I hear reports of you that make me long after you, God alone knows to what extent; and so wherever you wander my affection follows you, and wherever I remain, my desire encircles you. But when you beg me by your messengers, urge me by your letters, importune me by your gifts to keep you in remembrance, then *let my tongue stick fast to the roof of my mouth if I remember thee not* (Ps. 136.6), if I find in anyone but Gondulph the very perfection of friendship. How should I ever forget you? How could he perish from memory who is impressed upon my heart as a seal on wax?

Now tell me: why do you complain with such a mournful face that you never receive a line from me? Why do you ask with such affection that I should write frequently, when you have me always with you in thought? When you keep silence, I realize that *you love me*; and when I make no sign, *surely thou knowest that I love thee* (John 21.16)? You are constantly present in my mind because I never for a moment doubt you, and I hereby swear to you that you can feel equally certain of me.

St Anselm of Canterbury (c. 1033–1109)

The Best Medicine

What happiness, what security, what joy to have someone to whom you dare to speak on terms of equality as to another self; one to whom you need have no fear to confess your failings; one to whom you can unblushingly make known what progress you have made in the spiritual life; one to whom you can entrust all the secrets of your heart and before whom you can place all your plans! What, therefore, is more pleasant than so to unite to oneself the spirit of another and of two to form one, that no boasting is thereafter to be feared, no suspicion to be dreaded, no correction of one by the other to cause pain, no praise on the part of one to bring a charge of adulation from the other. 'A friend,' says the Wise Man, 'is the medicine of life.' Excellent, indeed, is that saying. For medicine is not more powerful or more efficacious for our wounds in all our temporal needs than the possession of a friend who meets every misfortune joyfully, so that, as the Apostle says, shoulder to shoulder, they bear one another's burdens. Even more – each one carries his own injuries even more lightly than that of his friend. Friendship, therefore, heightens the joys of prosperity and mitigates the sorrows of adversity by dividing and sharing them. Hence, the best medicine in life is a friend.

St Aelred of Rievaulx (1109–67)

To Blessed Diana d'Andalò

Beloved, since I cannot see you with my bodily eyes nor be consoled with your presence as often as you would wish and I would wish, it is at least some refreshment to me, some appeasement of my heart's longing, when I can visit you by means of my letters and tell you how things are with me, just as I long to know how things are with you, for your progress and your gaiety of heart are a sweet nourishment to my soul – though you for your part do not know to what ends of the earth I may be journeying and even if you knew you would not have messengers to hand by whom you could send something to me. Yet whatever we may write to each other matters little, beloved: within our hearts is the ardour of our love in the Lord whereby you speak to me and I to you continuously in those wordless outpourings of charity which no tongue can express nor letter contain.

O Diana, how unhappy this present condition of things which we must suffer: that we cannot love each other without pain and anxiety! You weep and are in bitter grief because it is not given you to see me continually; and I equally grieve that it is so rarely given me to be with you. . . .

These things we must bear with patience . . ., for with what measure our trials are meted to us, so shall be measured our joy, poured out on us by God's Son Jesus Christ, to whom is honour and glory and strength and empire for ever and ever.

Blessed Jordan of Saxony (c. 1190–1237)

To His Daughter

'Mistrust him, Meg, will I not, though I feel me faint. Yea, and though I should feel my fear even at point to overthrow me too, yet shall I remember how Saint Peter with a blast of a wind began to sink for his faint faith, and shall do as he did, call upon Christ and pray him to help. And then I trust he shall set his holy hand unto me, and in the stormy seas hold me up from drowning. Yea, and if he suffer me to play Saint Peter further, and to fall full to the ground, and swear and forswear too (which our Lord for his tender passion keep me from, and let me lose if it so fall, and never win thereby): yet after shall I trust that his goodness will cast upon me his tender piteous eye, as he did upon Saint Peter, and make me stand up again, and confess the truth of my conscience afresh, and abide the shame and the harm here of mine own fault. And finally, Marget, this wot I very well, that without my fault he will not let me be lost . . . And therefore, mine own good daughter, never trouble thy mind, for any thing that ever shall hap me in this world. Nothing can come, but that that God will . . . And if anything hap me that you would be loth, pray to God for me, but trouble not yourself: as I shall full heartily pray for us all, that we may meet together once in heaven, where we shall make merry for ever, and never have trouble after.'

St Thomas More (1478–1535)

To St Jane Frances de Chantal

In order to cut short all the rebuttals which may be taking shape in your mind, I must tell you that I have never understood that there was any bond between us carrying with it any obligation but that of charity and true Christian friendship, what St. Paul calls 'the bond of perfection'; and truly, that is just what it is, for it is indissoluble and never weakens. All other bonds are temporal, even that of a vow of obedience which can be broken through death or other circumstances; but the bond of love grows and gets ever stronger with time. It cannot be cut down by death, which, like a scythe, mows down everything but charity. 'Love is strong as death and firm as hell,' says Solomon. So there, dear sister (allow me to call you by this name, which is the one used by the apostles and the first Christians to express the intimate love they had for one another), this is our bond, these are our chains which, the more they are tightened and press against us, the more they bring us joy and freedom. Their strength is gentleness; their violence, mildness; nothing is more pliable than that; nothing, stronger. Think of me as very closely bound to you, and don't try to understand more about it than that this bond is not opposed to any other bond either of a vow or of marriage. Be totally at peace on that score. Obey your first director freely, and call on me in charity and sincerity.

St Francis de Sales (1567–1622)

To Katharine Asquith

The Faith, the Catholic Church, is discovered, is recognised, triumphantly enters reality like a landfall at sea which at first was thought a cloud. The nearer it is seen, the more is it real, the less imaginary: the more direct and external its voice, the more indubitable its representative character, its 'persona', its voice. The metaphor is not that men fall in love with it: the metaphor is that they discover home. 'This was what I sought. This was my need.' It is the very mould of the mind, the matrix to which corresponds in every outline the outcast and unprotected contour of the soul. It is Verlaine's 'Oh! Rome – oh! Mère!' And that not only to those who had it in childhood and have returned, but much more – and what a proof! – to those who come upon it from over the hills of life and say to themselves 'Here is the town.'

Hilaire Belloc (1870–1953)

To Maurice Bellière

I completely agree with you that 'the heart of God is saddened more by the thousand little indelicacies of His friends than it is by the faults, even the grave ones, which people of the world commit.' But my dear little brother, it seems to me that it is only when his friends, ignoring their continual indelicacies, make a habit out of them and don't ask forgiveness for them, that Jesus can utter those touching words which the Church puts on his lips in Holy Week: 'These wounds you see in the palms of my hands are the ones I received in the house of those who loved me.' For those who love Him, and after each fault come to ask pardon by throwing themselves into His arms, Jesus trembles with joy. He says to His angels what the father of the prodigal son said to his servants: 'Put his best robe on him and put a ring on his finger, and let us rejoice.' Ah! my brother, how the goodness of Jesus, His merciful love, are so little known! It is true that to enjoy these riches we must be humbled and recognize our nothing-ness, and that is what so many are not willing to do. But my little brother, that is not the way you behave, so the way of simple love and confidence is just made to order for you.

St Thérèse of Lisieux (1873–97)

Letter to Jesus

Dear Jesus,

I have been criticized. 'He's a bishop, he's a cardinal', people have said, 'he's been writing letters to all kinds of people: to Mark Twain, to Péguy, and heaven knows how many others. And not a line to Jesus Christ!'

Here is my letter. I write it trembling, feeling like a poor deaf mute trying to make himself understood . . .

When you said: 'Blessed are the poor, blessed are the persecuted', I wasn't with you. If I had been, I'd have whispered into your ear: 'For heaven's sake, Lord, change the subject, if you want to keep any followers at all. Don't you know that everyone wants riches and comfort? Cato promised his soldiers the figs of Africa, Caesar promised his the riches of Gaul, and, for better or worse, the soldiers followed them. But you're promising poverty and persecution. Who do you think's going to follow you?' You went ahead unafraid, and I can hear you saying you were the grain of wheat that must die before it bears fruit; and that you must be raised upon a cross and from there draw the whole world up to you.

Today, this has happened: they raised you up on a cross. You took advantage of that to hold out your arms and draw people up to you. And countless people have come to the foot of the cross, to fling themselves into your arms.

Pope John Paul I (1912–78)

DYING WE
LIVE

In Weakness Strength

He withdrew from them, about a stone's throw away, and knelt down and prayed. 'Father,' he said, 'if you are willing, take this cup away from me. Nevertheless, let your will be done, not mine.' Then an angel appeared to him, coming from heaven to give him strength. In his anguish he prayed even more earnestly, and his sweat fell to the ground like great drops of blood.

Luke 22:41–4

The Joyful Giver

It is not enough to help the poor. We must help them with generosity and without grumbling.

And it is not enough to help them without grumbling. We must help them gladly and happily.

When the poor are helped there ought to be these two conditions: generosity and joy.

Why do you complain of giving something to the poor? Why do you display bad temper in the practice of almsgiving? If they see you in that frame of mind, the poor would prefer to refuse your gift. If you give with a brusque demeanour, you are not being generous but lacking gentleness and courtesy. If your face reveals a feeling of hostility, you cannot bring comfort to your brother or sister who is living in the midst of hostility.

Afterwards, you will be happy to see that they do not feel ashamed or humiliated just because you have helped them joyfully. Nothing actually causes shame so much as having to receive something from someone else.

By showing great joyfulness you will succeed in enabling your brother or sister to overcome their sensitivity. They will understand that in your opinion receiving is just as beautiful as giving.

By showing bad temper, on the other hand, far from cheering them up you will be depressing them even further.

If you give gladly, even if you give only a little, it is a big gift. If you give unwillingly, even if you give a big gift, you turn it into a small one.

St John Chrysostom (c. 347–407)

Caring for the Sick

God tested the patience of Frances not only in the external events that happened to her, but it was also his will to try her in her body by many illnesses. It is a well-known fact that she was tried by long and serious illnesses. Yet she was never seen to show the slightest impatience, or the slightest dissatisfaction with any service done for her no matter how clumsily it was done.

Frances gave proof of her steadfastness when her sons, whom she dearly loved, died prematurely. She bowed to the will of God with serenity of spirit and gave him thanks for all that happened. That same steadfastness enabled her to endure the evil-tongued detractors who spoke ill of her way of life. Never did she show the slightest antipathy for those whom she knew spoke evil of her and of what she did. Instead, she repaid evil with good and prayed unceasingly to God for them.

God had chosen her for sanctity, not simply for her own sake, but so that she might direct his gifts to her towards the spiritual and bodily welfare of her neighbour. He gave her such an abundance of loving-kindness that anyone who had dealings with her immediately felt himself captivated by love and admiration for her and was ready to do whatever she wished.

St Frances of Rome (1384–1440)

Serving by Suffering

There is a useful method for strengthening hearts which lack courage. This is to give them the privilege of seeing the poor, of being shown Our Lord Jesus Christ not only in holy pictures painted by great artists but of being shown Jesus Christ and his wounds in the person of the poor.

The sons of noblemen must learn what it means to be hungry and thirsty or to live in an attic without clothing or furniture. They must be able to see dire poverty in the guise of sick children, of children who are weeping. They must be able to see them and to love them.

⚜

In our eyes the poor man, whom we help, will never be the creature whom many consider useless. We believe that, by suffering, he is serving God and is therefore serving society just as much as someone who prays. In our eyes he is performing an act of reparation, a sacrifice which brings down graces on all of us. We have less confidence in the protection offered by a lightning-conductor on the roof than in the prayer of the poor woman and her children who sleep on straw near the top of the building.

Blessed Frédéric Ozanam (1813–53)

Free Education

Mary was the eldest of eight children born to Scottish immigrants. Of her early years she writes: 'My life as a child was one of sorrow, my home, when I had it, was a most unhappy one'.

At sixteen Mary became the main provider and after some years started to teach in Penola in south-east Australia – a Church school where the education was free to all children. The success of the school was immediate. Mary was joined by other dedicated women and the Sisters of St Joseph were formed – the first Order to be founded by an Australian.

However the more conservative Catholics were unsure of the vigorous new Order and some of the bishops found it impossible. The freshness of the vision and its practical interpretation were unsettling! The Bishop of Adelaide declared Mary excommunicated and disbanded the Order. However the excommunication was ruled invalid and Mary's next step was to beg her passage to Rome where Pope Pius IX approved and blessed the Constitution of the Sisters.

On her return to Australia, shelters for the elderly and the homeless were opened. The schools spread through the bush and across to New Zealand. Mary died in Sydney and is known as the Australian People's Saint.

Blessed Mary MacKillop (1842–1909)

A Golden Chain

O Jesus, here I am before you. You are suffering and dying for me, old as I am now and drawing near the end of my service and my life. Hold me closely, and near to your heart, letting mine beat with yours. I love to feel myself bound for ever to you with a gold chain, woven of lovely, delicate links.

The first link: the justice which obliges me to find my God wherever I turn.

The second link: the providence and goodness which will guide my feet.

The third link: love for my neighbour, unwearying and most patient.

The fourth link: the sacrifice that must always be my lot, and that I will and must welcome at all times.

The fifth link: the glory that Jesus promises me in this life and in eternity.

O crucified Jesus, 'my love and my mercy now and for ever'. 'Father, if thou art willing, remove this cup from me; nevertheless not my will, but thine be done' (Luke 22:42).

※ ※

Love one another, my dear children.
Seek rather what unites,
Not what may separate you
    from one another.
As I take leave, or better still
As I say 'till we meet again'
Let me remind you of the
    most important things in life.
Our blessed Saviour Jesus; His good news;
His holy Church: truth and kindness . . .
I shall remember you all
And pray for you.

Pope John XXIII (1881–1963)

Your Merciful Love

I often have the impression, and I hope I am not being presumptuous in thinking so, that Jesus keeps me as it were on a leash. There are times when I feel very strong and sure of myself, especially in public, and this is important in front of others. But there are other moments which those around me do not know of, when I am overwhelmed with a feeling of utter weakness and impotence. In these moments of weakness when Jesus pulls upon the leash as it were, to remind me of my nothingness, I say to Him 'Jesus, I abandon myself to Your Merciful Love' but I do not always say it with complete and utter confidence. Pray then, my beloved friend, that Jesus will give me the grace to believe, that He will give me total faith, that He will never forsake me. I am, as it were, like St. Peter trying to walk on the surface of the water . . .

I can say only 'May His Will be done.' My tour of duty as Governor General [of Canada] is to be of five years' duration. It will be for Jesus to decide how long I will be able in weakness to serve Him and to serve my country.

Georges Vanier (1888–1967)

Everyone Is Lovable

Love never gets out of date. Love, therefore, all things, and all persons in God.

> So long as there are poor, I am poor;
> So long as there are prisons, I am a prisoner;
> So long as there are sick, I am weak;
> So long as there is ignorance, I must learn the truth;
> So long as there is hate, I must love;
> So long as there is hunger, I am famished.

Such is the identification Our Divine Lord would have us make with all whom He made in love and for love. Where we do not find love, we must put it. Then everyone is lovable. There is nothing in all the world more calculated to inspire love for others than this Vision of Christ in our fellow man: 'For I was hungry, and you gave me to eat; I was thirsty, and you gave me to drink: I was a stranger, and you took me in: Naked, and you covered me: sick and you visited me; I was in prison, and you came to me.'

Fulton Sheen (1895–1979)

The Hand of God

For me Jesus Christ is *everything*. . . . He was and he is my ideal from the moment of my entrance into the Society [of Jesus]. He was and he continues to be my way; he was and he still is my strength. I don't think it is necessary to explain very much what that means. Take Jesus Christ from my life and everything would collapse – like a human body from which someone removed the skeleton, heart, and head. . . .

In Lourdes, I acquired an awareness of the power of God as he intervenes in history.

In Marneffe, after our expulsion from Spain, I lived in a community of 350 persons who wondered each evening if they would have enough food for the following day. And each day, we had enough.

In the Yamaguchi prison, I was alone for thirty-five days, wondering why I was there, for how long, and if, in the end, I might be executed. When this 'experience' was over, you could not help but believe in a special Providence.

And immediately after the explosion of the atomic bomb in Hiroshima – shouldn't I remember how we were able to feed and care for so many wounded?

When, in the following years, I travelled throughout the world seeking men and collecting funds for Japan, I was the witness to a rare generosity and to extraordinary sacrifices. One might give many reasons for this, but as for me, I saw in it the hand of God.

Pedro Arrupe (1907–91)

Repentance

It seems a characteristic of one's later years that whilst the wrongs one has suffered fade in one's memory towards vanishing point, the wrongs one has inflicted on others stand out ever more distinctly. It is not that one is consumed with guilt over sins long since confessed but rather that the undoubted effects and the suspected effects of one's actions upon others really strike to the heart. But it is a joy-bringing revelation as well because it reveals how one's heart is longing as never before for repentance. Old age, therefore, as many cultures teach and as Christendom once knew, is the age of repentance. And in that joyful repentance there is also a deep poignancy because, inevitably, many of those one feels to have harmed, in one way or another, are dead. As a result direct reparation towards them is no longer possible. However the burning regret that one cannot now make reparation towards them only intensifies one's desire and determination to behave with all the more kindness and compassion towards anyone who comes across one's path during whatever time is left.

At the same time, if that desire and determination are not themselves to become a burdensome duty but a source of joy, then they have to be accompanied by a real hope that in some way our acts of kindness and compassion will, within the economy of salvation, touch those who have gone before us even though we ourselves can no longer touch them directly. That is a matter of hope – not of hopefulness.

Donald Nicholl (1923–97)

To Love Deeply

Do not hesitate to love and to love deeply. You might be afraid of the pain that deep love can cause. When those you love deeply reject you, leave you, or die, your heart will be broken. But that should not hold you back from loving deeply. The pain that comes from deep love makes your love ever more fruitful. It is like a plough that breaks the ground to allow the seed to take root and grow into a strong plant. Every time you experience the pain of rejection, absence, or death, you are faced with a choice. You can become bitter and decide not to love again, or you can stand straight in your pain and let the soil on which you stand become richer and more able to give life to new seeds.

The more you have loved and have allowed yourself to suffer because of your love, the more you will be able to let your heart grow wider and deeper. When your love is truly giving and receiving, those whom you love will not leave your heart even when they depart from you. They will become part of your self and thus gradually build a community within you. . . . Yes, as you love deeply the ground of your heart will be broken more and more, but you will rejoice in the abundance of the fruit it will bear.

Henri J.M. Nouwen (1932–96)

Love Me as You Are

I know your misery, the inner struggle of your heart. I also know the weaknesses of your heart. I am aware of your cowardice, your sins and your falls. I still tell you 'Love me as you are.' If you wait to be an angel before you give me your love, you will never love me. Even if you often fall again into sins you are ashamed of, even if you are poor in the practice of virtue, I do not allow you not to love me. Love me as you are! Yes, give me your heart at all times and in whatever dispositions you may be, in fervour or in dryness, faithful or unfaithful, love me as you are. I want the love of your poor heart. If you want to be perfect before giving me your heart, you will never love me. What can prevent me from turning every grain of sand into a shining radiant archangel of great nobility? Don't you believe that I could bring into being thousands of saints, more perfect and loving than those I have created? Am I not the Almighty God? But if I choose to be loved, here and now, by your limited heart in preference to more perfect love . . . will you refuse . . .? can you refuse . . .?

Anonymous

Martyrdom

'Let us lay traps for the upright man, since he annoys us
and opposes our way of life,
reproaches us for our sins against the Law,
and accuses us of sins against our upbringing.
He claims to have knowledge of God,
and calls himself a child of the Lord.
We see him as a reproof to our way of thinking,
the very sight of him weighs our spirits down;
for his kind of life is not like other people's,
and his ways are quite different.
In his opinion we are counterfeit;
he avoids our ways as he would filth;
he proclaims the final end of the upright as blessed
and boasts of having God for his father.
Let us see if what he says is true,
and test him to see what sort of end he will have.
For if the upright man is God's son, God will help him
and rescue him from the clutches of his enemies.
Let us test him with cruelty and with torture,
and thus explore this gentleness of his
and put his patience to the test.
Let us condemn him to a shameful death
since God will rescue him – or so he claims.'

Wisdom 2:12–20

United in Death [I]

The day of their victory dawned, and they made their way from the prison to the amphitheatre, with cheerful faces and in dignified manner, as though they were on the way to heaven. If they were trembling at all, it was from joy, not fear.

Perpetua was first tossed by the cow and she fell on her back. Then she stood up, and when she saw that Felicity had been crushed to the ground, she went and gave her her hand to help her up; and so they stood, side by side. Now that the cruelty of the people was appeased, they were recalled to the Sanavivaria Gate. There Perpetua was supported by a certain Rusticus, a catechumen at that time, who was keeping close to her. She began to look round her, as though she had been roused from a sleep, so deeply had she been in spiritual ecstasy, and she said, to the astonishment of all, 'When are we to be thrown to that cow or whatever it is.' And when she was told that this had already been done, she would not believe it until she noticed a number of marks of violence to her body and clothes. Then she summoned her brother and the catechumen, and spoke to them saying, 'Stand firm in your faith, and love one another. Do not let your sufferings be a stumbling-block to you.'

Saturninus at another gate was also giving encouragement to Pudens, a soldier. 'It has happened', he said, 'exactly as I supposed and foretold. Up till now, I have not been touched by a beast. And now you can believe me with all your heart. I shall go forward there and with one bite of the leopard I shall be finished off.'

SS Felicitas and Perpetua (d. 203)

United in Death [II]

And at once as the show was ending, Saturninus was thrown to the leopard, and with one bite was so drenched with blood that as he came back, the people called out in witness to his second baptism, 'Well washed! well washed!' Indeed he was saved who had been washed in this fashion.

Then he said to Pudens, the soldier, 'Farewell, and remember me and the faith. Do not let all this disturb you, but rather be strengthened by it.' Then he asked for the ring from Pudens' finger. He dipped it in his wound, and gave it back to him for a legacy, as a pledge and memorial of his blood. Then he became unconscious, and was thrown with the others into the place where their throats were to be cut.

When the people demanded that they be brought into the open, to make themselves party to the murder by watching with their eyes the sword being plunged into the bodies, the Christians rose up of their own accord and crossed over to where the people wanted. Then they kissed each other, so that their martyrdom could be brought to fulfilment by the ritual kiss of peace. The rest of them received the sword without moving and in silence, especially Saturninus, who as the first to ascend, was the first to yield up his life. For he was waiting again for Perpetua. But Perpetua, that she might taste something of the pain, was struck on the bone, and she cried out. And she herself guided the fumbling hand of the novice gladiator into her throat. Perhaps such a woman could not be otherwise killed, a woman who was feared by an unclean spirit, unless she herself gave consent.

SS Felicitas and Perpetua (d. 203)

As Bridegrooms to their Marriage

Early in the morning of 4 May 1535, a spectacle was witnessed inside the gates of the Tower of London, never before seen in the history of England, or of any Christian country in Europe. Three monks in their white habits were being led out from their prisons, to be dragged on hurdles to the place of execution at Tyburn. They were very cheerful. Thomas More, looking out from the window of his cell, turned to his daughter, Margaret, who was visiting him at the time, and said: 'Lo, dost thou not see, Meg, that these blessed Fathers be now as cheerfully going to their deaths as bridegrooms to their marriage?'

❦

'Campion's Brag'

Touching our Societie, be it known to you that we have made a league – all the Jesuits in the world, whose succession and multitude must overreach all the practices of England – cheerfully to carry the cross you shall lay upon us, and never to despair your recovery, while we have a man left to enjoy your Tyburn, or to be racked with your torments, or consumed with your prisons. The expense is reckoned, the enterprise is begun; it is of God, it cannot be withstood. So the faith was planted: so it must be restored.

St Edmund Campion (1540–81)

Japanese Jesuit [I]

When the crosses had been erected, it was wonderful to see how steadfast all were in response to the encouragement given by Father Pasius and Father Rodríguez. Father Commissarius remained almost immobile, his eyes fixed on heaven. Brother Martin continually gave thanks to God, singing psalms with the versicle, 'Into your hands, O Lord.' Brother Francis Blanco also gave thanks to God in a loud voice, while Father Gonsalvez, raising his voice a little, recited the Lord's Prayer and the Hail Mary.

Our brother, Paul Miki, seeing that he was standing in the most honoured pulpit of any he had ever been in, first of all declared to the onlookers that he was both a Japanese and a Jesuit. He told them that he was dying because he had preached the gospel, and that he gave thanks to God for such a singular privilege. Then he added the following words, 'Since I have now come to this moment, I do not think there is anyone among you who would believe that I would willingly tell a lie. I tell you openly, then, that there is no other way of salvation than that of the Christians. Since that way teaches me to forgive my enemies and all who have done me violence, I willingly forgive the king and those who have a hand in my death, and I entreat them to seek the initiation of Christian baptism.'

St Paul Miki (c. 1564–97)

Japanese Jesuit [II]

Then, looking to his companions, he began to encourage them in this last agony. On the face of each of them there appeared a great joy, and this was especially true of Louis. When one of the other Christians cried out that soon he would be in Paradise, he responded with such a joyful movement of his hands and his whole body that he attracted the attention of all the onlookers.

Anthony, who was beside Louis, with his eyes fixed on heaven, called on the most holy names of Jesus and Mary, and then sang the psalm, *Laudate, pueri, Dominum*. He had learned this at the catechetical school in Nagasaki, for among the tasks given to the children there had been included the learning of some psalms such as these.

The others kept repeating, 'Jesus, Mary', and their faces showed no sign of distress. Some of them, indeed, were encouraging the bystanders to lead good Christian lives. By these actions and by others like them, they gave ample proof of their willingness to die.

Then the four executioners began to take their spears out of the sheaths that the Japanese use. When they saw those terrible spears, all the faithful cried out, 'Jesus, Mary'. What is more, a sad lamentation assailed heaven itself. The executioners despatched each of them in a very short time with one or two thrusts.

St Paul Miki (c. 1564–97)

Martyrdom of Love [I]

One day Saint Jane said this: 'My dear daughters, most of our holy Fathers, the pillars of the Church, were not martyrs. Why was this, do you think?'

After each one of us had had her say, she went on: 'I think it is because there is such a thing as a martyrdom of love: God keeps his servants alive to work for his glory, and this makes them martyrs and confessors at the same time. I know this is the sort of martyrdom the daughters of the Visitation will suffer, that is, those of them who are fortunate enough to set their hearts on it.'

A sister wanted to know just how this martyrdom worked out in practice.

'Give God your unconditional consent,' she said, 'and then you will find out. What happens is that love seeks out the most intimate and secret place of your soul, as with a sharp sword, and cuts you off even from your own self. I know of a soul cut off in this way so that she felt it more keenly than if a tyrant had cleaved her body from her soul.'

We knew, of course, that she was speaking about herself.

St Jane Frances de Chantal (1572–1641)

Martyrdom of Love [II]

A sister wanted to know how long this martyrdom was likely to last.

'From the moment we give ourselves up wholeheartedly to God until the moment we die,' she answered. 'But this goes for generous hearts and people who keep faith with love and don't take back their offering; our Lord doesn't take the trouble to make martyrs of feeble hearts and people who have little love and not much constancy; he just lets them jog along in their own little way in case they give up and slip from his hands altogether; he never forces our free will.'

She was asked whether this martyrdom of love could ever be as bad as the physical kind.

'We won't try to compare the two and look for equality; but I do not think the martyrdom of love is less painful than the other, because "love is strong as death", and martyrs of love suffer infinitely more by staying alive to do God's will than if they had to give up a thousand lives for their faith and love and loyalty.'

St Jane Frances de Chantal (1572–1641)

St Andrew Kim Taegon and Companions

The Christian community in Korea is unique in the history of the Church by reason of the fact that it was founded entirely by lay people. In less than a century [from 1784] it could already boast some ten thousand martyrs from the thirteen-year-old Peter Yu to the seventy-two year old Mark Chong. Men and women, clergy and laity, rich and poor, ordinary people and nobles, many of them descendants of earlier unsung martyrs – they all gladly died for the sake of Christ.

Listen to the last words of Teresa Kwon, one of the early martyrs: 'Since the Lord of heaven is the Father of all mankind and the Lord of all creation, how can you ask me to betray him? Even in this world anyone who betrays his own father or mother will not be forgiven. All the more may I never betray him who is the Father of us all.'

And what did the seventeen-year-old Agnes Yi say when she and her younger brother were falsely told that their parents had betrayed the faith? 'Whether my parents betrayed or not is their affair. As for us, we cannot betray the Lord of heaven whom we have always served.' Hearing this, six other adult Christians freely delivered themselves to the magistrate to be martyred. Agnes, her parents and those other six are all being canonised today. In addition, there are countless other unknown humble martyrs who no less faithfully and bravely served the Lord.

The Korean Martyrs (1784–1839)

St Charles Lwanga and Companions

'Who are these clothed in white robes, and whence have they come?' (Rev. 7:13) This verse of scripture comes to mind as we add to the glorious list of saints triumphant in heaven these twenty-two sons of Africa. Who are they? They are Africans, first of all. By their colour, race and culture they are true Africans, descended from the Bantu race and the peoples of the Upper Nile.

Yes, they are Africans and they are martyrs. 'These are they who have come out of the great tribulation'. Twenty-two martyrs were recognised but there were many more and not only Catholics. There were also Anglicans and some Muslims.

These African martyrs open a new epoch. Africa is rising free and redeemed, bathed in the blood of these martyrs. Christianity found in Africa a special predisposition, and in this we do not hesitate to see a mysterious design of God, a vocation proper to Africa, a promise of historical significance. Africa is a land of the gospel. Africa is the new homeland of Christ. The straightforward and logical simplicity and the unwavering fidelity of these young Christians of Africa are clear evidence of this.

The Uganda Martyrs (1885–7)

The Seed of Liberty

'I have often been threatened with death. I have to say, as a Christian, that I don't believe in death without resurrection: if they kill me, I will rise again in the Salvadorean people. I tell you this without any boasting, with the greatest humility. As pastor, I am obliged, by divine command, to give my life for those I love, who are all Salvadoreans, even for those who are going to assassinate me. If the threats are carried out, even now I offer my blood to God for the redemption and resurrection of El Salvador. Martyrdom is a grace of God I don't think I deserve. But if God accepts the sacrifice of my life, may my blood be the seed of liberty and the sign that hope will soon become reality. May my death, if accepted by God, be for the freedom of my people and as a witness to hope in the future. You can say, if they come to kill me, that I forgive and bless those who do it. Hopefully they may realise that they will be wasting their time. A bishop will die, but the Church of God, which is the people, will never perish.'

Oscar Romero (1917–80)

A-Dieu

When an 'A-Dieu' takes on a face.
If it should happen one day — and it could be today —
that I become a victim of the terrorism which now seems ready to engulf
all the foreigners living in Algeria,
I would like my community, my Church, my family,
to remember that my life was *given* to God and to this country.
I ask them to accept that the Sole Master of all life
was not a stranger to this brutal departure.
I ask them to pray for me —
for how could I be found worthy of such an offering?
I ask them to be able to link this death with the many other deaths
which were just as violent, but forgotten through indifference and anonymity.
My life has no more value than any other.
Nor any less value.
In any case it has not the innocence of childhood.
I have lived long enough to know that I am an accomplice in the evil
which seems, alas, to prevail in the world,
even in that which would strike me blindly.
I should like, when the time comes, to have the moment of lucidity
which would allow me to beg forgiveness of God
and of my fellow human beings,
and at the same time to forgive with all my heart the one who would strike
   me down.

Christian de Chergé (1937–96)

Death and Eternity

Do not let your hearts be troubled.
You trust in God, trust also in me.
In my Father's house there are many places to live in;
otherwise I would have told you.
I am going now to prepare a place for you,
and after I have gone and prepared you a place,
I shall return to take you to myself,
so that you may be with me
where I am.

John 14:1–3

Ground by Lions' Teeth [I]

For my part, I am writing to all the churches and assuring them that I am truly in earnest about dying for God – if only you yourselves put no obstacles in the way. I must implore you to do me no such untimely kindness; pray leave me to be a meal for the beasts, for it is they who can provide my way to God. I am his wheat, ground fine by the lions' teeth to be made purest bread for Christ. So intercede with him for me, that by their instrumentality I may be made a sacrifice to God.

All the ends of the earth, all the kingdoms of the world would be of no profit to me; so far as I am concerned, to die in Jesus Christ is better than to be monarch of earth's widest bounds. He who died for us is all that I seek; he who rose again for us is my whole desire. The pangs of birth are upon me; have patience with me, my brothers, and do not shut me out from life, do not wish me to be stillborn. Here is one who only longs to be God's; do not make a present of him to the world again, or delude him with the things of earth. Suffer me to attain to light, light pure and undefiled; for only when I am come thither shall I be truly a man. Leave me to imitate the passion of my God. If any of you has God within himself, let that man understand my longings, and feel for me, because he will know the forces by which I am constrained.

St Ignatius of Antioch (c. 35–c. 107)

Ground by Lions' Teeth [II]

It is the hope of this world's prince to get hold of me and undermine my resolve, set as it is upon God. Pray let none of you lend him any assistance, but take my part instead, for it is the part of God. Do not have Jesus Christ on your lips, and the world in your heart; do not cherish thoughts of grudging me my fate. Even if I were to come and implore you in person, do not yield to my pleading; keep your compliance for this written entreaty instead. Here and now, as I write in the fullness of life, I am yearning for death with all the passion of a lover. Earthly longings have been crucified; in me there is left no spark of desire for mundane things, but only a murmur of living water that whispers within me, 'Come to the Father'. There is no pleasure for me in any meats that perish, or in the delights of this life; I am fain for the bread of God, even the flesh of Jesus Christ, who is the seed of David; and for my drink I crave that blood of his which is love imperishable.

I want no more of what men call life. And my want can come true, if it is your desire. Pray, then, let it be your desire; so that in your turn you also may be desired. Not to write at more length, I appeal to you to believe me. Jesus Christ will make it clear to you that I am speaking the truth; he is a faithful mouthpiece, by which the Father's words of truth find utterance. Intercede for me, then, that I may have my wish; for I am not writing now as a mere man, but I am voicing the mind of God. My suffering will be a proof of your goodwill; my rejection, a proof of your disfavour.

St Ignatius of Antioch (c. 35–c. 107)

Farewell

But because the day when my mother was to quit this life was drawing near –
a day known to you, though we were ignorant of it – she and I happened to be
alone, through the mysterious workings of your will, as I believe. We stood
leaning against a window which looked out on a garden within the house where
we were staying at Ostia on the Tiber, for there, far from the crowds, we were
recruiting our strength after the long journey, in preparation for our voyage
overseas. We were alone, conferring very intimately. Forgetting what lay in the
past, and stretching out to what was ahead, we inquired between ourselves in
the light of the present truth, the Truth which is yourself, what the eternal life
of the saints would be like. Eye has not seen nor ear heard nor human heart
conceived it, yet with the mouth of our hearts wide open we panted thirstily
for the celestial streams of your fountain, the fount of life which is with you,
that bedewed from it according to our present capacity we might in our little
measure think upon a thing so great.

St Augustine of Hippo (354–430)

The Seventh Day

After this age God shall rest as on the seventh day, when God shall make that same seventh day which we shall be, to rest in Himself. Furthermore it would take up a long time to discourse now exactly of every one of those several ages. But this seventh shall be our sabbath, whose end shall not be the evening, but the Lord's day, as the eighth eternal day, which is sanctified and made holy by the resurrection of Christ, prefiguring not only the eternal rest of the spirit, but also of the body. There we shall rest and see, we shall see and love, we shall love and we shall praise. Behold what shall be in the end without end! For what other thing is our end, but to come to that kingdom of which there is no end?

St Augustine of Hippo (354–430)

Hope of the World

O God that art the only hope of the world,
The only refuge for unhappy men,
Abiding in the faithfulness of heaven,
Give me strong succour in this testing place.
O King, protect Thy man from utter ruin
Lest the weak faith surrender to the tyrant,
Facing innumerable blows alone.
Remember I am dust, and wind, and shadow,
And life as fleeting as the flower of grass.
But may the eternal mercy which hath shone
From time of old
Rescue Thy servant from the jaws of the lion.
Thou who didst come from on high in the cloak of flesh,
Strike down the dragon with that two-edged sword,
Whereby our mortal flesh can war with the winds
And beat down strongholds, with our Captain God.

꽃꿏

'I pray Thee, merciful Jesus, that as Thou hast graciously granted me sweet draughts from the Word which tells of Thee, so wilt Thou, of Thy goodness, grant that I may come at length to Thee, the fount of all wisdom, and stand before Thy face forever.'

St Bede the Venerable (c. 673–735)

To His Mother

Not long will last that separation: there we shall see one another again and be happy without ever growing tired, united together with our Redeemer, praising Him with all our strength, and singing for ever His mercies. I do not at all doubt that, leaving aside all that the reasoning of human nature says, we shall easily open the door to faith and to that simple and pure obedience to which we are held by God, offering Him freely and promptly that which is His, and all the more willingly the dearer to you is the thing that He takes from you, believing firmly that what God does is all of it well done, taking away what He first had given us, and for no other reason than to put it in a safe and sure place, and to give to it what we all desire for ourselves. I have said all this for no other reason than to satisfy the desire I have that Your Most Illustrious Ladyship and all my family may receive this my departure as a dear gift, and that you may accompany me and help me with your Mother's blessing to pass this gulf and reach the shore of all my hopes. I have done it with all the better will because I have nothing else left with which to give you some little proof of the love and filial reverence that I owe you. I end by asking once more very humbly for your blessing.

St Aloysius Gonzaga (1568–91)

The Fullness of Love

The mystery of Christ is the ultimate truth, the reality towards which all human life aspires. And this mystery is known by love. Love is going out of oneself, surrendering the self, letting the reality, the truth, take over . . . It is not something we achieve for ourselves. It is something that comes when we let go. We have to abandon everything – all words, thoughts, hopes, fears, all attachment to ourselves or to any earthly things, and let the divine mystery take possession of our lives. It feels like death, and it is, in fact, a sort of dying. It is encountering the darkness, the abyss, the void. It is facing absolute nothingness – or as Augustine Baker, the English Benedictine, said, it is 'the union of the nothing with the Nothing'. This is the negative aspect of contemplation. The positive aspect is, of course, the opposite. It is total fulfilment, total wisdom, total bliss, the answer to all problems, the peace which passes understanding, the joy which is the fullness of love.

Bede Griffiths (1906–93)

Shouting Hallelujah

Ruby Turpin lifted her head. There was only a purple streak in the sky, cutting through a field of crimson and leading, like an extension of the highway, into the descending dusk. She raised her hands from the side of the pen in a gesture hieratic and profound. A visionary light settled in her eyes. She saw the streak as a vast swinging bridge extending upward from the earth through a field of living fire. Upon it a vast horde of souls were rumbling toward heaven. There were whole companies of white-trash, clean for the first time in their lives, and bands of black niggers in white robes, and battalions of freaks and lunatics shouting and clapping and leaping like frogs. And bringing up the end of the procession was a tribe of people whom she recognized at once as those who, like herself and Claud, had always had a little of everything and the God-given wit to use it right. She leaned forward to observe them closer. They were marching behind the others with great dignity, accountable as they had always been for good order and common sense and respectable behaviour. They alone were on key. Yet she could see by their shocked and altered faces that even their virtues were being burned away. She lowered her hands and gripped the rail of the hog pen, her eyes small but fixed unblinkingly on what lay ahead. In a moment the vision faded but she remained where she was, immobile.

At length she got down and turned off the faucet and made her slow way on the darkening path to the house. In the woods around her the invisible cricket choruses had struck up, but what she heard were the voices of the souls climbing upward into the starry field and shouting hallelujah.

Flannery O'Connor (1925–64)

Mystery

The meaning of things, and their purpose
is in part now hidden
but shall in the end become clear.
The choice is between
the Mystery and the absurd.
To embrace the Mystery
is to discover the real.
It is to walk towards the light,
to glimpse the morning star, to catch sight
from time to time
of what is truly real
it is no more than a flicker of light
through the cloud of unknowing,
a fitful ray of light
that is a messenger from the sun
which is hidden from the gaze.
You see the light but not the sun.
When you set yourself to look more closely,
you will begin to see more sense
in the darkness that surrounds you.
Your eyes will begin to pick out
the shape of things and persons around you.
You will begin to see them
the presence of the One
who gives them meaning and purpose,
and that it is He
who is the explanation of them all.

Basil Hume (1923–99)

A New Heaven and a New Earth

Then I saw a new heaven and a new earth; the first heaven and the first earth had disappeared now, and there was no longer any sea. I saw the holy city, the new Jerusalem, coming down out of heaven from God, prepared as a bride dressed for her husband. Then I heard a loud voice call from the throne, 'Look, here God lives among human beings. He will make his home among them; they will be his people, and he will be their God, God-with-them. He will wipe away all tears from their eyes; there will be no more death, and no more mourning or sadness or pain. The world of the past has gone.'

Revelation 21:1–4

SOURCES

p. vii: St Laurence. Slightly edited from Butler's *Dictionary of Religious Biography* (Burns & Oates).

Father, Son and Holy Spirit

p. 4   St Basil. From the Treatise 'On the Holy Spirit', ch. 9.

p. 5   St Columbanus. Instruction 1 on Faith, 'Sancti Columbani Opera.'

p. 6   St Hildegard. First poem 'To the Trinity' is from '*Symphonia*': *St Hildegard of Bingen*, tr. by Barbara Newman (Ithaca & London: Cornell University Press, 1988). Second poem 'Antiphon for the Holy Spirit' from *Hildegard of Bingen: An Anthology*, tr. Robert Carver, ed. and intro. by Fiona Bowie and Oliver Davies (SPCK, 1990).

pp. 7–8   Richard of St-Victor. From Book 3 of *The Trinity* (New York: Paulist Press, 1979), taken from *The Twelve Patriarchs, The Mystical Ark, Book Three of the Trinity*, Classics of Western Spiritual Series (CWS) (Paulist Press, 1979).

p. 9   Dante. From Canto 33 of *The Paradiso*, tr. by Mark Musa (Indiana University Press, 1984).

p. 10   Julian of Norwich. From Ch. 59 of *Revelations of Divine Love*, taken from *All Shall be Well* by Sheila Upjohn (DLT, 1992).

pp. 11–12   Catherine of Siena. From *The Dialogues of Catherine of Siena On Divine Revelation*, ch. 167.

pp. 13–14   Elizabeth of the Trinity. Tr. by the Darlington Carmel in *Your Presence is my Joy* (Carmelite Convent, Nunnery Lane, Darlington DL3 7PN).

God's Love for Us

p. 16   Gregory of Nyssa. *On the Song of Songs*, ch. 2.

pp. 17–18   St Gertrude the Great. *Gertrude of Helfta*, tr. M. Winkworth, CWS Series (Paulist Press, 1993).

p. 19   Julian of Norwich. *Revelations of Divine Love*, ch. 5, taken from *All Shall be Well* by Sheila Upjohn (DLT, 1992).

p. 20   Julian of Norwich. ibid., ch. 86.

p. 21   Catherine of Siena. From *The Dialogue*, tr. Suzanne Noffke, CWS (Paulist Press, 1988).

p. 22   St John of the Cross. From *Centred on Love. The Poems of St John of the Cross*, tr. Marjorie Flower OCD © 1983 (The Carmelite Community, St Andrew's Rd, Varroville, NSW 2565, Australia), quoted by Iain Matthew OCD in *The Impact of God* (Hodder, 1995).

p. 23   Fulton Sheen. From *Lift Up Your Heart* by Fulton Sheen (Burns & Oates, 1950).

Our Love for God

p. 25   St Basil the Great. From *The Longer Rules of St Basil the Great*, taken from *The Ascetic Works of St Basil*, tr. Lowther Clarke (SPCK, © 1925).

p. 26   St Augustine. From *The Confessions of St Augustine* ch. X: 27:38, tr. Maria Boulding (Hodder, 1997).

p. 27   From the treatises of Baldwin of Canterbury, Tr. 10.

p. 28   St Bonaventure. From the works of St Bonaventure, Opusc. 3, 29–30. 47.

p. 29   'Teach us, good Lord' is commonly attributed to St Ignatius. 'Take, Lord, and receive' comes from *The Spiritual Exercises of St Ignatius*, tr. Louis J. Puhl (Chicago: Loyola University Press, 1951).

p. 30   St John of the Cross. Letter to Madre Leonor de San Gabriel, 8 July 1589, *Lamps of Fire: Daily Readings with St John of the Cross* ed. by Elizabeth Ruth Obbard (DLT, 1985).

p. 31   Charles de Foucauld.

p. 32   Fulton Sheen. From *Go to Heaven* (The Catholic Book Club).

p. 33   Bernard Lonergan. *Method in Theology* (DLT, 1972).

p. 34   A Carthusian. *The Wound of Love* (DLT, 1994).

Love of Neighbour

pp. 36–7   St John Chrysostom. From the homilies of St John Chrysostom, Homily 50.3.4.

p. 38   St Augustine. From St Augustine's Treatises on St John, Treatise 17:7–9.

p. 39   St Caesarius of Arles. From the sermons of St Caesarius of Arles, Sermon 25.1.

p. 40   St Francis. *The Life of St Francis* by St Bonaventure, taken in this translation from *Bonaventure*, tr. and intro. by Ewart Cousins, CWS (Paulist Press, 1978).

p. 41   St Catherine of Siena. Letter to Bartolomeo Dominici from *The Letters of Catherine of Siena*, vol. I, tr. Suzanne Noffke (Paulist Press, 1988).

p. 42   Teresa of Avila. Original source *The Way of Perfection* by Teresa of Jesus, ch. 41 paras. 7 & 8. This translation from *Living Water. Daily Readings with St Teresa of Avila*, ed. and intro. by Sr Mary ODC (DLT, 1986).

p. 43   St Vincent de Paul. From the writings of St Vincent de Paul, Ep. 2546.

p. 44   Jean-Pierre de Caussade. Taken from *The Flame of Divine Love. Daily Readings with Jean-Pierre de Caussade*, ed. by Robert Llewelyn (1984).

p. 45   Fr Damien of Molokai. From a letter to his brother Father Pamphile, November 1873, reproduced in *The Heart of Father Damien 1840–1889* by Vital Jourdan SSCC, tr. from the French by Rev. Francis Larkin and Charles Davenport (Milwaukee: Bruce Publishing Company, 1955).

p. 46   Thérèse of Lisieux. Original source *Autobiography of St Thérèse of Lisieux*, Ms C 15v. Taken from *By Love Alone. Daily Readings with St Thérèse of Lisieux*, ed. and intro. by Michael Hollings (DLT, 1986).

p. 47   Dorothy Day. First paragraph from *Dorothy Day Selected Writings By Little and By Little*, ed. and with an intro. by Robert Ellsberg (Orbis, 1983/1992). Second paragraph from *The Long Loneliness: Autobiography of Dorothy Day* (San Francisco: Harper and Row, 1952).

p. 48   Letter from Fr David Gibbs SJ, quoted in *Strange Vagabond of God: The Story of John Bradburne* by John Dove SJ (Gracewing, 1997).

God the Creator

p. 52   St Basil. From *St Basil on Prayer* II.5, reproduced in *The Sunday Sermons of the Great Fathers*, vol. 2 (London/New York: Longmans Green, 1958). © M. F. Toal esq.

p. 53   Celtic. From *Celtic Spirituality and Nature* by Dr Mary Low (Edinburgh and Belfast: Blackstaff Press), taken from *Carmina Gadelica*, vol. I, by Alexander Carmichael (Scottish Academic Press, 22 Montgomery St, Edinburgh), p. 231. Copyright is vested in Trustees of Professor J.C. Watson 1972.

p. 54   Hildegard of Bingen. First poem from *Symphonia: St Hildegard of Bingen* with intro., tr. and commentary by Barbara Newman (Ithaca and London: Cornell University Press, 1988). Second poem is 'Antiphon for Divine Love' from *Hildegard of Bingen, An Anthology*, tr. Robert Carver, ed. and intro. by Fiona Bowie and Oliver Davies (SPCK, 1990).

pp. 55–6   St Francis of Assisi. From *Francis and Clare Complete Works*, CWS (Paulist Press, 1982).

p. 57   St Thomas Aquinas. Sermon on the Apostles Creed 13–14. English translation in *The Three Greatest Prayers* (Newman Press, 1956). Second paragraph in the *Summa Theologica* by Thomas Aquinas, Part I.q.47.

p. 58   Ven. Marie of the Incarnation. From a letter written to Pope Pius XI in 1872, reproduced in *A Procession of Saints* by James Brodrick SJ (The Catholic Book Club, 1947).

p. 59   Gerard Manley Hopkins.

p. 60   Friedrich von Hügel. From *Essays and Addresses on the Philosophy of Religion*, vol. I (1921), reproduced in *Spiritual Counsels and Letters of Baron Friedrich von Hügel*, ed. Douglas V. Steere (DLT, 1964).

p. 61   Francis Thompson.

p. 62   Charles Péguy. From *Le Porche de la deuxième vertu, Le Mystère des Saints Innocents*. Translation © Dame Teresa Rodrigues OSB, Stanbrook Abbey.

p. 63   Teilhard de Chardin. From *The Hymn of the Universe* by Pierre Teilhard de Chardin, English translation (San Francisco: Collins and Harper & Row, 1965). © Georges Borchardt, Inc.

p. 64   Tony Walsh. From 'A Statement' in *Alone for Others. The Life of Tony Walsh* by Lucien Miller (Community Concerns Associates, 1987).

Jesus Born

p. 66   St Ephrem. From *St Ephrem the Syrian*, tr. and intro. by Kathleen E. McVey, CWS (Paulist Press, 1989). This section from Hymns on the Nativity 3.

p. 67   St Augustine. From unidentified Australian translation of Sermon 191.

p. 68–9   St Leo the Great. From the letters of Pope St Leo the Great, Ep 31, 2–3.

p. 70   St Anselm. Prayer to St Paul from *Prayers and Meditations of St Anselm*, tr. and with an intro. by Sr Benedicta Ward SLG (Penguin, 1973).

p. 71   Robert Southwell.

p. 72   Teilhard de Chardin. From *Hymn of the Universe* by Pierre Teilhard de Chardin, English translation (San Francisco: Collins & Co. and Harper & Row, 1965). © Georges Borchardt, Inc.

p. 73   Edith Stein. From *The Writings of Edith Stein*, tr. Hilda Graef (Paulist Press).

p. 74   Caryll Houselander.

p. 75   Raymond Brown. From Raymond E. Brown, *The Adult Christ at Christmas* (Collegeville: Liturgical Press, 1978).

Jesus Crucified and Risen

pp. 77–9   From the liturgy on Easter Saturday night, © Rite of *Holy Week* © 1972, International Committee on English in the Liturgy Inc.

pp. 80–82   Descent into Hell. From 'An ancient homily for Holy Saturday'.

pp. 83–4   Melito of Sardis. From reading from the homily of Melito of Sardis on the Pasch Nn 65–71, copyright The Editor, *The Way*, for Edward Maltesta (tr.) 'Homily of Melito of Sardis on the Pasch' nn. 65–71: from *The Way*, vol. 2, no. 2, April 1962.

p. 85   St Ephrem. From Sermon on Our Lord 3:4–9.

pp. 86–7   St Andrew of Crete. From Homily Or. 10.

pp. 88–9   Authorship of 'Dream of the Rood' has been unknown for something over 1000 years. This version was taken by Stanbrook from J.A.W. Bennett's *Poetry of the Passion 1982*.

p. 90   Catherine of Siena. From *The Prayers of St Catherine of Siena*, ed. Suzanne Noffke (Paulist Press, 1983).

p. 91   Charles Péguy. From *Le Porche de la deuxième vertu: Le mystère des Saints Innocents*, © Dame Teresa Rodrigues, Stanbrook Abbey.

pp. 92–4   Karl Rahner. From *The Eternal Year* (London: Burns & Oates, 1964).

The Coming of the Spirit

p. 98   Third Eucharistic Prayer. The New English translation of the *Order of Mass and Eucharistic Prayers*, copyright 1969, International Committee on English in the Liturgy Inc.

p. 99   Isaac of Nineveh. From *Isaac of Syria*, ed. and intro. by A.M. Allchin, tr. from the Syriac by Sebastian Brock (DLT, 1989).

p. 100   Diadochus of Photike. From *Spiritual Works*, 23 (SC 5b), taken from *A Patristic Breviary* by Thomas Spidlik (London: New City Press), tr. from Italian by Paul Drake.

p. 101   Bianco da Siena. Tr. R.F. Littledale, 1833–90.

p. 102   St Mary Magdalene of Pazzi. From her writings *On Revelation* and *On Temptation*.

p. 103   Gerard Manley Hopkins.

p. 104   Paul Claudel. Preface to *The Satin Slipper* by Paul Claudel (Sheed & Ward, 1931), tr. John O'Connor. The Preface was written by Paul Claudel in French and in English.

Our Lady

p. 107 Cyril of Alexandria. From the letters of St Cyril of Alexandria, Ep. 1.

p. 108 Cynewulf.

p. 109 St Hildegard.

pp. 110–11 St Aelred. Sermon 20.

p. 112 Dante. Tr. Ronald Knox.

p. 113 John Duns Scotus. The first thirteen lines cited by Berand de S. Maurice in *Duns Scotus* and the remaining lines from Opus Oxoniensus III, 20.10, by permission of the Abbot of Nunraw.

p. 114 Julian of Norwich. *Revelations of Divine Love*, ch. 60, taken from *All Shall be Well* by Sheila Upjohn (DLT, 1992).

p. 115 St Louis Marie de Montfort. From 'God Alone' in *The Collected Writings of St Louis Marie de Montfort* (Bay Shore, New York 11706: Montfort Publications, 1987).

pp. 116–17 St Bernadette. From a letter of St Bernadette Soubirous.

p. 118 Henri J. M. Nouwen. From 'Mary, Mother of Priests' from an address delivered in Toronto.

Saints and Angels

p. 120 St Gregory of Nazianzus. From *Oration* 28, tr. L. Wickham and F. Williams.

p. 121 St Martin of Tours. From *A Select Library of the Nicene and Post-Nicene Fathers of the Christian Church*, vol. XI (Grand Rapids, Michigan: Wm Eerdmans, reprinted January 1973).

pp. 122–3 St Patrick. From *The Confession of St Patrick*, taken from Confession, 34, 36, 37, 38, 39.

p. 124 Dionysius. From *The Celestial Hierarchy* (Paulist Press, 1987).

p. 125 Columba. From *The Life of Columba* by Adomnan, Pref. II and Book III.

pp. 126–7 St Gregory the Great. From the homilies of Pope St Gregory the Great on the Gospels, Hom. 34.8–9.

p. 128 Baldwin. From Tractate 15 in *Spiritual Tractates: Baldwin of Forde*, tr. D.N. Bell (Kalamazoo: Cistercian Publications, 1986).

pp. 129–30 Dominic. From selected sources of the history of the Order of Preachers.

p. 131 St Martin de Porres. From the homily of Pope John XXIII for the canonisation of St Martin de Porres, 6 May 1962.

p. 132 St Francis de Sales. From *Daily Readings with St Francis de Sales* (CTS, 1911).

p. 133 St Maksymilian. From *Saint of Auschwitz* by Diana Dewar (DLT, 1982), slightly edited.

Church and Sacraments

pp. 138–9 From the Instructions to the newly baptised at Jerusalem.

pp. 140–2 From the letter to Diognetus, N 5–6.

p. 143 St Boniface. From the letters of St Boniface, Letter 78.

p. 144 St Thomas Aquinas. From the works of St Thomas Aquinas, Opusc. 57:1–4.

p. 145   Thomas à Kempis. From *The Imitation of Christ*, Book IV ch. 1 and ch. 2, tr. Ronald Knox and Michael Oakley (Burns & Oates, 1959).

p. 146   Francis de Sales. Taken from *Athirst for God. Daily readings with St Francis de Sales*, ed. and intro. by Michael Hollings (DLT, 1985).

p. 147   Philippine Duchesne. From *Mother Philippine Duchesne* by Marjory Erskine (Longmans, 1926), quoted in *To Any Christian* by a Benedictine of Stanbrook (Burns & Oates, 1964).

p. 148   Teilhard de Chardin. From *Hymn of the Universe* by Pierre Teilhard de Chardin, English translation (San Francisco: Collins and Harper & Row, 1965). © Georges Borchardt, Inc.

pp. 149–50   Pope Paul VI. From a sermon preached in Manila, Philippines, 29 November 1970.

Pathways in Prayer

p. 152   St Ephrem. From the commentary of St Ephrem the Syrian on the Diatessaron (the four Gospels in a single narrative), 1:18–19.

p. 153   From *The Celtic Vision*, selections from the *Carmina Gadelica*, ed. Esther de Waal (DLT, 1988).

p. 154   St Bernard. A reading from the sermons of St Bernard De diversis 5:4–5.

p. 155   From *The Cloud of Unknowing*, ch. 6, ed. and with an intro. by James Walsh SJ, CWS (Paulist Press, 1981).

p. 156   Richard Rolle. From *Richard Rolle. The English Writings*, tr., ed and with an intro. by Rosamund S. Allen, CWS (Paulist Press, 1989). Margery Kempe. Taken from *The Mirror of Love. Daily Readings with Margery Kempe*, ed. and intro. by Gillian Hawker (DLT, 1988).

p. 157   Francis de Sales. Taken from *Athirst for God. Daily Readings with St Francis de Sales*, ed. and intro. by Michael Hollings (DLT, 1985).

p. 158   Rose of Lima. From the writings of St Rose of Lima.

p. 159   St Margaret Mary. From the Letters of St Margaret Mary Alacoque.

p. 160   Jean-Pierre de Caussade. Taken from *The Flame of Divine Love. Daily Readings with Jean-Pierre de Caussade*, ed. and intro. by Robert Llewelyn (DLT, 1984).

p. 161   St Jean Vianney. From the catechetical instructions of St Jean Vianney.

p. 162   St Thérèse of Lisieux. Taken from *By Love Alone. Daily Readings with St Thérèse of Lisieux*, ed. and intro. by Michael Hollings (DLT, 1986).

p. 163   Marthe Robin. From *Marthe Robin* by Raymond Peyret, tr. from the French by Clare Will Faulhaber (Alba House, 1981).

p. 164   John Main. From *Moment of Christ* by John Main (DLT, 1984).

Mystical Prayer

pp. 166–7   St Anselm. From *The Proslogion* by St Anselm, ch. 1, copyright The Clarendon Press, Oxford, for extracts from St Anselm's *Proslogion*, tr. M.J. Charlesworth © Oxford University Press, 1965.

pp. 168–9   St Bernard of Clairvaux. From the Sermons of St Bernard on the Song of Songs.

p. 170 Thomas à Kempis. From *The Imitation of Christ*, Bk 2, 1.1.

p. 171 St Teresa of Avila. From *Book of the Life* by St Teresa of Jesus, ch. 29, paragraph 13, tr. E. Allison Peers.

pp. 172–3 St John of the Cross. From *Dark Night*, tr. Marjorie Flower OCD © 1983 in the *Poems of St John of the Cross* (published by the Carmelite Community, St Andrew's Rd, Varroville, NSW 2565 Australia), reproduced in *The Impact of God* by Iain Matthew OCD (Hodder, 1995).

p. 174 Kateri Tekakwitha. First paragraph is slightly edited from Butler's *Dictionary of Religious Biography* (Burns & Oates). Second paragraph is from the contemporary biography by Father Cholenec.

p. 175 Marie-Adele Garnier. From an unpublished account by Marie-Adele Garnier dated 1888, © Trustees Tyburn Benedictine Congregation.

pp. 176–8 Thomas Dehau. Translated from the French in the journal *Jesus Caritas*, 1971.

p. 179 St Thérèse of Lisieux. Autobiography Ms C. 7v. Taken from *By Love Alone. Daily Readings with Thérèse of Lisieux*, ed. and intro. by Michael Hollings (DLT, 1986).

p. 180 Anthony de Mello. From *Sadhana: A Way to God* by Anthony de Mello (St Louis: Institute of Jesuit Sources, 1979).

Conversion and Call

pp. 184–5 St Anthony. From the *Life of St Antony* by St Athanasius, chs. 2–4.

p. 186 St Anselm. From *Occasional Sermons of Ronald A. Knox*, preached in the Church of St Anselm and St Cecilia, Kingsway, London (Burns & Oates, 1960), slightly edited.

pp. 187–8 St Ignatius. From the Acts of St Ignatius taken down by Luis Gonzalez, ch. I, 5–9.

p. 189 Mary Ward. A Prayer of Mary Ward, reproduced in *Till God Will: Mary Ward through her Writings*, ed. M. Emmanuel Orchard IBVM (DLT, 1985).

p. 190 John Henry Newman.

pp. 191–2 Francis Thompson.

p. 193 St Thérèse of Lisieux. From the *Autobiography of St Thérèse of Lisieux*, Ms B, 3r–3v, taken from *The Autobiography of a Saint*, tr. Ronald Knox, 1958, © the Executors of Ronald Knox.

p. 194 Dorothy Day. *From Union Square to Rome* by Dorothy Day (Preservation of the Faith Press, 1939).

p. 195 Thomas Merton. From *Cistercian Life* by Thomas Merton, p. 19.

States of Life

p. 197 St John of Damascus.

p. 198 St Bruno. Statutes 3.2. from *The Wound of Love* (DLT, 1994).

p. 199 St Hugh. From *Hugh of Lincoln* by Joseph Clayton (Burns, Oates & Washbourne, 1931).

p. 200 St Elizabeth. From a letter of Conrad of Marburg, St Elizabeth's spiritual director.

---

p. 201   Dante. *The Inferno*, tr. Dorothy L. Sayers (David Higham Associates, 1947).

p. 202   St Teresa of Avila. *The Way of Perfection* by Teresa of Jesus, paragraphs 2, 5, 6, taken from *Living Water. Daily Readings with St Teresa of Avila*, ed. and intro. by Sister Mary ODC (DLT, 1985).

p. 203   Brother Lawrence. Taken from *An Oratory of the Heart. Daily Readings with Brother Lawrence of the Resurrection*, arranged and intro. by Robert Llewelyn (DLT, 1984).

p. 204   Seventeenth-century Nun's Prayer.

p. 205   Madeleine Delbrêl. From *Madeleine Delbrêl. A Life Beyond Boundaries* by Charles F. Mann, taken from a review by Bill Griffin in the *Catholic Worker* newspaper.

p. 206   Joseph Bernardin. First paragraph from Cardinal Bernardin's homily for his installation as Archbishop of Chicago, 24.8.82.

Second paragraph from his final sermon to archdiocesan priests and religious, Oct. 7, 1996, at Holy Name Cathedral, five weeks before his death on 13 November, 1996, reproduced in *The Gift of Peace. Personal Reflections* by Cardinal Joseph Bernardin (DLT, 1997).

Marriage

p. 208   Nuptial Blessing.

p. 209   Tertullian. From *Tertullian's Treatises on Marriage and Remarriage*, tr. William Le Saint SJ, ACW (Ancient Christian Writers), (The Newman Press).

p. 210   St Augustine. From *On Marriage and Concupiscence* 1.10 (PL 44. 420), reproduced in *A Patristic Breviary* by Thomas Spidlik, tr. from Italian by Paul Drake (New City Press, 1992).

p. 211   St Bernard of Clairvaux. From *Letters of St Bernard to the Countess de Blois*, tr. and ed. Bruno Scott James (Burns & Oates, 1953), reproduced in *To Any Christian* by a Benedictine of Stanbrook (Burns & Oates, 1964).

p. 212   St Francis de Sales. Taken from *Athirst for God. Daily Readings with St Francis de Sales*, ed. and intro. by Michael Hollings (DLT, 1985).

p. 213   G.K. Chesterton. From 'Boy and Girl: The Problem of their Upbringing' in *The Daily Graphic*, 12 September, 1907.

p. 214   Catherine de Hueck Doherty. From *Dear Parents* by Catherine de Hueck Doherty (Madonna House Publications, Combermere, Ontario, Canada K0J 1L0, 1997).

p. 215   Frank Sheed. From *To Know Christ Jesus* (Sheed & Ward, an apostolate of the Priests of the Sacred Heart, 7373 South Lovers Lane, Franklin, Wisconsin 53132, USA, 1972).

p. 216   Margaret Grimer. From *Water into Wine* (DLT, 1986).

p. 217   © *Barbara Wood*, 1987.

pp. 218–19   William Johnston SJ. *Letters to Contemplatives* (Collins Fount, 1991).

Holy Living

p. 221 St Augustine. From the sermons of St Augustine, Sermon 256.

p. 222 St Francis. Prayer of St Francis.

p. 223–4 St Francis. Francis of Assisi: *Early Documents vol. I The Saint*, ed. Regis J. Armstrong OFM Cap., J. A. Wayne Hellmann OFM Conv., William J. Short OFM (London, New York and the Phillipines: New City Press), © 1999 Franciscan Institute of St Bonaventure, New York.

p. 225 Thomas à Kempis. From *The Imitation of Christ*.

p. 226 John Henry Newman.

p. 227 Caroline Chisholm. From *Caroline Chisholm* by Trelawney Saunders, taken from *The Emigrant's Friend* by Joanna Bogle (Gracewing Publishing).

p. 228 Dorothy Day. From *On Pilgrimage: The Sixties*.

p. 229 Margaret Sinclair. From *Margaret Sinclair* by F.A. Forbes (London: *Sands & Co.*, 1927), slightly edited.

p. 230 Carlo Carretto. From *Love is for Living* (DLT, 1976), taken from *God of the Impossible: Daily Readings with Carlo Carretto* (DLT, 1988).

p. 231 Mother Teresa. From *Something Beautiful for God* by Malcolm Muggeridge (HarperCollins, 1970).

Ministry

p. 236 St Catherine. From *The Prayers of St Catherine of Siena*, ed. Suzanne Noffke (Paulist Press, 1983), Prayer 19, Passion Sunday, 27 March 1379.

p. 237 St Angela Merici. From *The Spiritual Testament of St Angela Merici*.

pp. 238–9 St Francis Xavier. From the *Letters of St Francis Xavier to St Ignatius*, Book 4, Letters 4 (October, 1542) & 5 (January, 1544).

pp. 240–1 St Peter Claver. From the *Letters of St Peter Claver from Colombia*, Letter to his Superior, 31 May 1627. Originally in Spanish in *San Pedro Claver*, ed. A. Valtierra SJ (Cartagena, 1964.)

p. 242 Nano Nagle. Based on a letter from Nano Nagle to Miss FitzSimons. Early 1770.

p. 243 St Jean Vianney. A reading from *Sacerdoti Nostri Primordia* – encyclical of Pope John XXIII.

pp. 244–5 St John Bosco. From the Letters of St John Bosco, Letter 4.

p. 246 St Frances Cabrini. From a letter to 'mia figlia carissima', 23 May 1904, reproduced in *Mother Cabrini* by Mary Louise Sullivan MSC (Center for Migration Studies, 209 Flagg Pl; Staten Island, New York, 10304–1199, 1992).

p. 247 Frank Duff. From *Legio Mariae*, official handbook of the Legion of Mary, Dublin 1993 (Concilium Legionis Mariae, de Montfort House, Morning Star Ave., Brunswick St, Dublin 7).

p. 248 Dorothy Day. Dated February 1968. From *On Pilgrimage: The Sixties*.

p. 249 Shusako Endo. From his novel, *Silence*, tr. from the Japanese by William Johnston (London: Peter Owen Ltd, 1976).

Spiritual Guidance

p. 251   St Ambrose. From *Ambrose of Milan*, in Ps 1.33:CSEL 64, 28–30, taken from *Tradition Day by Day*, compiled and ed. by John E. Rotelle (Augustinian Press, Villanova, PA 19085 USA, 1994).

p. 252   St Benedict. From *The Rule of St Benedict*, ed. and tr. Abbot Justin McCann (London: Sheed & Ward, 1951), ch. 3.

p. 253   St Benedict. ibid., ch. 64.

p. 254   St Louis. From the spiritual testament of St Louis to his son.

p. 255   Meister Eckhart. First paragraph from DW 83, DP 42 (W. 96. II.333). Second paragraph from DW 56, DP 6 (W. 13b, 1. 117–8). Both reproduced in *Mysticism and Prophecy. The Dominican Tradition* by Richard Woods OP (DLT, 1998).

p. 256   St John of the Cross. First paragraph from *Living Flame* 3.46., tr. by Iain Matthew OCD in *The Impact of God* (Hodder, 1995). Second paragraph from *The Dark Night of the Soul*, ch. 9, taken from *Lamps of Fire. Daily Readings with St John of the Cross*, ed. and intro. by Elizabeth Ruth Obbard OCD (DLT, 1985).

p. 257   Richard Challoner. *Garden of the Soul* (1740). Jean-Pierre de Caussade. From *The Sacrament of the Present Moment*, tr. Kitty Muggeridge (HarperCollins, 1981).

p. 258   John Chapman. From *Spiritual Letters* (Sheed & Ward, 1935, second edn).

p. 259   Blessed Padre Pio. From letter of Passion Sunday 29 March 1914 to Raffaelina Cerase, taken from *Correspondence* Vol. II (Editions 'Padre Pio da Pietrelcina', 71013 San Giovanni Rotondo, Italy, 1997).

p. 260   Caryll Houselander. From *This War is the Passion* by Caryll Houselander (Sheed & Ward, 1943).

p. 261   Thomas Philippe. From *The Contemplative Life*, ed. Edward D. O'Connor CSC (London: HarperCollins, 1991).

p. 262   Thomas Merton. From *No Man is an Island* (Burns & Oates, 1955), taken from *The Shining Wilderness: Daily Readings with Thomas Merton* (DLT, 1988).

Spiritual Friendship

p. 264   St Gregory. From the *Discourses of St Gregory of Nazianzus*, Or. 43.

pp. 265–6   St Scholastica. From a reading from the *Dialogues of St Gregory the Great*, Book 2:33, 34.

p. 267   St Anselm. From *Patrologia Latina* 158, Ep IV, col. 1098, reproduced in *To Any Christian*, selected and arranged by a Benedictine of Stanbrook (Burns & Oates, 1964).

p. 268   St Aelred. From *St Aelred of Rievaulx Spiritual Friendship* (Kalmazoo: Cistercian Publications, 1977).

p. 269   Bl. Jordan of Saxony. From *To Heaven with Diana* by Gerald Vann, a translation of the letters from Jordan of Saxony to the Dominican prioress Blessed Diana d' Andalò. © The Dominican Order in England.

p. 270   St Thomas More. From a letter of St Thomas More to his daughter Margaret Roper, written in 1534.

p. 271   St Francis de Sales. Letter of 24 June 1604. From *Francis de Sales: Jane–Frances de Chantal. Letters of Spiritual Direction*, tr. Peronne Marie Thibert, CWS (Paulist Press, 1988).

p. 272   Hilaire Belloc. From a letter to Katharine Asquith from Hilaire Belloc.

p. 273   St Thérèse of Lisieux. From *Maurice and Thérèse* by Patrick Ahern (DLT, 1999), translated by Patrick Ahern.

p. 274   Pope John Paul I. From *Illustrissimi*, Letters of Pope John Paul I (HarperCollins, 1978), slightly edited.

In Weakness Strength

p. 278   St John Chrysostom. On the letter to the Romans 21:1ff. (PG 60), from *Patristic Breviary* by Thomas Spidlik (New City Press, 1992), tr. from the Italian.

p. 279   St Frances of Rome. From the *Life of St Frances of Rome*, Acta Sanct. Martii 2, 188–9.

p. 280   Bl. Frédéric Ozanam. First paragraph from Letter to Fr Pendola, 19 July 1853. Second paragraph from newspaper article 'Alms-giving', *Ere Nouvelle*, 24 December 1848. Both used in *Through the Eye of a Needle* by Frédéric Ozanam (St Pauls, 1989).

p. 281   Bl. Mary MacKillop. From leaflet 'The Australian People's Saint' (edited), used with permission of the Trustees of Sisters of St Joseph of the Sacred Heart.

p. 282   Pope John XXIII. First paragraph from *Journal of a Soul: John XXIII* (Geoffrey Chapman, a division of Cassell Ltd, 1980. Used by permission of Doubleday, a division of Random House, Inc.). The second paragraph is headed 'Thoughts in Solitude'.

p. 283   Georges Vanier. Letter to a Carmelite nun in 1959. From *In Weakness Strength: The Spiritual Sources of Georges P. Vanier. 19th Governor General of Canada* by his son Jean Vanier (Toronto: Griffin House, 1969).

p. 284   Fulton Sheen.

p. 285   Pedro Arrupe. *One Jesuit's Spiritual Journey. Autobiographical Conversations with Jean-Claude Dietsch* (St Louis: Institute of Jesuit Sources, 1986).

p. 286   Donald Nicholl. From 'Growing Old' (Priests and People, 1973).

p. 287   Henri J.M. Nouwen. *The Inner Voice of Love* (DLT, 1996).

p. 288   Anonymous.

Martyrdom

pp. 290–1   SS Felicitas and Perpetua. From the account of the martyrdom of the Holy Martyrs of Carthage, chs. 18–21.

p. 292   St John Houghton and companions. 'Campion's Brag', 1580, addressed 'To the Right Honourable the Lord's of her Majestie's Privy Council'.

pp. 293–4   St Paul Miki. From the account of the martyrdom of St Paul Miki and his companions by a contemporary author. Acta Sanct.

pp. 295–6   St Jane Frances de Chantal. From the memoirs of the secretary of St Jane Frances de Chantal, III, ed. 1853.

p. 297   Korean Martyrs. From the homily of Pope John Paul II at the canonisation, 6 May

1984, reproduced in *Osservatore Romano* (English ed.), 14 May 1984 (Via del Pellegrino 00120, Vatican City).

p. 298   Uganda martyrs. First paragraph from Angelus message of Pope Paul VI in *Osservatore Romano*, 7 August 1969. Second paragraph from homily at canonisation in *Osservatore Romano*, 18 October 1964.

p. 299   Oscar Romero. From *Homilias* vol. 4, 11 May 1978.

p. 300   Christian de Chergé. 'Association des Écrits des Septs de l'Atlas' (c/o Dom Andre Barbeau OCSO, Abbot Notre Dame d' Aiguebelle, 26230 Montjoyer, France).

Death and Eternity

pp. 302–3   St Ignatius. From the letter of St Ignatius to the Romans, rom 4, 1–2; 6, 1–8, 3.

p. 304   St Augustine. From *The Confessions of St Augustine*, Bk IX. 10.23, tr. Maria Boulding (Hodder, 1997).

p. 305   St Augustine. From *The City of God* by St Augustine.

p. 306   'O God that art the only hope of the world' sometimes attributed to Bede. From *The Oxford Book of Prayer*, ed. George Appleton (1985). 'I pray Thee, merciful Jesus' at the end of Bede's *Historia Ecclesiastica*.

p. 307   St Aloysius Gonzaga. From a letter of St Aloysius Gonzaga to his mother, 10 June 1591, in 'The Vocation of St Aloysius Gonzaga' from *To any Christian*, selected and arranged by a Benedictine of Stanbrook (Burns and Oates, 1964).

p. 308   Bede Griffiths. From 'Prayer', a talk at Kreuth, Germany, 7 April 1992, reproduced in *Beyond the Darkness. A Biography of Bede Griffiths* by Shirley du Boulay (Rider, 1998).

p. 309   Flannery O'Connor. From 'Revelation' in Flannery O'Connor's collection of short stories *Everything that Rises Must Converge* (Farrar, Straus and Giroux, 1956)

p. 310   Basil Hume. 'Mystery' taken from *The Mystery of the Incarnation* by Basil Hume (DLT, 1999).

pp. 3, 15, 24, 35, 51, 65, 76, 97, 105, 106, 119, 137, 151, 165, 183, 196, 207, 220, 235, 250, 263, 277, 282, 301, 311 taken from the New Jerusalem Bible. © DLT and Doubleday & Co Inc, 1985.

pp. 4, 5, 11–12, 16, 25, 27, 28, 36–7, 38, 39, 43, 68–9, 80–2, 83–4, 85, 86–7, 101, 102, 107, 116–17, 122–3, 125, 126–7, 129–30, 138–9, 140–2, 143, 144, 152, 154, 158, 159, 161, 168–9, 170, 184–5, 187–8, 197, 200, 221, 237, 240–1, 244–5, 254, 264, 265–6, 279, 290–1, 293–4, 295–6, 302–3 taken from The Divine Office. © A. P. Watt Ltd on behalf of The Hierarchies of England, Wales, Ireland and Australia and Canada.

Every endeavour has been made to trace the copyright owners of each extract. There do, however, remain a few extracts for which the source is unknown to the compiler and publisher. The publisher would be glad to hear from the copyright owners of the extracts and due acknowledgement will be made in all future editions of the book.

AUTHORS AND TEXTS

St Aelred of Rievaulx (1109–67) Son of a Saxon priest. Cistercian abbot from 1147. Feast day 12 January.

St Aloysius Gonzaga (1568–91) Italian Jesuit novice. Died of plague in Rome aged 23. Feast day 21 June.

St Ambrose (c. 339–97) Bishop of Milan and instrumental in the conversion of St Augustine. Doctor of the Church. Feast day 7 December.

St Andrew of Crete (c. 660–740) Theologian. Reputed to have invented the canon as a musical form. Feast day (E. Church) 4 July.

St Angela Merici (c. 1474–1540) Italian foundress of the Ursulines, the first congregation for the education of girls. Feast day 27 January.

St Anselm (c. 1033–1109) Italian/French Benedictine monk and reluctant Archbishop of Canterbury from 1093. Doctor of the Church. Feast day 21 April.

St Antony of Egypt (c. 251–356) Hermit, 'desert father' and the founder of monasticism. Feast day 17 January.

Arrupe, Pedro (1907–91) Basque superior general of the Jesuits (1965–81). Ministered to atomic bomb victims at Hiroshima in 1945.

St Augustine (354–430) Bishop of Hippo in North Africa. Theologian and monastic founder. Doctor of the Church. Feast day 28 August.

Baldwin of Canterbury (d. 1190) Monk of Forde. Archbishop of Canterbury from 1184.

St Basil the Great (c. 330–79) Cappadocian Father. Bishop of Caesarea from 370. Feast day 2 January (with St Gregory of Nazianzus).

St Bede the Venerable (c. 673–735) 'The Father of English History'. Benedictine monk of Jarrow. Feast day 25 May.

Belloc, Hilaire (1870–1953) French-born British poet and writer.

St Benedict of Nursia (c. 480–c. 550) 'Patriarch of Western Monasticism'. Italian founder of the Benedictines. Feast day 11 July.

St Bernard of Clairvaux (1090–1153) French Cistercian monk who exercised immense influence. Doctor of the Church. Feast day 20 August.

St Bernadette Soubirous (1844–79) At the age of 14 received 18 apparitions of Our Lady at Lourdes. Feast day 18 February.

Bernardin, Joseph (1928–96) Cardinal Archbishop of Chicago. Recipient of the Medal of Freedom in 1996.

Bianco da Siena (d. 1412) Italian mystical poet.

St Bonaventure (c. 1217–74) Italian Franciscan theologian. Minister General of the Order from 1257. Feast day 15 July.

St Boniface (c. 675–754) The 'Apostle of Germany', born in England. Martyred in 754. Feast day 5 June.

Bradburne, John (1921–79) English Franciscan tertiary. Died in Zimbabwe defending those suffering from leprosy.

Brown, Raymond (1928–98) Sulpician priest, born in New York. Outstanding New Testament scholar.

St Bruno (c. 1032–1101) German-born. With six companions, founded the Carthusian Order near Grenoble in 1084. Feast day 6 October.

St Caesarius (c. 470–542) Monk of the island of Lérins and Archbishop of Arles at the age of 33. Feast day 27 August.

Carretto, Carlo (1910–88) Italian youth leader who subsequently became a priest and a follower of Charles de Foucauld.

Carthusian Order Strictly contemplative Order of solitaries founded 1084.

St Catherine of Siena (c. 1347–80) Influential Italian Dominican tertiary and mystic. Doctor of the Church. Feast day 29 April.

Caussade, Jean-Pierre de (1675–1751) French Jesuit, known for his book *Self-Abandonment to Divine Providence.*

Celtic Tradition (c. 500–c. 800) Of the churches without institutional unity in the areas using Celtic languages.

Challoner, Richard (1691–1781) Vicar Apostolic from 1758 and thus responsible for the Catholic community in England.

Chapman, John (1865–1933) English Benedictine monk and author. Abbot of Downside from 1929.

Chergé, Christian de (1937–96) French Cistercian prior martyred in Algeria with six others.

Chesterton, Gilbert Keith (1874–1936) English author, journalist and champion of catholic orthodoxy.

Chisholm, Caroline (1808–77) Devoted her life to the care of women emigrating to Australia from England.

Claudel, Paul (1868–1955) Playright and diplomat. French ambassador to Washington (1926–33)

Cloud of Unknowing: anonymous fourteenth-century mystical work.

St Columba (c. 521–97) In Irish, Colum Cille 'dove of the Church'. Columba founded the monastery on Iona. Feast day 9 June.

St Columbanus (d. 615) Irish missionary. Worked in France, Germany and Italy. Feast day 23 November.

Curé d'Ars. St Jean Vianney (1786–1859) From 1818 renowned parish priest of Ars in France. Feast day 4 August.

Cynewulf (early 9th century) Anglo-Saxon religious poet.

St Cyril (d. 444) Patriarch of Alexandria and theologian. Opposed the teaching of Nestorius. Feast day 27 June.

Damien, Father (1840–89) Belgian missionary to leprosy sufferers on the Hawaiian island of Molokai.

Dante Alighieri (1265–1321) Italian poet and philosopher. Author of *The Divine Comedy*.

Day, Dorothy (1897–1980) Prominent American peace campaigner, journalist and social activist.

Dehau, Thomas (1870–1956) French Dominican theologian and spiritual director.

Delbrêl, Madeleine (1904–64) With her companions lived alongside the poor in the Paris suburb of Ivry.

Diadochus (mid 5th century) Bishop of Photike after 451.

Diognetus: the Epistle to (c. 2nd/3rd century) Letter from an unknown Christian to an otherwise unknown enquirer.

Dionysius the Pseudo-Areopagite (c. 500) So-called because the writings of the otherwise unknown author were at one time ascribed to the first-century convert Dionysius the Areopagite (Acts 17:34).

Doherty, Catherine de Hueck (1896–1985) Russian-born American foundress of the Madonna House lay apostolate in Canada.

St Dominic (c. 1172–1221) Spanish founder of the Order of Friars Preachers (1215). Feast day 8 August.

Dream of the Rood. Old English poem by an unknown author representing the feelings of the cross during the crucifixion.

Duff, Frank (1889–1980) Dublin-born founder of the Legion of Mary (1921).

Eckhart, Meister (c. 1260–c. 1328) German Dominican theologian. Accused of heresy 1326 and died denying the charges.

St Edith Stein (1891–1942) Jewish-born philosopher and Carmelite nun. Died in Auschwitz. Feast day 9 August.

St Edmund Campion (1540–81) One of the first Jesuits to return to England. Martyred at Tyburn. Feast day 1 December.

St Elizabeth of Hungary (1207–31) Daughter of the King of Hungary she devoted herself to the sick. Feast day 17 November.

Bl. Elizabeth of the Trinity (1888–1906) French Carmelite from Dijon. Feast day 8 November.

Endo, Shusako (1923–96) Japanese novelist.

St Ephrem the Syrian (c. 306–73) Bible scholar and hymn writer. Doctor of the Church. Feast day 9 June.

Exultet: Pascal proclamation sung on Holy Saturday night. Can be traced back to 7th/8th century.

St Felicitas (d. 203) African slave. Martyred at Carthage with St Perpetua. Their Feast day 7 March.

Foucauld, Charles de (1858–1985) French explorer and 'Hermit of the Sahara'. His Rule has attracted many followers.

St Frances Cabrini (1850–1917) Italian missionary to American immigrants. First US citizen to be canonised. Feast day 13 November.

St Frances of Rome (1384–1440) Widow. Founded a community of Benedictine oblates. Feast day 9 March.

St Francis of Assisi (c. 1181–1226) Deeply committed to the poor and founder of the Franciscans (1209). Feast day 4 October.

St Francis de Sales (1567–1622) Bishop of Geneva from 1602. Doctor of the Church. Feast day 24 January.

St Francis Xavier (1506–52) Basque 'Apostle of the Indies and of Japan'. One of the first Jesuits. Feast day 3 December.

Bl. Frédéric Ozanam (1813–53) French scholar and founder of the Society of St Vincent de Paul. Feast day 9 September.

Garnier, Marie-Adele (1838–1924) French foundress of the Benedictine Congregation, the Adorers of the Sacred Heart of Montmartre.

St Gertrude the Great (1256–c. 1302) German mystic and visionary. Nun of Helfta. Feast day 16 November.

St Gregory the Great (c. 540–604) Pope from 590. Sent St Augustine to England in 596. Doctor of the Church. Feast day 3 September.

St Gregory of Nazianzus (c. 329–c. 390) Cappadocian Father. Son of the Bishop of Nazianzus. Feast day (with St Basil) 2 January.

St Gregory of Nyssa (c. 330–c. 395) Cappadocian Father, Bishop of Nyssa. Brother of St Basil. Feast day 9 March.

Griffiths, Bede (1906–93) English Benedictine monk. In India became internationally known as a 'bridge' between east and west.

Grimer, Margaret (1933–95) Worked for many years with the Catholic Marriage Advisory Council in England.

St Hildegard of Bingen (1098–1179) German mystic and Benedictine abbess. Feast day 17 September.

Hopkins, Gerard Manley (1844–89) English Jesuit poet and Professor of Greek at Dublin.

Houselander, Caryll (1901–54) English writer, poet and artist.

St Hugh of Lincoln (c. 1140–1200) French Carthusian who became Bishop of Lincoln. Feast day 17 November.

Hügel, Baron Friedrich von (1852–1925) German/English theologian and philosopher.

Hume, Basil (1923–99) English Benedictine monk. Abbot of Ampleforth 1963–76. Cardinal Archbishop of Westminster (1976–99).

St Ignatius of Antioch (c. 35–c. 107) Bishop of Antioch. Martyred in Rome. Feast day 17 October.

St Ignatius of Loyola (c. 1491–1556) Spanish soldier. Founder of the Society of Jesus (1540). Feast day 31 July.

Isaac of Nineveh (d.c. 700) Monk and subsequently Bishop of Nineveh.

St Jane Frances de Chantal (1572–1641) As a widow she founded the Order of the Visitation in France. Feast day 12 December.

John XXIII (1881–1963) Pope from 1958. Convened the Second Vatican Council (1962–5).

St John Bosco (1815–88) Founded the Salesian Order near Turin for the care of boys. Feast day 31 January.

St John Chrysostom (c. 347–407) Patriarch. The name Chrysostom meaning 'golden mouthed'. Doctor of the Church. Feast day 13 September.

St John of the Cross (1542–91) Spanish mystic. Joint founder of the Discalced Carmelites. Doctor of the Church. Feast day 14 December.

St John of Damascus (c. 655–c. 750) Theologian and hymn writer. Doctor of the Church. Feast day 4 December.

Bl. John Duns Scotus (c. 1265–1308) Scottish Franciscan philosopher and theologian. Feast day 8 November.

Ven. John Henry Newman (1801–90) Established the Oratorians in England (1849). Cardinal 1879.

St John Ogilvie (1579–1615) Scots Jesuit. Martyred in Glasgow. Feast day 10 March.

John Paul I (1912–78) Pope from 26 August to 28 September 1978.

John Paul II (1920–) Pope from 1978.

Johnston, William (1925–) Irish-born Jesuit living and working in Japan. Prominent in Buddhist–Christian dialogue.

Bl. Jordan of Saxony (c. 1190–1237) German Master General of the Dominican Order from 1221. Feast day 13 February.

Julian of Norwich (c. 1342–after 1416) English anchoress and spiritual writer.

Bl. Kateri Tekakwitha (c. 1656–80) Native American convert who practised great personal austerity. Feast day 17 April.

Kempe, Margery (c. 1373–after 1438) English visionary, author and mother of fourteen children.

Knox, Ronald (1888–1957) English priest, scholar and translator of the Bible.

Korean Martyrs (1784–1839) The Korean Church was founded by laypeople and has more than ten thousand martyrs. Feast day 21 September.

St Laurence (d. 258) Deacon. Martyred in Rome. Feast day 10 August.

Lawrence, Brother (c. 1614–91) French Carmelite laybrother and mystic.

St Leo the Great (d. 461) Leo I, pope from 440. Doctor of the Church. Feast day 10 November.

Lonergan, Bernard (1904–84) Canadian Jesuit theologian, philosopher and economist.

St Louis of France (1214–70) King Louis IX, crowned 1226. Feast day 25 August.

St Louis Marie de Montfort (1673–1716). French missioner and founder. Author of *True Devotion to the Blessed Virgin*. Feast day 28 April.

Main, John (1926–82) Irish-born Benedictine monk and founder of the Christian Meditation movement.

St Maksymilian Kolbe (1894–1941) Polish Franciscan. Died in Auschwitz. Feast day 14 August.

St Margaret Mary Alacoque (1647–90) French Visitandine nun and promoter of devotion to the Sacred Heart. Feast day 16 October.

Ven. Margaret Sinclair (1900–25) Edinburgh working girl who became a Poor Clare in England.

Bl. Marie of the Incarnation (1599–1672) French missionary to the Huron in Canada. Feast day 30 April.

St Martin de Porres (1579–1639) Peruvian Dominican lay brother who cared for the poor. Feast day 3 November.

St Martin of Tours (d. 397) Bishop of Tours and a patron saint of France. Feast day 11 November.

Bl. Mary MacKillop (1842–1909) Foundress of the first Australian religious Order, the Sisters of St Joseph. Feast day 8 August.

St Mary Magdalene de' Pazzi (1566–1607) Italian Carmelite mystic. Feast day 25 May.

St Melito of Sardis (d.c. 190) Bishop. Feast day 1 April.

Mello, Anthony de (1931–87) Indian Jesuit author, retreat giver and spiritual director.

Merton, Thomas (1915–68) Influential American Cistercian monk and writer.

Nagle, Nano (1718–84) Prominent Irish educationalist and foundress of the Sisters of the Presentation of the Blessed Virgin Mary.

Nicholl, Donald (1923–97) English scholar. First rector of the Ecumenical Institute at Tantur outside Bethlehem.

Nouwen, Henri J.M. (1932–96) Dutch-American priest, writer, teacher and spiritual director.

O'Connor, Flannery (1925–64) Novelist. Born Savannah, Georgia.

Bl. Padre Pio (1887–1968) Italian Franciscan priest and mystic. Feast day 23 September.

St Patrick (5th century) Apostle to the Irish. Feast day 17 March.

Paul VI (1897–1978) Pope from 1963.

St Paul Miki (c. 1564–97) Japanese Jesuit martyr. Feast day 3 November.

Péguy, Charles (1873–1914) French poet and philosopher.

St Perpetua (d. 203) African martyr. Died in Carthage with St Felicitas. Their Feast day 7 March.

St Peter Claver (1581–1654) Spanish Jesuit missionary to black slaves in Colombia. Feast day 9 September.

Philippe, Thomas (1905–93) French Dominican theologian. Co-founder of the Communities of l'Arche (1964).

St Philippine Duchesne (1769–1852) First member of the Society of the Sacred Heart to go on mission from France to America in 1818. Feast day 18 November.

Rahner, Karl (1904–84) Influential German Jesuit theologian. Prominent at the Second Vatican Council.

Richard of St-Victor (d. 1173) Scots theologian who lived and taught at the Abbey of St-Victor in Paris.

St Robert Southwell (1561–95) English Jesuit poet and martyr. Feast day 25 October.

Robin, Marthe (1902–81) Mystic who greatly influenced twentieth-century French religious communities.

Rolle, Richard (c. 1300–49) English hermit and spiritual writer.

Romero, Oscar (1917–80) Archbishop of San Salvador from 1977. Murdered while celebrating Mass in his diocese.

St Rose of Lima (1586–1617) Peruvian of Spanish origin. Dominican tertiary. Feast day 23 August.

St Scholastica (c. 480–c. 543) Benedictine nun. Sister of St Benedict. Feast day 10 February.

Sheed, Frank (1897–1981) Australian-born writer and publisher.

Sheen, Fulton (1895–1979) American Archbishop. Popular writer, preacher and radio and television speaker.

Teilhard de Chardin, Pierre (1881–1955) French Jesuit theologian and scientist.

St Teresa of Avila (1515–82) Spanish mystic and joint reformer of the Discalced Carmelites. Doctor of the Church. Feast day 15 October.

Teresa of Calcutta (1910–97) 'Mother Teresa'. Born of an Albanian family in Skopje (subsequently Macedonia), foundress of the Missionaries of Charity (1948).

Tertullian (c. 160–c. 225) African Church Father.

St Thérèse of Lisieux (1873–97) French Carmelite. Co-patroness of France. Doctor of the Church. Feast day 1 October.

St Thomas Aquinas (c. 1225–74) Italian Dominican philosopher and theologian. Doctor of the Church. Feast day 28 January.

Thomas à Kempis (c. 1380–1471) Dutch Augustinian canon. Author of *The Imitation of Christ*.

St Thomas More (1478–1535) Martyr. Lord Chancellor of England (1529–32). Feast day (with St John Fisher) 22 June.

Thompson, Francis (1859–1907) English mystical poet.

Uganda Martyrs (1885–7) Protestants and Catholics from the age of 15 (St Kizito) were martyred by the ruler, Mwanga. Feast day 3 June.

Vanier, Georges (1888–1967) Soldier and diplomat. Governor General of Canada from 1959 to 1967.

Vann, Gerald (1906–63) English Dominican preacher and author.

St Vincent de Paul (1581–1660) French servant of the poor. Founded the Vincentian Fathers and the Daughters of Charity. Feast day 27 September.

Walsh, Tony (1898–1994) Taught native American children and founded Labre House for the homeless of Montreal.

Ward, Mary (1585–1645) English educationalist and foundress of the Institute of the Blessed Virgin Mary.

Wood, Barbara (1946–) English writer. Her work includes a biography of her father, the economist E.F. Schumacher.

INDEX

CROSS COUNTRY

CROSS COUNTRY

ENGLISH BUILDINGS AND LANDSCAPE
FROM COUNTRYSIDE TO COAST

PETER ASHLEY

A John Wiley and Sons, Ltd, Publication

THIS EDITION FIRST PUBLISHED 2011
© 2011 JOHN WILEY & SONS LTD
Registered office
JOHN WILEY & SONS LTD, THE ATRIUM, SOUTHERN GATE, CHICHESTER, WEST SUSSEX, PO19 8SQ,
UNITED KINGDOM

FOR DETAILS OF OUR GLOBAL EDITORIAL OFFICES, FOR CUSTOMER SERVICES AND FOR
INFORMATION ABOUT HOW TO APPLY FOR PERMISSION TO REUSE THE COPYRIGHT MATERIAL
IN THIS BOOK, PLEASE SEE OUR WEBSITE AT WWW.WILEY.COM.

EXECUTIVE COMMISSIONING EDITOR: HELEN CASTLE
PROJECT EDITOR: MIRIAM SWIFT
ASSISTANT EDITOR: CALVER LEZAMA

ISBN 978-0-470-68611-9 (HARDBACK)
ISBN 978-1-119-97105-4 (EBK)
ISBN 978-1-119-97106-1 (EBK)
ISBN 978-1-119-97102-3 (EBK)

COVER DESIGN, PAGE DESIGN, LAYOUTS AND MAPS BY JEREMY TILSTON
PRINTED AND BOUND IN ITALY BY PRINTER TRENTO SRL

THE FRONT COVER ILLUSTRATION IS TAKEN FROM A PRE-WAR CHILDRENS' PICTURE BOOK
CALLED *MOTORS*. THE BOOK IS A TREASURE STORE OF 1930S' TRANSPORT ILLUSTRATIONS BY AN
ARTIST CALLED DOUGLAS LIONEL MAYS (1900–91). THERE IS NO PUBLISHER OR PRINTER
MENTIONED. THE AUTHOR FOUND IT TUCKED AWAY IN THE DARK AT THE BACK OF AN
ANTIQUE SHOP IN LECHLADE, GLOUCESTERSHIRE.
ALL PHOTOGRAPHS © PETER ASHLEY
P 53 ILLUSTRATION FROM *THE WITCH'S HAT* © TONY MEEUWISSEN

PREVIOUS PAGE
Cross-country lane between Blaston and Horninghold, Leicestershire

DEDICATION

For Teresa, with love.

ACKNOWLEDGEMENTS

I am extremely grateful to Mike Goldmark for his help and considerable support on *Cross Country*. My heartfelt thanks go to him and all at the Goldmark Gallery in Uppingham.

Stephen Allen, George Ashley, Wilfred Ashley, Kathy Ashley, Tom Barr, Lucy Bland, David and Ruth Bull, Helen Castle, Christopher Clark, Teresa Cox, English Heritage, Rupert Farnsworth, Ron Flaxman, Jay Goldmark, Abigail Grater, Leigh Hooper, Stuart Kendall, Calver Lezama, Maria Mitchell, Matthew Mitchell, National Trust, Roger Porter, Biff Raven-Hill, Neil Sharpe, Margaret Shepherd, David Stanhope, Gerald Stickler, Chris Strachan, Miriam Swift, Jeremy Tilston, Ken and Hazel Wallace, Gill Whitley, Philip Wilkinson.

Contents

TOP LEFT
Wheal Coates engine house, Cornwall

MIDDLE LEFT
Sunrise on Meon Hill, Warwickshire

BOTTOM LEFT
Romney, Hythe & Dymchurch Railway locomotive
Hurricane *at Dungeness, Kent*

TOP RIGHT
Vita Nova at Roa Island, Cumbria

MIDDLE RIGHT
Bell push, Winchcombe, Gloucestershire

BOTTOM RIGHT
Fonthill gateway, Wiltshire

15 x 30g Servings

This pack is sold by weight not volume, settling of contents may occur during transit.
*Approximate quantity per 30g serving

© 2008 Kellogg Company
®, ™ Kellogg Company
Kellogg Marketing and Sales Company (UK) Limited, Manchester M16 0PU.

£2.29

...ST

and see if YOU can...

n Bett...

...ice
...ispie...
...igina...

wels

Absorbent

...i-Purpose

...8t Pack

FSC

3 for £1.19

3 for £1...

HP®

BAKED
BEANS

IN A RICH TOMATO SAUCE

3 for £1.19

HP®

BAKED
BEANS

IN A RICH TOMATO SAUCE

3 for £1.1...

HP®

BAKED
BEANS

IN A RICH TOMATO SAUCE

3 for £1.19

HP®

BAKED
BEANS

IN A RICH TOMATO SAUCE

3 for £1.19

HP®

BAKED
BEANS

IN A RICH TOMATO SAUCE

3 for £1.19

HP®

BAKED
BEANS

IN A RICH TOMATO SAUCE

CROSS COUNTRY
INTRODUCTION

I ONLY went abroad for the first time when I was 30 — to Paris on a British Midland Viscount with curtains at the windows — and, although I have indeed enjoyed occasional foreign forays, it has been England that has taken up so much of my time and attention. The trouble is I have, like my father before me, an insatiable appetite for interesting-looking things, particularly in the countryside, and rural England is stuffed to the gills with them. I also have a problem in that I like going on about it to anyone who'll listen, and so have made people fall off bar stools with the constant recounting of my travels, trying to keep their attention with the 'glittering eye' of a bucolic Ancient Mariner. If I lived abroad, like a dear friend of mine who sits on a mountainside in Piedmont staring at a Hornby coal truck, I'd be called an anglophile.

Anglophile. That's the word we use to describe someone who loves England, but it tends to be the label attached to those from other lands who find this remarkable, beautiful country so absorbing, and perhaps somehow better than the one they were born in. What is it that they find so much suited to their taste and sensibilities? It could be social: 'Your policemen are so wonderful'; it could be political (although often that's difficult to understand); and, of course, it could be the roseate view that's somehow bound up with looking at exported English period television dramas. So it's also the sense of history, of which we have an awful lot by anybody's standards. It could be all of these things, but perhaps it's more likely to be topographical. If your view of life is the downtown shopping mall in Birmingham, Alabama, you may want to see the Bull Ring shopping centre in Birmingham, West Midlands. Those who hanker after a taste of the 'Old Country' may inevitably be drawn to the stereotypical whistle-stop tour: London, Bath, Stratford-upon-Avon, York and then off to Edinburgh, the passing countryside a blurred panorama outside an air-conditioned coach window. England reduced to a set of postcards or, more likely, files of images on a camera memory chip that will never be printed out. No, I think the true anglophile looks further than the next hotel stopover.

◄◄ OPPOSITE
Pyramid selling, Holt, Norfolk

▲ ABOVE
Roadside sign, Bradwell-on-Sea, Essex

My Australian friend Bob landed at Heathrow in 1975 with a wife and three children, promptly bought a black London cab and, once he'd stopped total strangers jumping in the back, they headed out into the Great Unknown. On driving through the village of Tur Langton in Leicestershire, he spotted my old Riley under a row of trees, its resting place after I'd shot a piston through the cylinder block between Northampton and Market Harborough. He knocked on my door, made me a derisory offer, we went to the pub. I started to show Bob and his family England. Well, my England. I made them shiver by fenland dykes, showed them a priest's skull in a glass case in Crowland Abbey complete with stab wound (someone later nicked it, it's probably now a conversation piece ashtray in Spalding), and the various design styles of pub interiors. They all ended up living here, went back to Australia, but now can't keep away. Bob and Liz both fit my definition of true anglophiles, dear folk who don't just love England, but will always look beyond the obvious, will always check out the detail.

England for me started at my front gate. The unadopted road I was born on was an eclectic mix of Victorian and Edwardian houses, many with their sumptuous gardens infilled with interwar semis. At the bottom of the lane was an equally 1930s pub, where a yellow delivery dray delivered Hole's Newark Ales on Tuesdays, and opposite was a post office with a little toy-shop annexe. Beer and Dinky Toys,

▲ **ABOVE**
Leicestershire countryside near Medbourne

➤➤ **OPPOSITE**
Bell rope, Old Romney, Kent

❦ **BELOW**
Sumo wrestler clearing a hedge in North Norfolk

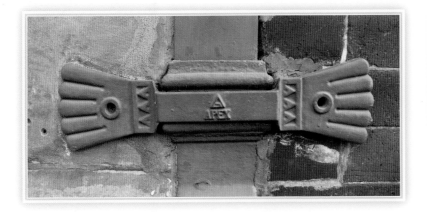

it was a good start. This was my world in microcosm, until I realised a large Midlands city was next door. From the front seat of a Leicester Corporation bus, I just stared out at the city. Shops, houses, pubs and factories, and the smaller things: the sun blinds and gilt lettering on shopfronts, the dark wooden floor in Woolworths, the white-sleeved policeman on point duty whom my mother once threatened to turn me over to.

The other way was open countryside. A Georgian farmhouse in a fold of sheep pasture, a limestone grange at the end of an avenue of chestnuts, an orange brick bridge across a reed-swamped canal. I couldn't get enough, cycling furiously down lanes strewn with straw and cattle dung. An annual holiday was like going to Africa. My father would send off for town guides, a habit I picked up as a teenager, filling my bedroom shelves with what Bury St Edmunds or Truro had to offer. Trains took us to places I'd only seen in books on Beautiful Britain, I saw photographs and watercolours of unknown towns and villages framed under the string luggage racks. Being with my father, we also ended up in places that were decidedly not subjects for artists: white-painted concrete bungalows dangerously near the edges of cliffs, caravans that tipped alarmingly when you sat on the Elsan. As soon as I got my first transport – a Ford Thames van with more rust than paint – I bought a *Bartholomew's Atlas* and set off, a trail of blue exhaust smoke drifting over the neighbouring counties, going further and further until breaking down in either Norfolk or the Cotswolds.

I had to read about the places I'd seen. Never one to take a guidebook around in a glove box, I avidly mugged up on them once I finally got home. First the Leicestershire and Rutland edition of Pevsner's indispensable *Buildings of England* series, and WG Hoskins' little paperback volumes on the same Midland counties. Two keys then turned in locks, finally opening doors into all the boundless possibilities that were waiting for me in England. Two films – first Tony Richardson's inimitable *Tom Jones* (1963), and then, a few years later, John

⬆ **ABOVE**
Norman Kerr's Cartmel bookshop, Cumbria

◤ **ABOVE LEFT**
Drainpipe bracket, Ludlow, Shropshire

◄ **OPPOSITE**
Gate lock, Bayfield Hall, North Norfolk

Schlesinger's *Far From the Madding Crowd* (1967). Henry Fielding, Thomas Hardy, the landscapes of Dorset and beyond. For a suburban chap like me this was rocket fuel.

❦ BELOW
Beach life, Littlestone-on-Sea, Kent

Six months after I'd seen Schlesinger's film at the Odeon Marble Arch, I walked into an eccentric Leicester bookshop and saw on a shelf *Dorset: Shell Guide.* As I picked it up, it fell open at John Piper's weather-soaked photograph of Waddon Manor, the location used in the film as William Boldwood's farm. I just had to find it, and the next Easter I stood in a windy Dorset field above Chesil Beach, seeing a handful of miles away the pale stone of Waddon intermittently lighting up in bright sunshine like some Holy Grail on the hillside of Corton Down. If this could be got from just one *Shell Guide*, I thought, I have to get the rest.

Anyone who seriously collects books knows the symptoms. The sweaty palms at book fairs, the taking home of treasures in Marks & Spencer's carrier bags saying

you've only been out buying vests. Macmillan's *Highways and Byways* series in blue cloth covers with gilt titles, Batsford books with Brian Cook's railway poster covers, eccentric *Vision of England* books from publisher Paul Elek, books with the whiff of petrol – *Shell and BP Shilling Guides*, National Benzole paperbacks, Esso Road Maps. My father introduced me to HV Morton; I couldn't resist SPB Mais. Edward Thomas and John Betjeman lit blue touch papers with poetry and prose, the latter inspiring me beyond reason with his 1970s television films *A Passion for Churches*, *Metroland* and *The Queen's Realm*. I discovered JJ Hissey, and although I gobbled up his books I found he does have his detractors, possibly because his prose is so drenched in his overwrought ivy-after-rain fantasies. Hissey made journeys around England in everything from dog carts to early Daimlers, but who else will go on about what the oak panelling was like in a country inn in 1897? The trouble is it doesn't stop. Every time Professor Aubrey Manning comes on the television with his *Talking Landscapes* programmes I rush to find a blank videotape.

❦ BELOW
Field barn at Cranoe, Leicestershire

Maybe now's the time, for whatever reason, to discover England again. Nowhere else on earth has such rich variety in so few square miles: descending from the lush green pastures of High Leicestershire and across Cambridgeshire fens to Norfolk flint-bound coasts in an hour and a half, or from the deeply wooded Kentish High Weald to willow-fringed Romney levels and bare Dungeness shingle in a matter of minutes. Landscape, culture, accents, it all changes as quickly as the vernacular architecture. This is what makes England so utterly unique: the thousand differences between counties, the look of buildings built from the underlying geology that changes every few miles, the sheer local flavours. Increasingly, I feel that it's this that should not only be enjoyed, but celebrated. The thing about England is that we tend to stick with what we know in the narrowest sense – striding energetically up a Lakeland fell, downing a Cotswold cream tea, staring at a north Norfolk seal sunbathing on a sandbank. All of which is perfectly OK, it's just that we can miss the detail, forget to look round the corners or simply not take the time to see again what's really around us. There is so much satisfaction in looking beyond the name on an eighteenth-century slate gravestone and appreciating the stunning hand-cut lettering, or picking up a piece of orange sea-washed brick on the shore and wondering about the house it came from.

◄◄ **LEFT**
RAF war memorial, Bradwell-on-Sea, Essex

▼ **BELOW**
Afternoon delights, Winchcombe, Gloucestershire

In a way, this is why I've directed my enthusiasms into *Cross Country*. For some time now, I've concentrated on either English buildings or on the nostalgic visual touchstones that created such a memorable past for many of us. For this, particularly the buildings, I travelled the length and breadth of England and scooted around the coast on mad frenzied itineraries. So I needed to sit down, pour myself a beer and take stock; to recall parts of the country that held particular appeal. With a lifetime of English journeys behind me I had, of course, a few but very distinct favourite areas in mind: the north Norfolk coast, even my own end of Leicestershire, but equally I wanted to find out about the less well-known, the places that for me had hitherto been photographs in books or snippets of film. Criticised for appearing never to go much further north than Nottingham, I spent a decent amount of time in southwest Cumbria. An unexpected lunchtime dealing with oysters in an estuarial shack excited me to the possibilities of the shredded Essex coast.

What *Cross Country* isn't, is a guidebook. Certainly not a gazeteer. This collection of essays and photographs are simply my accounts of certain places as I found them over a couple of years of new journeys around England (plus a brief but necessary crossing of the Welsh Border). My impressions, my discoveries. Conversations, remembrances, things I heard in pubs and jotted down and, of course, the unplanned and unexpected. You will find out far more about medieval churches and eighteenth-century houses in a Penguin (or Yale) *Buildings of England* guide; a fuller account of villages and towns in a Betjeman/Piper-edited *Shell County Guide*. Just think of me as the coach driver (a 1946 AEC Regal, obviously), sitting up front as we bowl along country lanes, steering round corners with one hand, pointing out things with the other.

What you will need, however, is a good, detailed map. I mainly used those orange Ordnance Survey *Explorers*, or my trusty torn and beer-stained magenta *Landrangers*. In each chapter, I have tried to keep to a coherent route that can be easily followed, but in the spirit of this book I wouldn't want it to be prescriptive. As you will see, there will be diversions. Which is part of the fun. I don't use a satnav, and I hope that if you embark on these journeys with one, you will turn it off when you get within range of the starting blocks. Assuming you're not driving a petrol tanker that's going to get wedged on a hump-backed bridge, one of the great benefits of driving unaided about England is that you can easily get lost. Don't worry, that's when you start to make discoveries for yourself: a forgotten church behind dark yews, an obsolete signpost in a hedge, an eccentric pub at a crossroads. That's what I've done, and my constant travels around England have been among the most revealing and fascinating experiences I could possibly have had. I do hope that you will find the places, buildings and landscapes of *Cross Country* equally rewarding on your own journeys; and that they will give you as much pleasure.

▲ ABOVE
Portland Garage, Weobley, Herefordshire

◄◄ OPPOSITE
Abandoned stone quarry, Ford,
Gloucestershire

SQUIRRELS & GRAPES
SOUTHWEST CUMBRIA

THE VERY WORDS 'Lake District' are sufficient to guarantee one of two polarised reactions – either that this northwest corner of England is the epitome of picture-postcard loveliness as seen on countless book jackets and jigsaws, or that it's the ultimate symbol of overkill tourism saturating an area of great natural beauty. Mountainous fells and woodland reflected in mirror-surfaced lakes, Kendal Mint Cake and Beatrix Potter, the combinations are irresistible. Intrepid late eighteenth- and early nineteenth-century tourists found it savage, unkempt country, and couldn't wait to either put it all down on canvas or dose up on laudanum and write yards of poetry. The railways helped, of course, and, as soon as the tracks met up with lake steamers, the rugged untamed landscape came under the Victorian idea of landscape gardening; which meant planting foreign species of pine and building slate and granite hotels with pristine lawns to wander about on reading Wordsworth.

Even in 1927, HV Morton was describing, in his marvellous and prescient *In Search of England*, how his blue Bullnose Morris was held up in a traffic queue, a train of motor vehicles playing a hot metallic follow-my-leader up the east side of Windermere. Sound familiar? It's the congregating in one place that's so depressing. Bowness on a rainy weekday in July, with every café full, every pavement crowded with bewildered holidaymakers wondering just when the sun's going to come out. To really get to grips with the Lake District you need to walk out and up, Wainwright guide in hand, good shoes on feet. However, if you're not into thermal underwear and Thermolite walking poles, take a look towards the coastal margins.

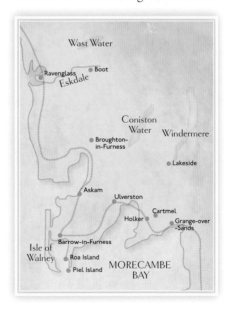

◄◄ OPPOSITE
Waterside Cottage, Cartmel

◥ ABOVE
Furness Railway bench end, Ulverston

This tour could just about be accomplished either by motoring or, almost, by catching trains. A big letter 'C' with the top stroke made by Eskdale, the quietest and least-frequented Lakeland valley; the bottom by the southern coastal peninsulas of Furness facing south out over Morecambe Bay. The down stroke is the estuaries and coast of the Irish Sea with its curious mixture of the rusting remnants of industry and exquisite beach landscapes. Through it all runs the Furness Railway, started here in the mid-nineteenth century, primarily to bring mineral resources to the coast and the rest of England. They emblazoned their activities with the usual flamboyant coat of arms, but curiously used a Lakeland squirrel eating grapes for their platform seat supports. Red squirrels must have been rife here before the greys got the boot in, but grapes? Probably to do with those Romans, who took full advantage of the accessible shores.

The start of our tour is high at the top of Eskdale, where the precipitous 'road' descends from the Wrynose Pass at Hardknott. A word of advice about this motoring nightmare: whichever way you approach this succession of impossibly steep and tight bends, make sure you're not in an articulated lorry and that you've not got a caravan in tow.

◄◄ OPPOSITE
Eskdale from Hardknott Roman Fort

❦ BELOW
Bath house, Hardknott Roman Fort

The Romans knew what they were doing when they decided on Hardknott for the location of their fort. Charmingly called Mediobogdum, it sits at the head of the valley, commanding a virtually uninterrupted view down what is now Eskdale, to their port at Ravenglass and the sea. What a posting for a legionary. After a reasonably short march (*sinister dexter, sinister dexter*) from the galleys they arrived at this bluff of land with its backdrop of dark brooding hills. A three-acre site with corner turrets, one of the first but welcome sights for the travel-worn soldier was the stone bath house, positioned outside the fort walls and consisting of the obligatory hot, warm and cold rooms. (*Caldarium, tepidarium* and *frigidarium* if you want to impress the children.) The fortress itself is obviously restored, but a course of slate in the walls shows where the original line of the remains was. Dating from Hadrian's time, around AD 122, it's part of a chain from his eponymous cross-country wall through Ambleside to this hillside. It was abandoned early in the third century.

To be up here in stormy weather is a rare treat, particularly if the skeletal wet remains of dead sheep lie in the ruins of a tower (very Ted Hughes), but to see a bright line developing out at sea to the west, the sun gradually lighting up Eskdale field by field, fell top by fell top, is to experience something almost spiritual. As the rough stone walls light up against the steep slopes of Bull How and Yew Crag, I always feel like singing a hymn, very loudly. To walk down into Eskdale is like coming indoors, under the trees arching over the lane between stone walls, into the bar of The Woolpack Inn and a welcoming pint of mild ale brewed just next door.

A little further down the road in Boot is a turning into a narrow track. You know it's going to be good because, very soon, you pass a George VI postbox attached to two lengths of iron and painted blue because it's for private use. At the end of the track is the church of St Catherine's, typical of religious meeting places in the dales, hunkered down against the weather with just a small bellcote rising above the roofline. No towers and spires here. Some of the tombstones are in pink sandstone with a local vernacular of incised lettering and curious angel heads; one, with sculpted clasped hands, tells of members of the Tyson family all dying in Canada. Inside, an 1894 window of pale stained glass signed by Savells of Albany Street, London, depicts an almost photographic likeness of Theodora Lewin Taylor. Outside, one hears the sound of the River Esk rushing over stepping stones. The quiet dignity of a funeral here, heads bowed as the prayerbook words are uttered over the lowering of a coffin – 'Man that is born of woman hath but a short time to live ...', and the thundering of the river providing evidence of the continuity of life.

A little further on is Dalegarth Station, the eastern terminus of the Ravenglass and Eskdale Railway (the 'Ratty') that runs for seven miles from here and through Miterdale to the coast. The navvies building it would fly down to Ravenglass in the evenings on one of those gangers' trolleys, fill themselves full of beer, and then pump themselves back up at closing time. Opened in 1875, the 15-inch gauge railway ferried iron ore down to the port at Ravenglass, but two years later it was bankrupt, finally closing in 1913. At various times, the little trains still ran, carrying both granite blocks and passengers, and local poet Norman Nicholson talks of being able to jump off a slow-moving train to grab wild roses and goldenrod from the embankments and then getting back on again. Presumably such an activity is now discouraged. In 1940, writer and social campaigner Doreen Wallace in her *English Lakeland* remembers the London Midland & Scottish Railway, calling it 'the smallest railway in the world', and by September 1960 the preservation society was rewarded by a local landowner and a Midland stockbroker stepping in with the necessary cash, thereby securing its future.

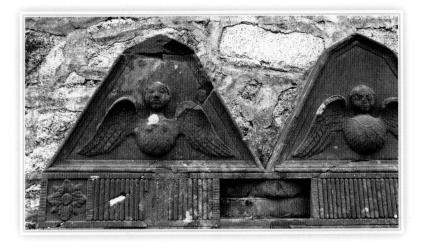

The indefatigable Doreen Wallace lived at a yellow Tudor manor farm near Diss and, when a sale was forced on her, she hung the Tithe Act from a gallows in the garden and set fire to it. She got into trouble for quite a few things she wrote, but her words about Eskdale are as true now as in 1940, that there are 'no flamboyant hotels and no shanties with picture postcards for sale'. I like that 'shanties'. The road has a tendency to narrow down severely, resulting in nervous moments when you think that opposing wing mirrors will engage and bodywork scrape against wet walls with ferns sprouting from the fertile crevices. Stone barns and farmhouses are glimpsed through the trees, willowherb and saxifrage stand sentinel next to imposing granite gateposts. Dark plantings of fir stir in the breeze on the ridges, and modern-day preoccupations are only really seen when a cagouled walker strides by in the rain, or a 4x4 is encountered outside a self-catering cottage, numerous mountain bikes being unloaded off the back bumper.

The road comes out on to the A595 at Gubbergill, and on turning left the tiny lost port of Ravenglass is reached after two and a half miles. Ravenglass: I always think it sounds like something in *Treasure Island*, but this was the Roman port of Glannoventa. It's not difficult to envisage the galleys riding at anchor here, sunlight flashing on the spread-eagled aquilas, the legionaries preparing to disembark prior to their slog up to Hardknott (*sinister, dexter*). On the slight rise behind, is another impressive Roman souvenir – the Bath House reached by a lane that runs due south next to the railway. They say that at 12 feet high, these are the tallest Roman remains still extant in Britain. Somehow the Jewry Wall in Leicester never gets considered, but these walls and arches are certainly impressive. Seen now in a slightly manicured setting, this was the leisure centre for the occupiers of the nearby fort, and, I shouldn't wonder, a few local cognoscenti too. Remarkably preserved are the niches that would have had little statues of their gods in them. Lit by citronella tea lights perhaps. On a rainy day, the grassy ground around the walls fills up with water, so you can have your own, albeit unheated, footbath up here.

Back down on the shore, Ravenglass is essentially only one street of cottages and houses, finishing at a shore strewn with stones and pieces of orange sea-rubbed brick. The frontages are much as one would expect in any Cumbrian village: rendered, painted, hollyhocks around doors. (And here the curious sight of a National petrol pump in a front garden, still with a price disc saying 1/5 a gallon. That's about 7p.) At the back of the western side of the street, it couldn't be more different. Yards and gardens protected by high walls from the sea, rusting or rotting steps and ladders reaching down to the foreshore. Storm doors and drain covers battened down, washing lines strung out between bleached posts. You want to hurry back to the tea shop, to watch rain lashing the windows, little yachts bobbing up and down where the galleys rose and fell with the tides, or smugglers swung lanterns out in the dark. Ravenglass sees the outfall of three rivers: the Irt, Mite and Esk, and still received trading vessels up to the mid-nineteenth century. Now it will be the odd tourist turning up for teacakes, and gulls wheeling and screaming over the terracotta chimney pots. At one time, Ravenglass was reckoned to be the breeding ground of around two-thirds of England and Wales's black-headed gull population.

There are two stations in Ravenglass; the terminus of 'the Ratty' narrow-gauge railway and, at its side, the station serving the village on the Lancaster to Carlisle line that winds so spectacularly through Furness in the south and up the Cumbrian coast through Whitehaven and Workington. From Ravenglass, our road runs southwards after circumnavigating the Esk Estuary over Muncaster Bridge, the fells rising to our left, the Irish Sea and a long straight stretch of the railway running on reclaimed Ice Age mud to our right. The road then turns northeast and travels through the Whicham Valley in order to round the first of the Furness estuaries. The head of the Duddon Channel is marked for both motorists and railway passengers by the big airy signal box at Foxfield, but well worth a detour here is the village of Broughton-in-Furness.

Broughton still has the atmosphere of a little town at the hub of its community. Farmers in beaten-up Landrovers arrive to drop off or pick up tyres from a little back-street garage, a corner shop sells apples from brassbound wooden cases and birdseed from green tin buckets. On a warm summer's evening, the Market Place echoes to the conversation of drinkers outside the Manor Arms, as figures scurry to meetings in the cream corrugated iron Parsonage Room. The sharp contrast of colours used on the houses on one side of the Market Place may not be to everyone's taste, but in bursts of direct low light, they line up as dramatically as a set of scenery flats.

⚘ **ABOVE**
Garage, Broughton-in-Furness

➥ **OPPOSITE**
Steps to the shore, Ravenglass

⚘ **BELOW LEFT**
Houses, Broughton-in-Furness

⚘ **BELOW**
Brick and pebbles, the Ravenglass shore

Road and railway line swing across eastwards, but a loop in both through Askam takes in Barrow-in-Furness. This is the outpost, the runt of the litter, the poor music-hall joke – 'Barrow's like a mortuary with the lights left on', but it really does deserve a closer look, a rummage about beneath the surface. Now dominated by the massively out-of-scale submarine 'shipyard' building, in 1843 there were only 32 cottages and two pubs facing Walney Island across the Piel Channel. However, mineral ore brought down from the fells by the 7th Duke of Devonshire (1808–91) resulted in an iron and steel industry that quickly expanded into shipbuilding. Dark red tenement buildings rose up on Barrow Island, manufacturers Vickers created their own enclave of housing on Walney. Docks resounded to the blast of steam whistles and workers streamed out of factory gates in their thousands. The Duke and his compatriot, James Ramsden, created a new community with new buildings that used the red Furness brick for not only the tenements but chapels, libraries and a classic fire station.

Tough people, tough lives. A police uniform outfitter said that Barrow men had the largest chest sizes of anyone in the country. Shipbuilding dominated Barrow life, champagne bottle launchings of everything from battleships to liners – the last being the original cruise ship *Oriana* in 1960. Vickers even built ill-fated airships here. The absorbing Dock Museum, built over a graving dock, tells it all and shows us the proof. Among the most jaw-dropping artefacts are the big glass and mahogany cases holding ships' models, with mid-blue painted battleships built for Japan showing every minute bolt screwing down a capstan, every safety railing in thin gold wire.

Now it seems that everything is going on behind enormous closed doors, or even underwater I suppose. Workers clocking in, soldering motherboards into Tridents and then, perhaps after looking at the weather outside through a periscope, running out for a quick trolley dash round Tesco Extra next door. Rivets must come into it somewhere, but there is also a sad air here of past greatness replaced by punishing deprivation. The housing estates you could find anywhere, but in Barrow they seem incongruous, turning their backs to the sea that surrounds them. A sea that is always just over a dune or across a pavement. On the eight-miles-long Walney Island, you can walk past iron and timber sheds clustered together as if in rusty conversation, and then enter an open landscape reaching out to Biggar and the white lighthouse on the nature reserve in the south, acrobatic flights of dunlins looping over the intervening creeks and marshes.

South of the town, a lane runs past a curious forgotten beacon light at Rampside and on to the Roa Island causeway. Wrecked and not-so-wrecked ships lie at angles on the shore, anchor chains lie across mud. At the end, the parking spaces are marked out for the lifeboat crew and, next to their state-of-the-art station high above the water, a jetty leads down to the ferry for Piel Island. A short but exhilarating boat journey across Bass Pool, past red buoys and moored yachts with the tide thumping the boat sides, saltwater spraying your back, brings you to another jetty, the ferryman probably having done a spot of fishing as he brought you over. The ferry will return, he promises, and on disembarking, a grassy path through Oxford ragwort takes you first in front of an inn and then past a row of four atmospheric pilot houses that appear to cower against big racing clouds.

The southern tip is dominated by the silhouette of Piel Castle. It appears to grow out of the landscape, and indeed the stones of the beach built the keep and corner towers, with the local red sandstone brought over for the details. You can immediately see why a castle was built in this position. Apart from anyone else wanting to keep out undesirables, the rich monks of Furness Abbey needed a place of safety and a monitoring point for cargo going in and out of the Walney Channel. Once Henry VIII had dissolved the abbey, the castle was left to fall into the ruinous state we see today, but it's well cared for, and in 1920 the whole island was given by the 7th Duke of Buccleuch to the people of Barrow as a memorial to the dead of the First World War: local workers who had been sent to war in local ships. But this is now a Famous Five paradise, with sea, blue mussel-shelled shores and dark interiors just begging to be the backdrops for children's adventures.

➸ **OPPOSITE**
Beacon, Rampside

❦ **BELOW**
Vita Nova *at Roa Island*

ABOVE
Dunes and beach at Sandscale, on the Duddon Estuary

OPPOSITE
Piel Island, pilot cottages

To the north of Barrow town centre is another wild expanse to explore, the dunes of the Sandscale Nature Reserve. From the car park (with its green hut selling ice cream), you can walk right round the peninsula on the Cumbrian Coastal Way. However, be warned: this is no sanitised path with pictures of flora and fauna and environmentally friendly recycled signposts every five minutes. You can walk round the peninsula on the fringes of the dunes among marram grass and clusters of blue sea holly, or on the beautiful empty beach that gives breathtaking postcard views over Duddon Sands to the western Lakeland fells; but venturing into the core of the peninsula can be very disorientating and paths marked on the map difficult to find. One big sand dune can look very much like another, and on following a post-and-wire fence I had a Ray Bradbury moment, fully expecting to walk over a sandy rise to find the fence suddenly stopping, the skeleton of the erector slumped over his last post, hammer still in hand. A silver birch bent by the westerly wind looked so out of place it had to mark the way, and indeed it did. On cresting the dune by the tree, a gap opened out to the northern beach again. A big 99 Flake has never been so welcome.

Before we leave Barrow and rejoin our road eastwards, Furness Abbey is certainly worth a detour, hidden in the appropriately named Vale of Nightshade that encloses the deep pink ruins. Extensive, impressive and appearing to be carved straight out of the sandstone cliffs that surround it, the abbey was once one of the most important in England. King Stephen (1135–54) gave land for Cistercian monks to build here, and bundled it with not only the surrounding acres but vast estates in Cumberland, Lancashire and Yorkshire, and one as far away as

Lincolnshire. What wealth. At the time of the Dissolution, the monks ran their own ships and traded in the local iron, and the whole enterprise brought in an income of £900 a year. That's about £300,000. No wonder Henry VIII wanted to get his pudgy hands on it all.

For all the magnificence of what is undoubtedly an important and edifying corner of our heritage, my eye kept wandering to the old custodian's ticket office next to the outer railings. Superseded now by a retail opportunity that looks like a health centre, this little building seemed so much less pretentious and, well, honest. This says Ministry of Works, the contemporary administrators. A roll of pink paper tickets at one end, a coal fire at the other, and perhaps a small stack of plain white paper-covered books with the royal coat of arms and the legend *Ancient Monuments: Northern England*. A little girl running around the cloisters said: 'Can we see the Witch's House now?', and ran up to peer through the dusty windows.

Just down the lane, and past the excellent tea rooms that do a good line in chocolate cake, is the hidden Bow Bridge over the Mill Beck. I have repeatedly torn my trousers on barbed wire trying to get a shot of this medieval three-arched bridge, and on every occasion rain has formed big pink-blushed puddles in the adjacent field. It's always worth opening the iron gate, with its closure relying on a loop of baler twine, to see another demonstration of how those loaded monks liked to put a bit of panache into their architecture.

☗ **ABOVE**
Original Ministry of Works ticket office, Furness Abbey

◄◼ **OPPOSITE**
Furness Abbey and quarry face

⚘ **BELOW**
Saucy Ulverston

Closing the circle we join the A590 at Thwaite Flat (look out for Rainbow Bungalow on the right) and head for Ulverston, home to a lighthouse memorial to Sir John Barrow (1764–1848), Secretary to the Admiralty and a founding member of the Royal Geographical Society that – at the time of writing – is shrouded in Christo-style restoration wrappings. Ulverston appears to appreciate its past; on one of the shopping streets a well-lettered sign for Abbey Sauce is still extant on a wall, and down a side street is the restored dark sandstone Furness Railway station. Finished off in green and red paint, this is how town stations should be, a building to be proud of, imbued with civic pride. The iron supports of the platform seats are fashioned from the ubiquitous squirrels and grapes, and there's a waiting room with wooden wall seats. The only really jarring note is the livery of the trains that arrive and depart under the glass canopies, in this case First TransPennine Express (*sic*); this week's franchise. It is a source of increasing dismay that railway companies – and buses for that matter – show no consideration for the environment their trains run in when agreeing colour schemes.

▲ **ABOVE**
Bow Bridge, Furness Abbey

The railway makes a shortcut across the Cartmel Sands over the Leven Viaduct (if you're a passenger, then hope that the tide's in so you get the impression of sailing on a train), but motorists must plough on up past Greenodd Sands before turning down on to the Cartmel Peninsula. The lane is long but rewarding, dim tunnels of trees, sheep grazing on green fields once swept by high tides. A couple of lattice-windowed cottages with bright blue paint announce the estate village of Holker. The Cavendishes' great Victorian Elizabethan Holker Hall – the family home for over four centuries – and Joseph Paxton's park are off to the right behind walls with blue doors, the village a delightful amalgam of school, barns and cottages, all smartly lined in pristine blue paint. Our road goes off to the left at the Rose & Crown in Cark, winding through to the tiny town of Cartmel. The countryside is quieter here, certainly less traffic, and these gentler green hills enfold buildings that look so at home in the landscape. Low-built farmhouses, white-walled cottages, everything in scale.

Cartmel is a delightful small village presided over by an impressive twelfth-century priory with the top half of its tower set on the diagonal in order to cleverly spread the enormous weight more effectively. Built in the twelfth-century Transitional style, that is between Early and Late Norman, it escaped the Dissolution when the local population of fisherfolk and cockle gatherers complained that this was their only church. This may seem odd for a village that's at least three miles from the

sea, but wasn't always so. A characterfully lettered signpost on the corner of a lane gives distances 'over sands', a reference to the routes to Ulverston and Lancaster that avoided much longer road journeys. Sit for a while in the church and, if you're lucky, girls may start practising madrigals, their voices lifting up and around the big round-headed arches.

▲ **ABOVE**
Barns below Hampsfield Fell, near Cartmel

🍇 **BELOW**
Estate cottages, Holker

LANCASTER
OVER SANDS **15** MILES
ULVERSTON
OVER SANDS **7** MILES

 GRANGE

CARK

I only knew three things about Cartmel before I first came here: there was a betting scam at the racecourse in 1974, my brother chose it for his honeymoon, and Mavis Riley of *Coronation Street* retired here to a less dramatic Cartmel street. The Cartmel Racecourse is so near to the village that you can almost touch the white rails from a stone wall that must provide a free vantage point for watching races. There's a surprise on every corner: a tin Raleigh Cycles sign, a classic barber's shop with hot towels next to a Spar, the slate-floored Cartmel Gallery and a bookshop that used to be a Martins Bank in Doreen Wallace's day and is about the size of two telephone boxes. (Buy your HV Mortons here.) The little market place has a fourteenth-century gatehouse tucked in next to the bookshop, a market cross, a village pump and slabs for slapping fish down on. Norman Nicholson said it all looks remarkably like the stage set for an Edwardian musical comedy. I know what he means, I once stayed in an eccentric hotel on the square and shared a room with a rocking horse and a row of black books on a dressing table that turned out to be every individual book of the Bible. I recall that as Obadiah's a bit thin he was lumped in with Joel and Amos.

Just down the road is Grange-over-Sands, the 'grange' bit being a reference to this being the site of big granary barns for those enterprising Furness monks. Created largely by the railway, it reminds me of Great Malvern without Elgar – grey stone, a bandstand and the Victorian planting of evergreen trees and shrubberies. And once again an impressively restored 1857 station for the Furness Railway that sits almost in Morecambe Bay and has its companion Grange Hotel opposite. Beware taking photographs on the platforms, as you will be immediately suspected of terrorism under a new dictat from 'head office'. Just down on the narrow promenade is one of those coin-in-the-slot telescopes. Usually, the clockwork mechanism of such things cuts off just as I've got it focused, but here I managed to get a superb view across the bay to where I was able to pick out both the Art Deco Midland Hotel in Morecambe and the preposterous Ashton Memorial on its hill behind Lancaster.

Back up to Haverthwaite via Lindale, it's always worth a look at yet another railway: the Lakeside & Haverthwaite at the side of the busy A590. You might catch the little oddly named saddle tank *Repulse,* pulling a rake of blood 'n' custard carriages (I think all franchisees of today should be made by law to adopt either this or Maunsell Green as their livery) up to Lakeside on the bottom end of Windermere. Which is where we came in, with HV Morton's Morris overheating in a queue on the opposite bank. After everything else on this tour, Lakeside comes as a bit of a shock. Passengers disembark from a real steam train to see a plastic coin-operated locomotive doing virtually nothing for 50p. Gin palace launches nose up to a posh hotel, children hire bikes to ride about the car park, and tawdry souvenirs are sold next to an aquarium that's in a building as out of character here as the timeshares and condos down the road. Out on the lake, though, it's pretty much as it's been for 150 years or so, big-sailed yachts tacking against towering hills reflected in blue water. The Lake District: beautiful, commanding, inspiring. The annual rainfall is just under 200 inches, but the rain clears quickly from the coastal fringes, lighting up Barrow at the same time as Walney Island, Ulverston as quickly as Cartmel. Hardknott takes a little longer as the sun's rays searchlight up from Ravenglass, but it's all worth the effort, all immeasurably worth the wait.

➤ **OPPOSITE**
Lakeside & Haverthwaite Railway, Haverthwaite

❧ **BELOW**
Yachting on Lake Windermere

BOOKS & MAGPIES
HEREFORDSHIRE & SHROPSHIRE

My love affair with this part of the country started with my bank giving me an Access card in 1978. Although obviously a clerical error, I nevertheless immediately set off for a weekend in the west, starting with a favourite bookshop in Malvern and ending up in the Feathers Hotel in Ludlow for one night and the Green Dragon Hotel in Hereford the next (where I saw magician Paul Daniels getting into a gold Jaguar XJS with his initials on the door). When not waving my 'flexible friend' about, I did my own vanishing trick, disappearing into the deep recesses of border country.

The inspirations had been manifold. I'd been reading *Kilvert's Diary* and following the television adaptation, so had to see Hay-on-Wye and Llanthony Priory. I had discovered watercolour artist SR Badmin's mouthwatering Shell poster of Shropshire, just bought *Highways and Byways in the Welsh Marches* and *A Shropshire Lad*, and someone had said 'Ludlow's nice'. Above all, it was probably Alfred Watkins' *The Old Straight Track* that did it, the result of the Hereford brewer's vision of invisible lines connecting ancient sites, hilltop notches and landmark firs across this very countryside. I of course got hooked on the whole idea, frantically devouring John Michell's cosmic AA handbook *The View Over Atlantis* and staring misty-eyed into blue distances. But the 'feel' of this countryside, be it the melancholy of Capel-y-ffin in the Black Mountains on a winter's afternoon, or the fey charms of magpie Stokesay Castle on a spring morning, is always with me, always drawing me back.

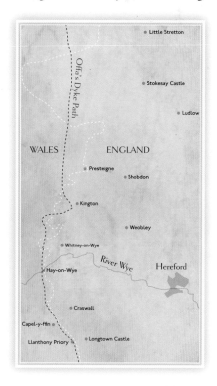

In the same way that you try to stick to a footpath, but keep seeing things over the hedge where you shouldn't go, well, that's how it is when you write about the borders from the English side: half the time you don't really know which country you're in. So I went into Golesworthy's shop in Hay-on-Wye to buy maps and asked where I was. 'Wales' was the unequivocal answer, although when I looked at my new map it looked like the border was only a few doors down the street. Anyway, if you love reading, you will know that Hay is made of books. Almost 40 bookshops in all, here you should be able to get everything from a fine copy of the Ladybird book of *What To Look For In Winter*, to a signed fifth impression of Len Deighton's *The Ipcress File*. You can watch men with pebble glasses still searching for their particular Holy Grail – finally finding the yellow cloth first edition of Bram Stoker's *Dracula* and then expiring outside the baker's.

You will almost certainly find a copy of *Kilvert's Diary*. The Rev Francis Kilvert was curate over on the other side of the Wye at Clyro, and finally vicar at Bredwardine to the east of Hay, where he died prematurely of peritonitis at the age of 39 in 1879, a few days after he returned from his honeymoon. His diaries (1870–9) give a unique unhindered view of Victorian rural life, a searchlight illuminating the everyday minutiae of friends, parishioners and landscape that was never intended for publication. We are so lucky to have anything at all of these totally absorbing, brilliantly written daily entries. His new wife disposed of much of what he'd written; what was left was edited into three volumes in the late 1930s by William Plomer, whose transcripts were promptly incinerated in the London Blitz. The actual surviving diaries were inexplicably destroyed by the prudish relatives that owned them, and, as if not to be left out, the 1977–8 superb television series of 18 15-minute films was apparently lost by the BBC. Put the diary in your pocket for the early stages of our tour (you can get an abridged single volume), and make sure someone doesn't steal it or set fire to it, and don't give it to anyone from the BBC to look after. Kilvert will be our unseen companion for a while.

> *I ... met no-one else till I came to Hay Bridge where the long empty sunny white road stretched away over the river to the town, the picturesque little border town with its slate-roofed houses climbing and shining up the hill crested by the dark mass of the old ivy-grown castle with its huge war-broken tower.*
> (*Kilvert's Diary*, Good Friday, 15 April 1870)

Kilvert would still recognise Hay, even though his often-used local railway running next to the Wye has long been dismantled. In and out of the bookshops you will still find the other life essentials: bread, ironmongery, coloured postcards on racks, and the stamps to send them off with. The castle dominates the town, still the home of the man who started the whole book thing when he opened his first shop in Hay's old fire station in 1961. In 1977, he proclaimed himself king of the new independent state of Hay and proceeded to go about with a lavatory cistern ballcock for an orb. I wonder what Kilvert would have made of that.

⬆ **ABOVE**
Hay-on-Wye

◄ **OPPOSITE**
Postcards from the edge, Hay-on-Wye

⬇ **BELOW**
Penguin Kilvert's Diary, with Timothy Davies in the BBC series

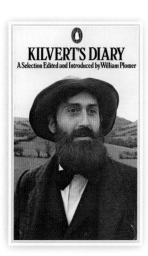

The Black Mountains have been described as a hand, the fingers the mountain ridges reaching down to touch a line between Longtown and Abergavenny. The back of the hand is gloved with trees sloping down to the road between Hay and Talgarth, with bald high spots at Castell Dinas, Lord Hereford's Knob (really) and Hay Bluff. We climb up from the town to this dramatic incline, and, avoiding hang gliders running and jumping into hopeful air currents, descend into the Vale of Ewyas via the Gospel Pass. The road is impossibly narrow, enclosed by trees and ragged rocks that on my last visit appeared to be about to collapse where the underlying pink soil had been eroded by flash floods scouring the banks. Very slowly, we carefully reach the widening gap between fingers of mountain into the nexus of the Afon Honddu, the English border above to the left, where Offa's Dyke follows the highest part of the ridge.

At the junction of the mountain streams the Nant Bwch and Honddu, we arrive at Capel-y-ffin: a pub, a handful of cottages and a tiny church and chapel next to the shallow water winding through the trees. Kilvert thought nothing of walking over the hills to Llanthony, just down the lane, and back to Clyro the same day. Certainly, he would still be at home in the tiny churchyard at Capel-y-ffin:

> ... I remembered the place perfectly, the old chapel short stout and boxy with its little bell turret, (the whole building reminded one of an owl) the quiet peaceful chapel shaded by the seven great solemn yews, the chapel house, a farm house over the way, and the Great Honddu brook crossing the road and crossed in turn by the stone foot bridge with its narrow gangway. Before the chapel house door by the brookside a buxom comely wholesome girl with fair hair rosy face blue eyes and fair clear skin stood washing at a tub in the sunshine, up to the elbows of her round white lusty arms in soapsuds.
> (Diary, 5 April 1870)

➤➤ **OPPOSITE**
Roadside, Vale of Ewyas

↙ **BELOW**
The 'owl' church at Capel-y-ffin

Typical Kilvert, continually being distracted by pretty girls. 'An angel satyr walks these hills.' He came here on this occasion hoping to see Father Ignatius, who was busy building a little white-painted monastery up a side lane as part of his attempt to revive monasticism. Much later, the lane saw the excess baggage train of the trouserless Eric Gill and his family arriving here from Sussex in August 1924. Sculptor, wood engraver, typographer, Gill would find Capel-y-ffin remote even by his spare economic standards. A station 10 miles away, a postman on horseback and a travelling doctor once a week. At least the stones for sculpting were just outside the door, as he said, 'at no extra charge'.

Barely a couple of miles further down the road is Llanthony Priory, surely one of the most dramatically sited ancient buildings in the country. A lane leads up, past a farmhouse, to where green lawns extend under the arches and towers of what is one of the earliest foundations of Augustinian canons. The original church disappeared, owing to it being 'fixed amongst a barbarous people', and what we see now are the remains of its successor, built 1180–1230. In and around the ruins is the Llanthony Priory Hotel, with its bar in the cellar and four bedrooms in one of the smaller towers. I stayed here once in the dead of winter, with a blazing fire in the dining room and a quick cold ascent up a stone spiral staircase to the comforts of a warm bed, a twig tapping at the old glass of a window pane like in the 1965 film *Doctor Zhivago*. Of course Kilvert turned up here with a mate, complaining about two tourists who not only upset him by waving lecturing walking sticks about but also because they'd ordered their dinners first, making him and his companion late back.

◄◄ **OPPOSITE**
Afon Honddu at Capel-y-ffin

❦ **BELOW**
Llanthony Priory

> ... *we had to wait till they had done, solacing ourselves with the Hereford Times and the Visitors' Book from which to the great and just indignation of the landlord* [Stout Beauchamp] *some of the British tourists had cut out and stolen half a year of entries from October 1865 to May 1866, including my last entry.*
> (Diary, 5 April 1870)

There you are, it was happening to everything Kilvert wrote even then.

At the end of the Vale of Ewyas, we turn back to go up the other side of Offa's Dyke, re-entering England at Lower Cwmcoched. After a few miles, we enter Longtown, and a surprise in a field of a Marcher castle. The border country is so rich in these motte-and-bailey castles, the strongholds of Norman barons who had to keep those recalcitrant Welsh in order. William de Lacy built here around the same time as the Augustinians were building in the next valley, war and peace in uneasy alliance. Arrived at through a ruinous gatehouse, the intimidating drum of a keep glowers from its mound, still dark even in sunshine. Another localised inspiration flashed up like a flickering lantern slide: the meticulous and literally spellbinding illustrations of Tony Meeuwissen, who painted the pictures for Irwin Dermer's *The Witch's Hat* while living in border Presteigne in the mid-1970s. One image in this stunning children's book has the remains of a round tower and arch with dark silhouettes of trees above a still lake, where a fish lazily catches an unsuspecting dragonfly. I had looked at it for 35 years until, quite recently, a friend turned it sideways and showed me that it was also a bearded face.

The countryside is more open here, and soon we pass a sign saying 'Craswall', the entrance to what must be one of the most stretched-out villages in Herefordshire, if not England. I discovered it from the other end one winter's afternoon, when the road over Hay Bluff was closed because of a heavy fall of snow. Sheep stared at me from the snowbound fields as I struggled on the ice, and as I took a sharp left at Craswall, I saw a little pub in what looked like a farmyard. Two farmers stood outside (in my imagination, if not in fact, wearing leather gaiters) and I think there were at least two chickens pecking about. Desperately wanting to stop,

◄◄ OPPOSITE
Longtown Castle

🗡 BELOW LEFT
Bull's Head, Craswall

🌷 BELOW RIGHT
'Face in the landscape' an illustration by Tony Meeuwissen from The Witch's Hat

the thought that I might get stuck up here prevailed and I continued my journey. Stuck? In a pub? Whatever next?

Driving back up northwestwards on a bright spring morning, it was very different. I was glad to see that there was still a pub, even gladder that it was open and everything I'd hoped for. The Bull's Head is dark but not gloomy, the wallpaper genuinely peeling rather than artfully torn, and the Wye Valley ale and Gwatkin's cider is served from their barrels through a traditional 'hole-in-the-wall' bar. Beattie Lewis's family ran this pub for 125 years, and Beattie was still serving beer and making jam sandwiches for walkers up until 1997. Her family came here in the 1870s when two brothers arrived from Somerset to repair the bells in Craswall Church. Outside, a trailer full of straw bales was temporarily parked by a solitary phone box, but a group of Scots pines on the right-angled corner, and their ancestors, had obviously landmarked this spot in the Herefordshire hills for centuries. I can envisage Alfred Watkins putting brewery paperwork into his saddle bag and staring thoughtfully up at them. I go back down to Hay, and then out on the road to Whitney-on-Wye, and into England again by the magpie-timbered Rhydspence Inn noted by Kilvert:

> The night was cool and pleasant as I walked home under the stars. About midnight I passed over the Rhydspence border brook, and crossed the border from England into Wales. The English inn was still ablaze with light and noisy with the songs of revellers, but the Welsh inn was dark and still.
> (Diary, May Day 1872)

◂◂ LEFT
Craswall Church

At Whitney, the Wye is crossed by that rarity, a wooden-planked toll bridge. The tariff board is dated 1796 and so was last valid in George III's time. It tells us that a dog pulling a cart would be charged 2d, about 50p now, but I don't imagine you see many dogs or carts on the bridge these days. Canoeists appeared to be negotiating the Wye in a continuous flotilla, each vessel buoyed-up with a big blue barrel as meandering courses were made past and under the willows. Staying on the main road you can either turn left at Golden Cross and make your way up through Eardisley to Kington, or make a small detour via Weobley.

Weobley is an archetype for magpie half-timbered building, and indeed opposite the Ye Olde Salutation Inn is a magpie called Magnus, sculpted in metal by Walenty Pytel as a millennium centrepiece. Weobley was very quiet, most of its shops were closed on a hot sunny afternoon, one permanently with just a few remnants of stock still visible through the window. I did like the garage (with extendable hose petrol pumps) that appeared to double up as a hairdressers, but it did seem to be a village hiding behind closed doors, a community self-conscious of its colour-plate status.

I had noticed there were brown signs on the verges around here indicating a 'Black & White Village Trail', bringing visions of Beautiful Britain calendar cottages being pointed out with a pipe stem from a Morris Oxford. There appears to be a resurgence of this kind of thing, of structuring our otherwise hopeless meanderings into themed itineraries. There is a 'Blossom Trail' and an 'Elgar Trail' just over in Worcestershire, packaging England into easily assimilated panoramas.

The idea of black-and-white half-timbered houses fits very well into this vague concept of an English Arcadia. It takes its place in popular culture alongside stagecoaches pulling up outside snowbound inns (nearly always a 'magpie'), church bells sounding through apple boughs and faux hand-painted canal hardware. In fact, the sharp contrast between wood and plaster is probably only as old as Brilliant White on the colour chart. Ye Olde oak timbers were originally left alone, turning a wonderful silvery grey with age, and the infilling would nearly always be brushed with antique whites, creams and pale yellows. (In Suffolk, they delighted in mixing the wash with pig's blood to give a delicious rose pink.) Blame the Victorians for pasting on dark unnecessary preservatives that increased the contrast and therefore a perceived 'picturesqueness'.

◄◄ FAR LEFT
Redundant petrol pump, Presteigne

◄◄ LEFT
Presteigne books

►► OPPOSITE
St John the Evangelist, Shobdon

Kington is in the shadow of Hergest Ridge, which I seem to recall is also the name of a Mike Oldfield album with a dog on the cover. The country town has been here on the English side of Offa's Dyke for over a thousand years, a Marcher stronghold on the banks of the River Arrow (probably aptly named) and haunt of the Saxon kings that gave it the name. Position is all for towns like this, and quite apart from its Border location, this was wool-trading country where sheep were brought over from Wales on a drover's road for the English fattening pastures and markets. Thirty years ago, I came here on a Saturday afternoon, and the High Street was bustling with shoppers crossing between butchers and bakers, but on this Saturday the sunlit streets were strangely empty, just a couple of girls with a pram and an old lady sweeping the pavement outside her terraced cottage. But there were many things to delight: kitchen utensils strung up on a length of twine in the window of an ironmongers, and in another shop, balls of pink wool proudly arranged around a Stylecraft knitting pattern. Much to my immense pleasure and that of my itching screwdriver, there was still what appeared (it was closed) a functioning tobacconist that displayed two heavyweight enamel signs for Capstan cigarettes, curved to fit around double bay windows. These fabulous items of 'street jewellery' were once commonplace, but thanks to people like me in the 1970s up ladders held steady by shopkeepers, they are now rarely seen in situ. Where they are still in their original positions, they add much to the character of the country townscape, something of a degree of permanence, even though the product they advertise may well have disappeared.

🌲 **ABOVE**
Lucton School

Back over the border once again, the little town of Presteigne was showing more signs of life, and a man I chatted to outside a pub said, 'There's not a lot to it, you can go either straight up that way', nodding up the street, 'or straight down that way', nodding down the street. Presteigne was once the county town of Radnorshire, but now it's Powys and has to be called 'a unitary authority' for some reason. The Jacobean magpied Radnorshire Arms Hotel was humming with a wedding reception spilling out on to the stone patio, where loud laughter wore morning suits and girls with long red fingernails held king-size cigarettes away from red satin dresses. Round the corner, at the back of an antiques shop with dusty relics in the window, a room lit by just one light bulb was crammed from floor to ceiling with books. The door was not only wedged open, it looked like it was never closed, the floor covered with leaves. It was as if a lorry backed up to it once a week and tipped books out like coal into a cellar. An ironic handwritten notice asked for the room to be kept tidy.

Moving eastwards from Presteigne, we're quickly back in Herefordshire and pulling off the road for Shobdon church, marked by another heritage brown sign. What is so special about a church that appears to be nothing out of the ordinary on the outside? The Bateman family grafted a new nave on to the thirteenth-century tower in 1756, the original arches being re-erected on top of a nearby hill – the Shobdon Arches folly. There's a clue in the ogee arch over the church's west door, and when you walk in be prepared to have your breath taken away. Everything you see looks like it's been made out of white and blue icing, a perfect Rococo and Gothic interior in the fashionable style of Horace Walpole's Strawberry Hill 'Gothick'. Walpole was a pal of the Hon Richard Bateman, who undertook the rebuilding, of whom he was said to have been glad to have weaned off *chinoiserie*, another contemporary fad. Shobdon's pews have fancifully decorated bench ends, everywhere are flowing ogee arches. There's an imposing triple-decker pulpit and a reading desk that looks like a heavenly sleigh waiting for winged horses to return it to paradise. All it needs is a periwigged congregation, dressed all in white with sepulchral pale make-up and dark eyeglasses, and Handel being played on an out-of-tune spinet. This interior must be high on *Brides* magazine's top 'My Perfect Day' wedding backdrops. What a contrast it would make to red-satined Presteigne girls. The more the merrier, this fragile survivor currently needs a lot of cash dowries to preserve it as it is.

From Shobdon, we go over Mortimer's Cross and on the right see the stunning frontage to Lucton School. As with all our public schools, there are obviously newer extensions behind it, but the orange brick north range of 1708 is intact. Above a hooded central doorway, and below a clock and bell turret, is an arched niche where a white statue of founder John Pierrepont stands, as if about to leave for evensong at Shobdon.

Oh I have been to Ludlow fair / And left my necktie God knows where,
And carried half way home, or near, / Pints and quarts of Ludlow beer:
Then the world seemed none so bad, / And I myself a sterling lad;
And down in lovely muck I've lain, / Happy till I woke again.
(A Shropshire Lad, AE Housman, 1896)

◄◄ **OPPOSITE**
Church Street, Ludlow

❦ **BELOW**
Ludlow from Whitcliffe Common

With or without a necktie, Ludlow comes as a very refreshing stopover. Much has been written about this Shropshire border town and, ever since I first came here and woke up in the Feathers Hotel with that Access card under my pillow, I have continually returned with a camera of one sort or another. It's not that it's necessarily a front cover contender for the Beautiful Britain calendar, although its groupings of visual charms are self-evident. It's more that this classic English market town on the River Teme still exudes the possibility that people love being townspeople here, and would probably like to keep the more thrusting excrescences of 'modern' life at bay for a few decades yet. It took Tesco years and yards of planning applications to get in here, but one of the many overt joys of Ludlow is that there are still so many original and independent shops. Not Olde Worlde pastiches, not a Ludlow preserved in Heritage Aspic, but real, local retailers. Five proper butchers, an ironmonger that stacks rat traps and rockery forks up in the windows, sun-blinded fruiterers and bakers, and a café with fancy cakes in the window and fancy girls dishing them up. A bric-a-brac market in the square on Sundays means you can buy old Penguins and Dinky Toy army lorries as the bells from St Laurence's church cascade down over the rooftops. After you've been to morning service, of course.

↟ ABOVE
Broadgate, Ludlow

An old man in Broad Street stopped me and said that if I was around in the evening I'd hear the bells do *The Conquering Hero Comes*, and it took me a few steps further up the street to realise he was referring to Housman: 'Or come ye home of Monday, / When Ludlow market hums / And Ludlow bells are playing / The conquering hero comes.' St Laurence is the largest parish church in Shropshire, its crossing tower dominating the town centre at 135 feet tall, and its counterpoint is the magnificent castle, built only about 20 years after the Norman Conquest.

The castle, church, town and river put me in mind of a beautiful book I loved taking out of the library as a child: *A Valley Grows Up*, where I could see the progression of a town from prehistoric settlement to Victorian market town in a series of illustrations painted from the same fictitious viewpoint by Edward Osmond. That's one of the delights of Ludlow, that you can see a history of building through medieval, Georgian and Victorian buildings, quiet alleyways, street names and shop fascia lettering. Long may it be preserved but not pickled, may neckties be continually lost and found here.

Travelling north, we cross over the railway at Onibury, where a dear friend, as the daughter of the incumbent of St Michael's Church in the 1920s, hung on the crossing gate by the station waiting for her father's train, like Bobbie in E Nesbit's *The Railway Children*. Now looking across the fields to the left, is a sight that could be another illustration from a children's book. A lonely Scots pine appears to lean over an exquisite castle, with a tower flying a flag and a half-timbered upper storey at the other end jutting out as if to let down Rapunzel. This is Stokesay Castle, one of the finest fortified manor houses in England. Built around 1280 by Laurence de Ludlow, he took a great risk in putting such tall church-like windows in the Great Hall. Anything earlier than this would have had Welsh bricks thrown through them, but Stokesay is a very early example of things settling down a bit, and a house being enjoyed for what it is rather than the owner having to get up halfway through supper every night to go out and kill someone. English Heritage have done a good job here, having bought a nearby cowshed and turned it into the shop and toilet block. So from here you go up through the simply stunning gatehouse of 1640–1, an undoubted inspiration for Tony Meeuwissen with its carved timber and yellow-painted plaster. Here is how it should be, the repeat patterns of the framing left in dark silver oak. Across a grassy courtyard, surrounded by flowers, is the curiously shaped south tower. Come in April and find swallows building nests up in the roof and continually sweeping in and out of the unglazed windows. From the roof next to the billowing flag, we can look out over the empty moat and a pond under willows up to where a little brick cottage guards the crossing gates on the very rural railway line that winds across the borders from Shrewsbury to the south Wales coast. Every now and then, a little two-carriage train clatters through under the wooded hills.

⬆ ABOVE
Door detail, Stokesay Castle

⬇ BELOW
Gatehouse and south tower, Stokesay Castle

A wooden staircase goes up from the Great Hall to a half-timbered room sitting on the stone north tower, from where there is a superb view of the gatehouse and the adjoining church. The castle was, remarkably, left alone in the Civil War after Royalists were held under siege here, but not so the church, suffering much damage after Royalist horsemen held out against Parliamentarians in 1646. St John the Baptist has two items of note: a double-canopied box pew built in the restoration of the church for the use of the castle gentry (made high so that they could play cards during sermons and as a protection against flying Welsh bricks, possibly), and outside in the churchyard an intriguing war memorial. The soldier statue looks like Bruce Bairnsfather's Old Bill, the satirical First World War cartoon character, who is inexplicably holding a giant fish behind his back, which may be explained by the Shropshire Regiment having a naval ancestry. Among the inscribed names is a list of those from Stokesay that survived and presumably returned to these quiet acres. Ian McEwan's novel *Atonement*, with its equally thought-provoking take on the survival (or not) of its wartime protagonists, was largely filmed at nearby Stokesay Court.

Further on is Craven Arms, a village grown up around the railway, and one of a handful of inns in England that give their names to stations. (Sevenoaks' other station, Bat and Ball, comes to mind, and Elephant & Castle.) As the hills close in, we could get preoccupied with the hills of the Long Mynd above Church Stretton, but only in passing. Up on the nearest hill is the extraordinary sight of the Longmynd Hotel, a white slab of a building built as a hydro in 1900 when Church Stretton fancied itself as a spa destination, dominating everywhere above and

below. Most incongruous though, are the huge red cut-out letters on the roofline, designed as if someone had just come back from seeing the Hollywood sign above Beverly Hills.

On my last visit up here, another very old lady accosted me as I made for The Ragleth Inn in Little Stretton, admonishing us with one horny finger and pointing across the road with another. Intrigued, I followed her signals and found under the cherry blossom the delightful little half-timbered and exquisitely thatched church of All Saints. Another snapshot of Arcadia. Not one that excited Dr Pevsner or the *Shell Guide* explorers much, just a simple village church of 1903 styled in what we might call Mission Hut Magpie. Inside, I found a fat sleepy bumble bee slowly progressing across a red carpet, just as Kilvert found one on a Victorian Sunday morning in June: 'Very hot in morning church, and an enormous bumble bee crawled over the white cloth and everything else during the Holy Communion.' (Diary, Whitsun Day, 5 June 1870)

What companions we can have in the Borders. Kilvert striding out across the hills to visit the sick and preach sermons from mountain pulpits, Housman lying back to hear Ludlow bells and dream of Shropshire youth, Watkins' pin-holing X-ray visions of landscape and landmarks. Once we're in really good shape from our exertions, we'll be fit enough to take on Iain Sinclair's *Landor's Tower*, and feel the shock of connection again as he lines up his obsessions with Dodman staves across this truly enigmatic country.

BELOW LEFT
Blossom in Stokesay churchyard

BELOW
Stokesay war memorial

FLINT & SAMPHIRE
NORTH NORFOLK

BLACK PINES above salt marshes, ruinous churches alone in fields, orange brick and pale flint cottages. Shuttered halls standing out against fields of wheat, the clear glass of high medieval naves framing equally vast skies. And always the sea, a gunmetal-blue strip on the margins that continually reaches saltwater fingers down into creeks that hold fast-decaying hulks and green samphire in glistening mud. This is north Norfolk, both coast and hinterland, and I come here as often as I can.

For me it starts at King's Lynn, remembering as a child seeing the broad expanse of the Great Ouse from a Midland Red coach as it trawled around the town, thinking that at last we were at the sea. Our journey continued for another hour or so to Norwich and beyond, but later we were all taken up to Hunstanton in order for us to crouch in a caravan for a week. First by a push-and-pull train (I thought it must be something to do with *Doctor Dolittle*), wandering up through Royal Wolferton and Snettisham with the name sheared into the platform hedge. Then in my father's apple-green Ford Popular, with me nervously doing half the driving from the back seat. So that's the direction this tour is taking. From King's Lynn to Salthouse, using the coastal A149 and the inland A148 as loose boundaries, taking in both the sea-girt and inland parishes where we could end up just about anywhere. And lost probably, with only the sound of a lone combine harvester or the sea-like soughing of the wind through pines for company.

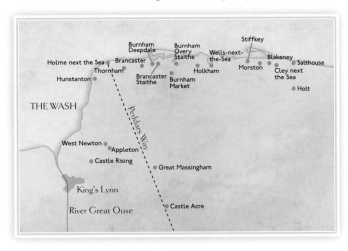

Some say this part of Norfolk gets more than its fair share of attention, and perhaps it's true. All of this large, bulbous county is deserving of scrutiny, from Broadland waters to the riverine boundaries with Suffolk, but the north Norfolk coast is particularly worth taking proper time out to enjoy in detail. Starting at King's Lynn, two very different buildings have always grabbed my attention: one a stunning hymn of praise to commerce that reminds us that this was once one of England's busiest ports, the other a passing nod to the surrounding fenland that supplied the ingredients for the products made at its feet.

Nikolaus Pevsner called Henry Bell's 1683 Custom House, 'one of the finest late C17 public buildings in provincial England'. And so it is, standing among the brick warehouses on Purfleet Quay in the guise of a classic English town hall, pale stone contrasting beautifully with a white-painted balustrade and crowning cupola. The arches on the ground floor were once open to the quay and King Charles II looks down from his niche. When I first saw the Custom House, it was towered over by a grain silo (now thankfully removed) and, like the film set it became in Hugh Hudson's film *Revolution* (1985), was until quite recently made even more impossibly cinematic by the rotting hulk of the schooner *Dania* marooned at its side.

On the coastbound busy bypass, you can see on the left a brick tower built as a cooling tank for the Campbell's Soup factory (prop. A Warhol). I don't know how long it will be here; Tesco's want to demolish it and the factory to extend the display area for oven chips. To find the Custom House, you must get down into the maritime heart of the town, but the soup dragon's tower always acts as a landmark to tell you you're at last in true Norfolk acres, and that the fens will now be replaced by the silhouettes of pines and a hint of the sea on the breeze. Out in the fields to the east of the main road at Bawsey, can be seen the first of many gaunt church ruins, and on a prominent rise in the ground behind Church Farm is St James, falling into decay as early as 1770.

Three miles to the north, a left-hand turning goes into Castle Rising. The village could be our first taste of Norfolk brick and flint, but here we will also see the very local carstone in rich gingerbread slices. A seam of this golden-brown stone runs in a narrow band up this coast, where it not only ends but also spectacularly reveals its natural state in the layer-cake strata of the cliffs to the north of Hunstanton. The houses and church of Castle Rising sit at the foot of the earthworks of the Norman castle, the keep of which is remarkably well

preserved. It gives credence to the couplet in an old local rhyme: 'Rising was a seaport town / When Lynn was but a marsh.' The silting up of harbours and their subsequent decay, or indeed total disappearance, are a recurring theme on this tour. Poor Queen Isabella, the wife of Edward II (the one who was despatched by a red-hot poker at Berkeley Castle), was imprisoned here for the last 27 years of her life. More fortunate are the female occupants of the nearby almshouses, who wear very fetching red cloaks and tall black hats like Welsh chapel-goers.

❦ BELOW
Castle Rising keep

Further up we can turn off at Butlers Cross and wander through West Newton to Appleton. On a corner is the fabulous carstone and iron water tower that served Sandringham and, by all accounts, stopped royal personages contracting typhoid fever again after a particularly nasty outbreak. Down on the far side of a farmyard is another ruined church. Not a great deal is left; just the remains of a typically Norfolk twelfth-century round tower and a stone slab recalling some seventeenth-century Pastons, later relations of the famous letterwriting family from the same county. No hymns and sung prayers now, just the plaintive bleat of sheep in the surrounding pastures.

This is how, so often, the Norfolk landscape is, beguiling lonely church ruins that throw up far more questions than answers. Who were the people that worshipped within these walls now open to the sky, what happened to them? Just in this one small corner of the county, the Ordnance Survey map spells out in little gothic letters: 'Church (Rems of)' for Appleton, Bawsey, Babingley, Bircham Tofts. Ruinous or not, round towers in west Norfolk are numerous: 17 in all. The reasons for the abandonment of churches were not always straightforward, although the fourteenth-century Black Death undoubtedly ravaged many parishes. In truth, there were probably simply too many of them. Farming settlements in these vast acres existed away from the traditional villages, and many of their places of worship were abandoned in the medieval period after drastic changes in agricultural practice.

New Hunstanton is largely a product of the railway. The Le Strange family had been around here for seaside donkey's years, and what is now Old Hunstanton was their place on the beach. The family head is the Hereditary Lord High Admiral of The Wash, who can apparently lay claim to anything on the beach or even in the sea if it's within the distance a man can ride a horse and throw a spear. So watch where you leave your girlfriend. Henry Le Strange joined forces with the Great Eastern Railway, opening the line up from King's Lynn in 1862, and developing the town we now know simply as Hunstanton. Old Hunstanton is where the cliffs end in sand dunes, each successive ridge of which sees a new row of pastel-coloured chalets appear as the sea recedes further away. Stand back and take a look at these cliffs, a sideways view of the earth with grass and soil at the top, white and red chalk and then the very local carstone above the beach itself. This is 3D geology, knowing that if you sliced another cross section, 50 yards back through the playing fields, it would all look virtually the same.

⌃ ABOVE
Beach chalet, Old Hunstanton

◂ OPPOSITE
Cliffs, Old Hunstanton

⚘ BELOW
Appleton church porch

Hunstanton must be unique in east-coast resorts, in that you can watch the sun setting over the sea. Facing west over The Wash, I clearly remember my father pointing out the illuminated Big Wheel at Skegness on the horizon. Now, our road turns at St Edmund's Point to follow a north-facing coast. Holme next the Sea is where they found that incredible timber 'henge' on the beach. The locals reckoned they had known about it for years, but archaeologists got very excited in 1999 when around 50 oak posts set in a circle became visible. A large chunk of oak sat in the centre. The people who preserved the *Mary Rose* got to work on it, and now bits of it are on display in a new museum in King's Lynn.

Was this strange monument once a marker at the end of what we now call the Peddars Way? Not now it isn't. This almost perfectly straight trackway takes off from Holme southeastwards and may have ended up in Colchester, so giving credence to the notion that it's Roman, but it isn't. Certainly the Romans used it to reach their fort at Branodunum (Brancaster), but no, the ghosts on the Peddars Way are much older. HV Morton sat beside it writing: 'Every time a leaf falls, every time there is a sudden rustle in the undergrowth I look up, half-expecting to see a figure not of this age coming towards me along the dead road' (*In Search of England*, 1927). I know how he feels. I heard ghostly rustlings on the Peddars Way near Great Massingham, and was mightily relieved to find it was only pigs shuffling about on the other side of the hedge.

The old track was used by everyone: coast-bound traders, military Romans, Walsingham pilgrims. Right on the line is Castle Acre, a village that grew up under the walls of both a Cluniac priory and a Norman castle, the bailey gate to the latter still surviving virtually intact and standing upright among the later houses and cottages. Although in ruins, the castle is a superb example of constructing in flint. Not the neat knapped stones that decorated churches with chequerboard flushwork, but massive piebald flints that look like they have fallen to earth as meteorites from another planet. The centre of Castle Acre village is usually quiet, with the trees moving opposite the eighteenth-century Ostrich Inn and reflecting in the windows. At one end of the village is an old butcher's shop, still displaying its name in a blue and white mosaic, and at the other end, a sign saying 'Blind Lane leading to Chimney Street', but this is a lengthy diversion from our intentions and also in the opposite direction.

Back up on the coast road, Thornham sees the start of the salt marshes that divide the villages from the sea. Instead of rivers and streams decanting straight into the ocean like the outfalls around The Wash, here they tend to run in parallel with the coast, creating with the sea tidal marshes until they finally find a way out, forming lateral islands like Scolt Head and Blakeney Point. Thornham is so typical of what is to come. Church, hall and cottages seem to ignore the sea, but the lane at the backs of gardens, bordered with green alexanders, opens out on to the marsh. As old locals might tell you: 'There's isn't much here except for the eyesight.' And that's the pleasure, discovering the detail that lies amid the gurgling creeks. A flint barn standing on its own with big timber doors telling of the storage of fishing gear and goodness knows what else, wooden staithes standing precariously on stilts as the incoming tide rapidly lifts boats and buoys. Tides that can no longer float the skeletal remains of leaning hulks, but still salt the samphire that grows with such abundance. Richard Mabey in his indispensable *Food for Free* tells us to pick the whole plant in August and September and serve as an asparagus-like starter. 'Leave the roots on and boil the plants upside down in a saucepan of water. Drain, and serve whole in a bowl, with molten butter.'

⬆ **ABOVE**
Thornham moorings

➤➤ **OPPOSITE**
Brancaster tool shed

◄◄ **LEFT**
Barn at Thornham

Out on the marsh at Titchwell, there's a nature reserve that will reward those with
the obligatory tripoded telescopes with sightings of marsh harriers and bearded
tits; at Brancaster, those with the mandatory check trousers can knock golf balls
about with exclusive abandon. More to my taste is to walk along the coastal path
to Brancaster Staithe with its lobster creels and little wooden fresh fish hut. Boats
lie about everywhere, and the muddy path leads to a collection of huts crowding
around a tiny harbour. Fishing and sailing detritus is stacked up on the quay, spent
ropes and lost tools are hung up in gravity-defying sheds, and a rusty marine
engine shares space with the red frame of a recycled Eastern Counties bus
timetable. At the mouth of the harbour is the gaunt and dangerous silhouette of
the wreck *SS Vina*. In the Second World War, the ship survived being used to
blockade Great Yarmouth harbour only to be towed here to provide target practice
for the RAF. It's a danger to shipping and paddling curiosity seekers alike, but the
only viable option is to blow it up. However, this would apparently take out every
window in Brancaster.

⬆ ABOVE
Cottage on the coastal path, Brancaster

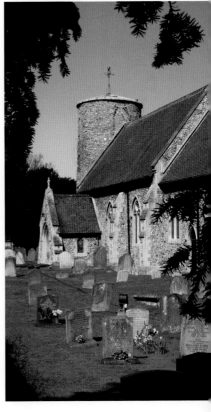

The Burnhams comprise seven Norfolk parishes. Our first encounter with one is on the coast road at Burnham Deepdale, and also our first face-to-face encounter with that Norfolk peculiar: the round church tower. There has been much conjecture over the reason for building them thus, and I have always thought it to be just a style thing in this part of the world. It has often been mooted that because of the lack of suitable local material for quoins (the stones used for right-angled corners), round towers were easier to build. They weren't. The shuttering required was far more difficult to construct, as was the junction of the tower with a nave wall. There are 179 round towers still standing in England, and amazingly about 140 of them are in Norfolk. Burnham Deepdale's St Mary's round church tower is Anglo Saxon, but most of the rest is an 1870s restoration by Frederick Preedy. Inside, you can still see a stunning Norman font depicting the Labours of the Months: June weeding, July scything, August binding a sheaf, etc. January and February involve the labours of drinking and keeping the feet warm. The vestry gave up two delights for me; early morning stained-glass colours streaming across a wooden cupboard door, and a peacock butterfly drowsily testing its wing flaps on the window sill.

⬆ ABOVE
St Mary's, Burnham Deepdale

⬉ ABOVE LEFT
Burnham peacock

The Burnhams are quiet now, except for during the holiday months when a tide of visitors runs through the villages, but the thirteenth century was its noisy, rumbustious and most prosperous time. Everything looked towards the sea, and ships could get as far as Burnham Thorpe, now three miles inland. The inevitable silting-up of the river courses and the rise of neighbouring ports at King's Lynn, Cley and Blakeney slowly strangled the trade. Burnham Thorpe still saw the birth of Nelson in the now demolished rectory, so England's great seafaring tradition is assured a place forever in this quiet corner of Norfolk.

Burnham Market (or Burnham Up Market) now trades in weekend colour magazine must-haves rather than in Dutch pantiles; time-worn *Rupert* annuals over Baltic timber. Retro retreaded England for the Twittering classes, the sheer quantity of four-wheel-drive behemoths lining up in the marketplace is like the starting grid of some bizarre style-over-substance Grand Prix. Thankfully, there is still the reality of Gurneys Fish Shop with its announcements of cod, bass and halibut: 'brill' as their well-painted sign says. Multi-coloured beach gear shares flinty paving next to dog-eared Penguins in a bargain box, and a film prop bicycle brings a Powell & Pressburger insouciance to the exterior of an outfitter to the gentry.

⌃ **ABOVE**
Gurneys Fish Shop, Burnham Market

◂◂ **OPPOSITE**
Jack Wills, Burnham Market

⚘ **BELOW**
Half the story, an enamel sign in Burnham Market

The coast road now does a dog-leg past Burnham Overy Mill and its attendant cottages. The red brick pantiled mill with its weatherboarded hoist and the bridge over the River Burn are both of 1790. The watermill was operated by Edmund Savory and, needing extra milling power, he built the windmill just a little further up the road in 1816. Early one summer's evening, I walked out into a boggy field at the side of the watermill and heard a sound like the sudden rustle of a silk dress. Right in front of me, a barn owl lifted up from the reeds like a pale ghost and beat a retreat to trees at the field edge.

If the tide is out at Burnham Overy Staithe, the boats lean precariously on their moorings, and now you can discover a rich pattern of rusty rings and chains among the strands of seaweed and discarded shells left drying out in the sun. Commercial shipping declined here in the mid-nineteenth century, after the arrival of the railways in Norfolk, the last cargo thought to have been loaded just after the First World War. I wonder if the work was watched by Richard Woodget, one-time captain of the clipper *Cutty Sark*, who retired here.

On the right-hand side of the road there now appears a long estate wall, the northern boundary of the Holkham Estate. Holkham is stuffed full of good things, from Thomas Coke's (pronounced 'Cook') simply prodigious eighteenth-century house of yellow gault brick, to a little thatched Ice House out in the park. The landscaping and surrounding countryside owes much to Coke's great-nephew, the 'Coke of Norfolk' who helped revolutionise agricultural practices. Much else

❦ **BELOW**
Chain reactions at Burnham Overy Staithe

⌂ ABOVE
Triumphal Arch, Holkham

has been innovatory here, including the invention of the bowler hat (made by the Bowler brothers for Lock's hatters), protective headgear given to the estate gamekeepers most likely by Edward Coke, younger brother of the second Earl of Leicester. The park and woodland they patrolled stretches out into blue distances, and everywhere are ilex trees. They say these evergreens are the result of statuary arriving at Holkham from Italy in boxes using ilex leaves, much as we would use bubblewrap. You can imagine them being unpacked and stray leaves gently blowing out into the park through an open door.

My favourite building here is the 1752 Triumphal Arch, near the southernmost gate lodges at New Holkham. Designed by Coke's right-hand man William Kent, and executed by Matthew Brettingham, it uses the ubiquitous gault brick, but this time is 'rusticated' by big eggs of flint. I first saw it as a painting by John Piper, the front cover of his and Richard Ingrams' *Piper's Places*, and it held my imagination until I could stand on the lane in front of it and feel its full impact. The little room above the main arch would be just the place to play a cello, looking down from that semicircular window at travellers going through underneath, with over two miles still to go to the Hall.

▲ **ABOVE**

Moorings and quayside, Wells-next-the-Sea

To the north, opposite the Victoria Hotel on the coast road, Lady Anne's Drive goes across to a break of Corsican pines planted by Thomas William Coke in the mid-nineteenth century. Wooden duckboarding laid across the sandy floor among the trees brings you to Holkham Bay, a vast tract of beach that stretches out to the sea. Here are big sand dunes, ideal places for family picnics, but watch the tide, which instead of predictably progressing in an orderly straight line tends to fill up a channel behind you. I find this calm and shallow water makes a good launch site for tin Sutcliffe clockwork liners.

It is possible to walk from here round to Wells-next-the-Sea, where one of the first sights will be a row of colourful beach huts on stilts. Rounding the corner for the walk down into the town, you will see the lifeboat station, once an 1895 picturesque jumble of cream and maroon corrugated iron, now encased in a smart, but thoughtful, modern shell in the same colours. Wells will be where you encounter the most people on this tour, tripping over the chains lying on the quayside in order to eat ice cream, or wolfing down fish 'n' chips in a café that doesn't give you a plate to eat it from. The harbour has a covered hoist stretching out over The Quay from a warehouse, a trademark for Wells except that it's now loft apartments, and at the end the location for the pub that the amateur treasure seeker stayed in for the wonderfully atmospheric film the BBC made in 1972 of MR James's *A Warning to the Curious*. Walk up away from the harbour and the half-hearted amusement arcades and the town itself are rewarding, with good Georgian building in the lanes and a marvellous post office built in carstone, the material most likely brought here from westernmost Norfolk by the railway that ran up from Fakenham through Walsingham.

Stiffkey (or Stewkey) is archetypal north Norfolk: a ruinous Old Hall of the 1580s built by Sir Nicholas Bacon (now being repaired) below the churchyard, a classic village school in flint with brick quoins and decoration and an old Methodist chapel overflowing with period lighting. This last is a veritable Aladdin's cave of white globe shades, green bell shades, blue ribbed frill shades. Everything for your oil lamp, plus desirable little period home accessories like oval house numbers. I couldn't find mine. Stiffkey, with its marshes of purple sea lavender and its 'Stewkey Blues' cockles, is also famous for its errant rector, the Reverend Harold Davidson, who was summarily defrocked in 1932 for doing the Lord's work a little too intimately with London prostitutes. In the missionary position, you might say. He was shopped by one of them, a Miss Barbara Harris, and subsequently ended up displaying himself naked in a barrel at the circus, among other equally bizarre performances. Still protesting his innocence, he was killed by a lion called Freddie in Skegness.

Morston is where you get your boat to go to see the seals basking out on Blakeney Point, but more remarkable for me is the church tower. A massive hole in the side – caused by a lightning strike of 1743 – was repaired using red brick as opposed to the original pale stone, which gives it a very patched appearance, like a sticking plaster casually placed on an arm. Inside the church is an inscription to the Reverend Thomas Shorting, who preached his first sermon here and promptly died. My main reason for remembering Morston is that we once stayed in a B&B run by an elderly couple. Getting up in the middle of the night as a result of overindulgence in a nearby pub, I pulled the chain and the whole cistern came away from the wall. The accompanying noise brought the owner out from his room waving a rubber-tipped walking stick at me, thinking I was a burglar. Back in our room I had a pair of shoes thrown at me for good measure.

⚓ **ABOVE**
Moreton's Morston

I first stayed in Blakeney (no midnight rambling) in 1968. As I approached the village, an ink-blue sky with white gulls etched on it presaged a snowstorm that the next day threatened to keep me in Norfolk for a week. I only got out with the help of a spade lent by a publican's wife in Fakenham. Forty years later, I stayed in the burnt-orange pantiled King's Arms pub, listening to swifts as they screamed around the terracotta chimney pots. Blakeney, as with so many villages on this coast, was once a hive of maritime activity that has all but gone. Only small craft can now navigate the muddy channels, but a reminder of greater days stands up above the village at the church of St Nicholas. Looking like an offspring of the big west tower is another, polygonal tower on the northeast corner. It has always been said that this was a beacon for shipping, no doubt because it's so much shorter than the main tower. Perhaps both were lined up with each other as a navigational aid to boats coming into the Glaven Estuary, a device that could be used in daylight hours. The wooden louvres also tell of a small belfry, perhaps for a sanctus bell that marked the rituals progressing within, or rung by the sexton during burials.

⚓ **ABOVE**
Second tower, Blakeney church

➤ **ABOVE LEFT**
King's Arms, Blakeney

➤➤ **OPPOSITE**
Blakeney boat humour

Only just down the road, across the River Glaven, is Cley next the Sea. I find this little lost town somehow incredibly sad, as if a wraith had slowly come out of the sea on a moonlit night and stolen all the babies. My melancholia is perhaps not helped by my once being shown a room in a local hotel, attached to a very imaginative price tag, the westering sun illuminating what appeared to be someone in the other single bed, humped in true MR James ghost-story fashion.

The remnants of a quay lie down among the reeds near the 1810 windmill, a Norfolk showstopper that achieved national fame as one of the locations visited by BBC2's orange hot-air balloon in what was by far their most successful (and relevant) series of channel identities. The mill was converted into a holiday house for Miss Sarah Wilson in 1921. Reminders of past glories are everywhere, not least in the church of St Margaret, just to the south on the Holt road, with its magnificent porch that once gave out on to the thriving harbour on the Glaven Estuary, now just the quiet meadows of Newgate Green. In the town itself can be seen the old Custom House in the High Street, a carved St George and his dragon scrapping on the corner of the George Hotel and the enticing chalkboard of the Cley Smokehouse. Down on the beach, reached by another lane winding across the salt marsh, you can see them hauling the fishing boats up on to the shingle, just a

mile from the Smokehouse. It makes you want to run back and buy a pair of oak-smoked kippers for your breakfast.

Next door is Salthouse, a group of houses and cottages facing the marsh, with its church perched up on the hill above the village. Here in November 1897 came the Rage: a northwesterly wind that lifted the sea over the shingle bank, across the marsh and into the village. One woman said she saw 'the sea as high as houses, and all of a sudden that come slopping over'. Fires in grates hissing with saltwater, occupants left clinging to roofs as baulks of timber, poultry, clocks and haystacks floated by. It happened again, in 1953. 'We are lucky to be alive', said one man, a large buoy nestling cuckoo-like in his garden. Another said, 'We had just finished our tea when the sea broke the door and in swam my dog.' Up in the churchyard, looking down and across the marsh to the beach, you realise just how vulnerable this coast must be to incursions by the sea. A coast where, from any vantage point, the sails of schooners and square riggers would have been seen navigating the channels into the havens of the busy ports; Salthouse schoolboys carving images of flags, masts and rigging into the church choir stalls.

⬆ **ABOVE**
Salthouse church

🌷 **BELOW**
Choir stall ship, Salthouse church

We can now turn our back on the sea and take the road from Blakeney to Letheringsett and Holt, where we follow the Glaven through Glandford, noting the exquisite setting of Bayfield Hall and its church up on the opposite bank of the river. The local Pevsner guide will sniffily tell you that Holt has 'few houses of marked interest in the centre', while grudgingly admitting that the town is 'pleasant'. Destroyed by a disastrous fire in 1708, the town was rebuilt and, although apparently not stuffed with grandly architectural buildings, is nevertheless a very rewarding town to wander in for anyone with an eye for detail. Like Oundle or Uppingham, Holt enjoys the close proximity of a public school, in this case Gresham's, so caters accordingly. I come here to buy high-waisted trousers from a shop that sells such things along with moleskin waistcoats and striped ties with names like 'Brighton Line', but this need not detain us. Pevsner's right, it is a very pleasant town with a host of interesting shops, like the grocer that piles up pyramids of baked-bean cans in eye-catching displays.

↑ ABOVE
Food colouring, Holt

↖ ABOVE LEFT
Building detail, Holt

I would like to have been here when they rolled up the carpets in the Feathers Hotel on market day to accommodate Norfolk farming boots, but back in the present I really must travel on the North Norfolk Railway to Sheringham from its western terminus here in Holt. A few years ago, I was on the road between Weybourne and Sheringham on a very hot July day. Below a deep azure sky and beside a yellow cornfield studded at the margins with red poppies, a black tank engine pulled a rake of crimson carriages through the morning heat, the white exhaust smoke evaporating against the blue. This, and the memory of all that I had seen since leaving King's Lynn, combined to make this probably one of the most beautiful, atmospheric and satisfying of English coastlines.

SHEEP & SHINGLE
ROMNEY MARSH & DUNGENESS

BETWEEN Fairlight in Sussex and Sandgate in Kent runs the Royal Military Canal, and I'm going to take you around the country that lies to the southeast of it. The only other borders are the sea. The canal offers the first clue as to the nature of the Romney Marsh and the Dungeness Peninsula, built, along with the prodigious upturned-sandcastle Martello Towers, as part of the coastal defences should Napoleon consider paying us a visit. When you look at an Ordnance Survey map it's obvious why the canal was so important; at each end there are the natural defences of cliffs, and much higher ground rises immediately to the northwest — the original, and extremely old, coastline. Everything else is flat and looks like it's been reclaimed from the sea, which of course is how it happened, creating a distorted triangle of green marsh and bleak shingle that ends in a point at Dungeness.

Romney Marsh is a bit of a misnomer when describing the more gentle part of the area, because in fact apart from Romney there are the Walland, Denge and Guldeford Marshes. Nevertheless, for simplicity we will stick with Romney, and Dungeness is uniquely Dungeness. The Marsh just seems to drift effortlessly into this vast tract of shingle, as if the pastures just ran out of steam as they headed for the beach. The sea is now at bay, waves rising and falling along a 20-mile stretch of coastline, but you are always aware here that it would only need a succession of great storms for it all to dramatically change once again.

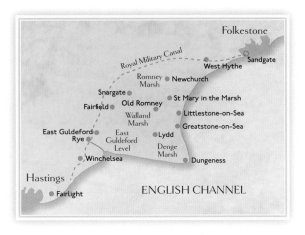

In the late 1950s, I had my first holiday that did not involve being buffeted about on the Lincolnshire coast. My excitement knew no bounds as we travelled down to St Pancras and over to Charing Cross, where we piled into the compartment of a green Southern Region electric train. It was hot, and I shall never forget the train moving out on to the bridge over the Thames and a sudden breeze coming off the water and into the open carriage windows: '... all sense / of being in a hurry gone', as Philip Larkin had it in *The Whitsun Weddings*. We finally got out at Sandling station, just short of Folkestone, and a cream and green Bedford coach took us squeakily down a tree-lined lane to Hythe. Within a couple of days, I was sitting behind my father as we canoed down the Royal Military Canal, he with a Brazil nut toffee on the go and me staring at the back of his check sports jacket and hoping we wouldn't capsize. It came back to me as I drove down off the steep escarpment, that was once coastal cliffs, and came across an ornate bridge over the canal at West Hythe.

The Royal Military Canal was sanctioned by William Pitt in 1804, on hearing from a defecting French general that Napoleon was amassing a flotilla of 1500 barges in preparation for an invasion over La Manche. First thoughts were to flood the marsh, but the prospect of compensating so many farmers put the government off. As it would now I expect. The thought that Napoleon could very easily land at Dungeness quickened the pace of the navigation, and the next four years saw navvies building not only the canal but guard houses, gun emplacements on corners and a service road on the north side. It came into its own again in the Second World War, when a succession of pillboxes were erected to face the threat of German invasion, but in the end they weren't needed. However, an unexpected bonus has been its utility as a very useful drainage channel. Controlling water flow is very important on such low-lying land, and in the summer the canal can be used as a reserve tank. The Marsh is now 80 per cent arable, but there are still invaluable wetlands where Romney Marsh sheep spot the fields between dykes and banks of willow. As Tom Shoesmith says to Dan in Kipling's *Puck of Pook's Hill*: 'Ah, but the diks an' the water-lets they twists the roads about as ravelly as witch-yarn on the spindles.'

⌃ ABOVE
Royal Military Canal, West Hythe

◂◂ OPPOSITE
Romney Marsh at Fairfield

Below West Hythe, the road arrives at a junction at Botolphs Bridge Inn, where a big corrugated iron mobile shepherd's hut sits under an electricity pole. Avoiding the temptation to hitch it to our towbar, we will cross another canal subsidiary that runs out into the Channel at a sluice gate and progress in a straggly fashion westwards, echoing the military canal to our right and glancing up at the ramparts of Lympne Castle on the escarpment above us. Imagine it. Where once gulls screamed around the castle walls and waves crashed below, herons now stand on the banks of the canal and kingfishers flash through the willows. We are now on the Marsh proper: narrow lanes lined with breaks of willow, the undersides of leaves flashing silver in the breeze, remote cottages and scattered farms with names like Tontine, perhaps denoting a will where a group of potential owners all had to die until only one was left to take possession. Shades of the dastardly deeds in Bryan Forbes' 1966 film *The Wrong Box*.

Newchurch is a group of houses gathered around a village pond and the first of a number of simply extraordinarily atmospheric Romney Marsh churches, dedicated to St Peter and St Paul. Some have been over-restored, most are not, or at least have been altered with great sensitivity. Essentially, they will be medieval, but often with Georgian box pews and sets of black oval plaques with texts lettered in gilt, and numerous hiding places for the contraband smuggled in from the lonely shores. Kipling again: 'Brandy for the Parson, / 'Baccy for the Clerk.' The tower of ragstone Newchurch leans at an alarming angle, and on entering the churchyard I saw that a big family vault looked like it was about to be opened, showing the inner core of an arched brick vault. I was more disconcerted by seeing the figure of a beautiful woman dressed in black standing in the corner of the wide south aisle. Metaphorically splashing on Eau de Cologne, I went up to introduce myself, only

⬆ **ABOVE**
Newchurch glamour

⬆ **ABOVE LEFT**
Mobile shepherd's hut, Botolphs Bridge

to suddenly realise she was a shop window mannequin dressed up as a Newchurch museum piece. I really should've gone to Specsavers.

Travelling southwards, we soon arrive at St Mary in the Marsh, a tiny handful of cottages, farms and a pub opposite another church. When I arrived here, wind and rain were slanting down across the churchyard, but soon the first signs of impending sunshine lit up the pitch pine pews and the red tiled floor that contained fragments of long-forgotten memorial stones. Simple Early English, I found great calm within its walls, and thought about E Nesbit, author of *The Railway Children*, who spent her last years in the village and is remembered in the churchyard. Up on the north wall are the big colourful 1775 Royal Arms of George III, another common Marsh feature.

Across the road, I was directed by an elderly Marsh Man (more of him at Snargate) to a reconstructed shepherd's house that had been erected quite recently in a farmyard. The 'lookers', as the shepherds were called on the Marsh, were out in all weathers watching over vast flocks of sheep. These little brick huts were their shelters, lived in during lambing time when their families would bring food to

❦ BELOW
Shepherd's house, St Mary in the Marsh

⬆ **ABOVE**
St Mary in the Marsh

➥ **OPPOSITE**
Sound mirror, Greatstone-on-Sea

them, and latterly, as the looker got around in a car, used as a tool shed. Virtually all are gone now. I did find a wrecked house on the Marsh near Midley, just four low courses of brick rapidly succumbing to tall stands of nettles, the only sign now of any domestication being the remains of the whitewashed interior walls. The example in St Mary in the Marsh, admirably preserved by Dennis Cole for future generations, is also a sad reminder that so many have been irrevocably lost, even one, much loved by artists, violently bulldozed into the ground.

Our road slips into the back of New Romney, and on to the seafront at Littlestone-on-Sea. England is full of unsuccessful seaside resorts, the result of speculators looking for a fast buck from a holiday trade that never came in sufficient numbers. Here are reminders, the washed-up souvenirs of failed enterprise at Littlestone still expressed in tall villas bleached by the sun, standing accusingly as if forever waiting for guests to arrive in their hundreds from the railway station, an infant Hastings or Folkestone virtually stillborn. Richard Ingrams inimitably says in his book *Romney Marsh and the Royal Military Canal* that they: '... look as if they are inhabited by lunatics or ghosts'. It doesn't help that

apart from in the morning their fronts are in shadow, but on the foreshore Littlestone more than makes up for it, with colourful beach huts and sea holly competing on the hot shingle with rusty winches and upturned fishing boats, the leitmotifs of Dungeness.

Across the flatlands to the west of Greatstone-on-Sea can be found the remarkable sound mirrors, an early experiment in 1928 for detecting aeroplanes coming at us from over the Channel. Huge concrete dishes and a curved wall like a massive sea defence stand alone among gravel pits where visitors are discouraged. You can walk up to where a little swing bridge is locked against you, that keeps the mirrors isolated on a little gravelly island. They were so nearly destroyed by ignorant officials, but thanks to Herculean efforts by Lilian Madieson of Lydd, the Department of the Environment finally listed the structures in 1979. Although much derided, especially as their purpose was rapidly overtaken by the advent of radar in 1932, they did work to a very limited degree, microphones being placed in front of them attached at the other end to a pair of headphones worn in a concrete bunker.

▲ ABOVE
Beach huts, Littlestone-on-Sea

▼ BELOW
Dungeness eccentricity

ABOVE
Dungeness electricity

In front of us now will be the silhouettes of the Dungeness lighthouses, the ugly block of the nuclear power station and the strings of pylons emanating out across the horizon. There are a succession of lighthouses here: the base of Samuel Wyatt's 1792 light next to the 1904 Old Lighthouse and its successor, the 1961 torch built from self-coloured prefabricated concrete rings. I'm certain the Old Lighthouse is the one that author HE Bates was thinking of when he wrote his superb short story *The Lighthouse*, an intense evocation of heat, light and sandy eroticism. For dramatic effect he painted it white, but the light he describes on a sun-dazzled shore is unmistakable. There's a café too, not as hospitable as the tin one in the story, and certainly not as seductive. I once queued up here for a cuppa and suddenly realised that the blue-boiler-suited man in front of me was filmmaker Derek Jarman. I introduced myself, and was about to embark on a discussion with him about his set designs for Ken Russell's 1971 film *The Devils*, but he very wisely (and kindly) steered me towards his quest for plants that would attract bees and yet still be able to thrive on the discouraging shingle surrounding his black-tarred home down the road. Something of which I knew absolutely nothing.

The low-slung shacks of Dungeness have no real borders, what gardens they have are made of incredibly hardy plants clinging on for dear life among driftwood and bits of rusty iron. In reality, everywhere is shingle that builds and builds in ridges that look like ploughed furrows from the air, colonised by clumps of sea holly and viper's bugloss, and, remarkably at one point, a surprise patch of brilliantly coloured sweet peas growing by the hot tarmac. So tedious was the walking on this ever-shifting ground, the locals once wore wooden plattens on their feet, the shingle version of the snow shoe. The 'main' road is the old trackbed of the Southern Railway (SR), which last left passengers here in 1937 and presumably didn't mind the locals appropriating their rolling stock as starter homes. Many can still be seen at the core of the shacks. The SR's predecessor, the South Eastern Railway, used the shingle as track ballast on their system; however, it was not only deemed to be totally unfit for purpose, but was also the main cause of the 1927 Sevenoaks train disaster. The SR owned the Dungeness Peninsula before apparently flogging it to the Mayor of Lydd for £1 an acre, who then promptly charged all the carriage dwellers ground rent.

◄ OPPOSITE
Dungeness sweet peas

▼ BELOW
Dungeness carriage shacks c 1987

▲ ABOVE
*Romney, Hythe & Dymchurch Railway
locomotive* Hurricane *at Dungeness*

Amazingly, trains still run here: the Romney, Hythe & Dymchurch Railway (RH&DR) that comes down from Hythe to clatter behind gardens and between bungalows and houses, until looping the loop around the lighthouses. This is not the normal seaside miniature railway: a few yards along a promenade or a trip through flowerbeds in the park. No, the RH&DR is a proper railway, 13 and a half miles long, used by schoolchildren and with an impeccable war record of bringing supplies down to Dungeness. Captain JEP Howey and Count Louis Zborowski had the idea in the 1920s and, having failed to buy 'The Ratty' line in Eskdale, they ordered two Pacific locomotives, *Green Goddess* and *Northern Chief*, and decided on the Romney Marsh as their track bed. Zborowski was promptly killed in the Italian Grand Prix at Monza, but the line, at first only to New Romney, was opened in 1927. In those early years, everyone flocked to see this miniature masterpiece and have pictures of themselves standing like giants next to the locos and carriages. The Second World War saw it carrying equipment for Operation Pluto (the undersea fuel pipeline for the Allied invasion) and even an anti-aircraft gun, but it was quickly re-opened in 1946 by Laurel and Hardy. I can vouch for the sheer quality of an afternoon spent on this little railway, sitting sideways in the bar carriage *Gladys* with an RH&DR Celebration Steam Ale to hand and the door slid open to a sea breeze.

On my holiday I purloined my father's binoculars to look at the aeroplanes taking off from the nearby Ferryfield Airport near Lydd, just to the west of the sound mirrors. These were no ordinary aircraft. Silver City Airways channel-hopped with Bristol Freighters that carried a couple of cars and their occupants over to Le Touquet. The front snout lifted up to take the vehicles in, and they will be best remembered from the film *Goldfinger* (1964) when James Bond followed his quarry's Rolls-Royce over to the Continent. In an ever-increasing desire to make pots of cash by destroying the unique atmosphere of the Marsh (they've had a lot of success with an appalling wind turbine farm at Little Cheyne Court), they now want to turn this little airport into a major one. Doubtless they will call it 'London Lydd'.

From Lydd, we can go north again until we reach Old Romney, on what is really only one of two main roads on the Marsh that bring traffic in from outside or 'from up on the cliff', as they probably don't say. St Clement's Church can only be reached by a tiny lane at the back of the village, and I can't tell you how much it's worth the effort. A giant yew tree towers almost benevolently next to the mainly thirteenth-century church with its squat shingled spire, and I propped my camera on top of a big slate gravestone while waiting for the sun. Only when I reached out for it again did I realise it was Derek Jarman's, the simple slate slab just incised with his signature.

❦ **BELOW**
Church of St Clement, Old Romney

⬆ **ABOVE**
Old Romney church interior

Inside, one just wants to sit looking around from a pink Georgian box pew. Pink? In the early 1960s they made a film here, variously called *The Scarecrow of Romney Marsh* or *Doctor Syn* (1963), another adaptation of Russell Thorndike's novel of 1915, a tale of a smuggling parson also played by Peter Cushing as the eponymous *Captain Clegg* made at the same time. For the *Scarecrow* version (with Patrick McGoohan), Walt Disney and the Rank Organisation restored the pews and painted them a fetching ointment pink. The villagers so liked it, they kept them as we see them today. This was not the first time a film camera turned here. In 1947, Ealing Studios were on the Marsh shooting *The Loves of Joanna Godden*, a superior film with Googie Withers and a screenplay by HE Bates, music by Vaughan Williams and a poster by John Minton. What was there not to like?

Carrying on out of the back of Old Romney, we can travel by Sunnyside Farm, Five Vents Bridge and Yoakes Court Farm to Ivychurch. Rogues and thieves keep nicking the lead off the roof of St George's Church, and the last time it happened the vicar apparently quite rightly said that he'd like to have the perpetrators' heads on spikes. Perhaps they should employ a night watchman, like those employed to look out for eighteenth-century grave robbers. He (or she) could sit in the curious mobile shelter they keep in the church, once used to keep the rain off bewigged vicars at gravesides. I found the church strangely disorientating, with its screen running down the nave, but I liked the Commandment boards each side of the altar and the nine typical Marsh oval texts on the pillars. Equally impressive outside are the row of Butler tombs in their iron railing enclosure against the church wall.

We can now wander across the Marsh on tiny lanes until we come to Cuckold's Corner (now what happened here?), and turn for Snargate and the Church of St Dunstan's opposite the Red Lion pub. The rector here was once Richard Barham who wrote *The Ingoldsby Legends*, and on a lead plate in the church is a somewhat confusing embossed inscription 'J. Bourne, C. Warden- Warrington Romney plumber T. Apps carpenter and all his jolly men, 1780'. I bet those jolly men got even jollier over in the Red Lion.

I'll not go on about the Red Lion, other than to say that at the time of writing, which of course hints at possible change in the future, it fits perfectly into the idea of a particular kind of pub as expressed in (shameless plug) my previous book – an evocation of England past and present – *Unmitigated England*. When I wrote that chapter I hadn't been here, now I wish I lived down the road. Run by Land Army Girl Doris and her daughter, this is how all country pubs should be, and very decidedly are not. Sitting on his chair with a local pint I met my Marsh Man, such a kindly gentleman with a pipe in his waistcoat pocket and a profound knowledge of all aspects of the Marsh. He saw it all start to change dramatically during the Second World War, as the aerodromes were built and many roads were widened to service them. He told me about the lookers, and their sheep that didn't need close shepherding and virtually looked out for themselves. Too docile to even think of jumping the dykes, the lookers wouldn't have wanted any trouble from them. Not like in my home county of Leicestershire where they can't wait to get out of fields and down to the pub. He told me of the shepherds' houses, how a looker could expect to be held up in one for a considerable time, with just the sounds of the sheep on the wind and a fire in the little brick hearth for company, and how they had all but disappeared. He spoke of the old Marsh, where 'you were lucky if you saw two other people in a day', and how trustworthy everyone was. 'You could leave your gold watch on a gatepost and it'd still be there a week later.' (It reminded me that on tour for this book I'd left a camera on top of a roadside egg cupboard in farthest Essex, and it was found and kept for me by the eggman until I picked it up three hours later.) I later saw the Marsh Man bicycling slowly down a busy main road, cars rushing and hooting by him to the sea, and I thought how privileged I'd been to meet him, and for his account of a way of life now lost forever.

BELOW LEFT
Red Lion, Snargate

BELOW
Snargate

From Snargate, we cross over to Fairfield, not a village but another scattering of farms and cottages on one of the last areas of proper Marsh, that is: open wetlands bisected by dykes. At its heart is the little church of St Thomas a Becket, completely alone in the pastures and surrounded by water courses and slowly grazing sheep. One of the last opportunities, I imagine, to see the true marshland character. As I roamed the surrounding field, a man appeared on the horizon waving something at me. Thinking it was an irate farmer with a billhook, I thought of trying to jump the nearest dyke to get away, but on the still evening air I heard him say that he'd got the key to the church.

I shall never forget the sight that met us when we finally worked out how the door catch worked. The westering light of an early July evening lit the awe-inspiring crown-posts and tie beams holding up the steep red-tiled roof, a seventeenth-century font, and the ubiquitous box pews – all of them set in four-sided enclaves with seats all round that meant each of them must have provided accommodation for the individual families from surrounding farms. Some of them must have had their backs to the preacher in his eighteenth-century three-decker pulpit. Incredibly, all this was the subject of extensive restoration in 1913 by WD Caröe, but he was very wise, certainly at the time, to retain so many original fittings. It is odd, seeing what is a timber-framed building infilled with over-neat courses of early twentieth-century brick.

We can go back across to Brookland, where the church of St Augustine is remarkable anywhere, let alone on the Romney Marsh, for its detached campanile.

John Newman, in my well-thumbed copy of *The Buildings of England: West Kent and The Weald*, puts it exactly, saying it's 'like three candle-snuffers stacked on one another'. They say it was because the church couldn't take the weight on the somewhat unstable Marsh soil. The rest of the church is equally rewarding, having avoided the attentions of Victorian restorers, with a timber porch with stable-like doors, a lead font that has the Signs of the Zodiac round it where Sagittarius is depicted by acorns being knocked down for pigs, and yet another graveside shelter. Those Romney rectors and vicars certainly wanted to keep their wig powder dry.

The main road to Rye does some sharp turns and is very busy, but it's worthwhile seeing if you can park safely in East Guldeford and take the shady footpath across to the barn-like St Mary's Church. The twin roofs have a small timber bell-turret snuggling between them, but I couldn't get in to tell you how much restoration had been carried out in the early nineteenth century. As I came round the southwest corner, a Little Owl blinked at me from on top of a gravestone. The wide-eyed bird watched me for a few seconds and then lifted off to join the companion I could hear thrashing about in nearby foliage. The experience provides me with an excuse to tell of other watchers of these very special and immeasurably atmospheric places, and urge you to support the Romney Marsh Historic Churches Trust.

⬆ **ABOVE**
East Guldeford Little Owl

↖ **ABOVE LEFT**
East Guldeford

⬇ **BELOW**
Brookland

The storybook silhouette on the horizon is the town of Rye. So much has been written, eulogised, filmed and just talked about this hilltop East Sussex town that it's very difficult to know where to begin. I won't get into what does, or what doesn't, constitute a Cinque Port, but there are more than five and Rye's one of them. To get to grips with it, you must walk up into the town through one of the old gates and just keep turning off down streets and alleys (many of them keeping in character with cobbles), remembering all the time that the sea once came up to the walls and that it's all impossibly romantic. In just one place – Lamb House in West Street – lived novelists Henry James, EF Benson, and a scion of one of the great publishing firms, Brian Batsford. James lived here from 1897, Benson wrote the Mapp and Lucia books and set them in Rye (which he called Tilling), and more recently, Sir Brian Batsford, perhaps better known as Brian Cook, the illustrator of those fabulous Batsford book jackets of the 1930s.

The eclectic collection of buildings is a painter's paradise: brick, coloured renders, weatherboarding and tile hanging. The shops are traditional – pies from Simple Simon's – and there's something quirkily interesting around every cobbled corner, whether it's a brick water cistern or a gull nesting in guttering. Most visitors tend to congregate down by the black-tarred done-up warehouses on the quayside of the River Brede, those that make it up the hill stand and look at the quarter-boys performing like clockwork up on the wall of Rye's centrepiece church of St Mary's. Or inside, stare upwards at the 18-foot-long pendulum swinging across the church like something in Edgar Allan Poe.

⬆ **ABOVE**
Rye guardian

➼ **OPPOSITE**
Rye maritime

❦ **BELOW**
Rye retail

ABOVE
Rye churchyard at St Mary's

I once climbed up the stairs to the tower parapet with my mate Mr Hooper, after we'd had an excessively good lunch in The Mermaid. We'd arrived in Rye earlier, getting off a steam train that was plying the Marsh all day between Hastings and Ashford. Up at the top, we looked down over the red rooftops, seeing curls of smoke rising vertically from terracotta chimney pots and nudging each other when we saw our girlfriends coming out of a shop. The view to the southeast was artist Paul Nash's Shell poster of the river winding out to Rye Harbour. 'All we need now', I said, 'is for that steam train to come through again.' As I said it, we heard the shriek of a whistle and the big green locomotive and its rake of carriages came out of the late afternoon haze to the west, slowing up for Rye station just below. Hooper turned to me and said: 'Peter it won't get any better than this. Let's jump off now, holding hands.'

A road dusty with concrete goes out alongside the River Rother to Rye Harbour. Gates with barbed wire wrapped round them and signs saying 'Don't Even Think Of Coming In Here'; factories producing solvent or something, and then it opens out on to a higgledy-piggledy landscape of odd buildings with the Rother streaming one way or another through it all. A caravan park on one side with a Martello Tower overgrown with weeds to one edge, on the other a black-painted coastguard cottage, a pub, a bright blue lifeboat station and a window propped open with a Dan Brown hardback. On a scruffy area of shingle sits impotently an abandoned, wheel-less Southern Railway carriage.

Down at the water's edge, with an aperitif of samphire sprouting up out of the mud, is a good place to watch the tide coming in at incredible speed. On my last visit, there was the added attraction of seeing the harbour pilots untie their launches and then to see them spinning round with the current as if completely out of control. Which I assume was not the case, just a party piece they do to amuse themselves before the next drug smugglers come in.

 **ABOVE**
Abandoned Southern Railway carriage,
Rye Harbour

 BELOW
Rye baker's cart

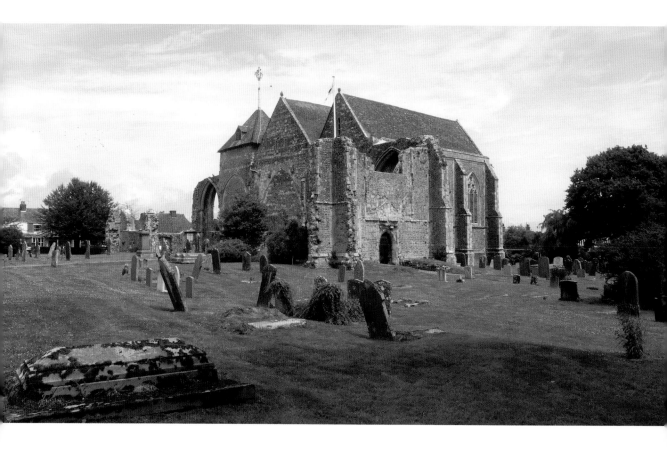

ABOVE
*Church of St Thomas the Martyr,
Winchelsea*

To the south of Rye, we find its companion. Quieter, more subdued, less overrun, Winchelsea is another hilltop town. Again approached up through one of three medieval gates, the town wasn't always here but down on the levels by the sea. The French kept coming over and giving it a good sacking, the sea came in every Wednesday and finally totally submerged it in 1288. So Winchelsea was reborn in the time of Edward I, up on the hill with a grid pattern of streets with more wine cellars underneath than you could shake an empty bottle at. These were essential for the wine trade with Gascony, but the French still kept coming and making a nuisance of themselves, and by the reign of Queen Elizabeth I the harbour had silted up and the trade disappeared.

Now, it appears to be just a handful of streets with very desirable houses around a large church that takes up a whole block of the grid. It was once even bigger, and I found it very curious to sit looking towards the altar with a huge windowless wall behind me. Out in the large churchyard under the trees you can find Spike Milligan's gravestone. I was disappointed to find that his wish to have 'I told you I was ill' engraved on it had not been granted. Unless its in the Oirish Gaelic that

most of the inscription's in. I kept thinking about those wine cellars, and discovered that a great many are still in existence throughout the town. Over 30 of them, all tunnel-vaulted and arched like church crypts. Perhaps Winchelsea meets down here at night, interconnections disguised behind big oaken barrels, baluster-stemmed glasses raised against the light of flickering candles.

We are at the end of our journey. We could just go down the sea lane to the beach, buying fish outside a cottage on the way back before climbing up again on to the High Weald. Or back through Rye and along the Military Road next to the canal to Appledore. This is what I did, stopping at the bridge and walking a few yards down the footpath next to the water. A movement to my right made me stop, and I found myself eye to eye with a Romney Marsh sheep. The staring competition was won by her as I looked away, down to the water. I saw my father, another toffee unwrapped, paddling his way through the algae, under the willows and out of sight. As John Piper wrote in a letter to Richard Ingrams about the Romney Marsh, 'What I really like about it is that it is all — 90% — atmosphere.'

ABOVE
Romney Marsh sheep, Appledore

WALLS & WOOL
NORTH COTSWOLDS

THE COTSWOLDS run from Bath up to Chipping Campden, a tract of limestone hills seen from the west as a steep escarpment called The Edge. From the east, the approach is less dramatic, with stone walling replacing hedges, and villages hiding in the deep clefts of the slowly rising plateau. These mostly Gloucestershire and Oxfordshire settlements and their outlying farms and houses have been the constant pull of the Cotswolds on outsiders since at least the eighteenth century, and their reasonable distance from the larger towns and cities has always attracted visitors. A water-taking spa enthusiast climbing up from Bath, a day-tripper from Birmingham, Bristol and Oxford, or a London commuter hammering down the M40, all find what repose they can in these enticing folds and ridges. A cream tea in Bourton-on-the-Water, a cider with the ghost of Laurie Lee up near Painswick, or perhaps just a light lunch in a dark pub: the Cotswolds are here to provide for even the most casual incursions.

We all know that this quintessential English landscape is so much more than just a day's drive out with a fish pie in the middle, as anyone who has chanced upon, say, Stanway, with its stunning Jacobean gatehouse and thatched cricket pavilion, will readily testify. So rather than try to describe the whole lot, I'm going to concentrate on the perhaps lesser-known northern Cotswolds, in particular a strip running from Winchcombe in the southwest to Mickleton and the last outlier of Meon Hill in the northeast.

My Winchcombe informant says that although his town is very much part of the Cotswolds, it has 'a toe in the Vale of Evesham'. Indeed it does. Coming up from Cheltenham, and after you've ascended the steep road over Cleeve Hill, the ancient settlement of Winchcombe is found in a coombe that appears to drift almost imperceptibly into the Vale. The little town amply repays a walk in and around its buildings, of stone predominantly, but, bearing in mind its position, also of half-timbering and brick.

On Gloucester Street is the Corner Cupboard Inn, with its still-intact West Country Ales ceramic plaque and a bust of Benjamin Disraeli above the porch. It depends whom you listen to, but the most likely reason for his austere presence is that some Victorian or Edwardian students relieved a Cheltenham householder of his ornament, an owner who came to think it actually suited its new location rather better. England's Prime Minister in 1868 and then 1874–80, he's there on an early twentieth-century photograph inside the pub, and hiding behind flowerpots in a 1939 British Pathé film.

Opposite is the Rabbit Box House, with the appropriate animal in stone crouching under a battlemented string course. Winchcombe once had an abbey, a great Benedictine monastery that has completely disappeared. Although in fact, in so many ways, it hasn't. Everywhere you go in the town you can look in, or at, a building like the Rabbit Box, and see something of the abbey. A stone frieze, a section of arch, a handful of floor tiles. Now virtually impossible to metaphorically piece back together into their respective locations, so thoroughly did Lord Chandos of nearby Sudeley Castle dismember the abbey in 1539. Every builder in Winchcombe at the time must have said, 'I'll have some of that', and, 'Ooh, that'll go nicely above the fireplace'.

The Perpendicular church of St Peter, which adjoined the abbey, has its fair share of monastic bits and pieces, including a large stone coffin found on the abbey site in 1815. On the tower, a gilded cockerel twists in the sun, perfectly in proportion against the sky until recently brought down for restoration to ground level, and everyone stood next to it because it's six feet tall. Across the road, a row of almshouses sits at right angles to the street. Making brilliant use of different coloured stone, the terrace was a philanthropic gesture by the brothers Dent, rich Worcester glovers who bought nearby Sudeley Castle in 1837. They employed George Gilbert Scott (he of the Midland Hotel at St Pancras) on numerous projects, including this Dent's Terrace in 1865.

At the foot of the escarpment to the north we find the Gloucestershire Warwickshire Railway, a beautifully preserved line that runs from Cheltenham Racecourse – in the natural amphitheatre of Cleeve Hill – up towards Broadway. The Honeybourne Line would like to make it back to Stratford, but for the time being the railway runs immediately below the Cotswold Edge, with a station at Greet for Winchcombe and one at Toddington, both done out in the splendid Great Western Railway (GWR) paintwork of dark and light stone. Here we will turn right and run up the escarpment on the Stow road to where we find a curious and utterly compelling war memorial on a corner above the village of Stanway. A limestone pillar is surmounted by Alexander Fisher's sculpture of St George in the process of killing a dragon who looks up in dismay at his nemesis. Designed by Sir Philip Stott, of whom more later, the lettering is by sculptor, typeface designer and stonecutter Eric Gill, and tells us that there really are people called 'Buggins'.

Down the lane is the remarkable gatehouse to Stanway House. Built in 1630–40, with its three beautifully shaped gables topped out with scallop shells it is sometimes ascribed to Inigo Jones, who is often credited for much that he didn't do. This is still a real showstopper, and a magnificent entrance to the late

◄◄ OPPOSITE
The Cotswold Escarpment from above Winchcombe, with Sudeley Castle

❧ BELOW
Stanway House

sixteenth- and early seventeenth-century Hall built for the Tracy family. There is a view of the western elevation from the churchyard, and you may remember the building, again faced in golden ashlar, being used to great effect in the Christopher Miles film *The Clandestine Marriage* (1999).

Large yews dominate the churchyard, where another perfectly matched gateway is found in the garden wall, decorated with oversize scallop shells and telling of a convenient entrance for the churchgoing family. In the north wall of the churchyard are inset many beautiful medieval pieces of carved stone including a coffin, ejected from the church during restoration but still surviving here as a potent reminder.

There is more. A fourteenth-century tithe barn, and up on the hill behind the house, a 1750 pyramid announcing a water cascade. Just outside the village on the Stanton road are two simple little buildings that never fail to please: thatched tennis and cricket pavilions. The idea for the latter is credited to Sir James Barrie, and built by John Oakey of Winchcombe of larch poles kept off the ground by staddle stones, usually used for keeping grain barns out of the reach of marauding vermin. Barrie was a frequent visitor to the house, and, it is said, had the idea for Tinkerbell in *Peter Pan* when he saw a flashing spectre on his bedroom ceiling that turned out to be moonlight reflecting off the church weather vane.

Following the lane out of Stanway, past the pavilions and under a particularly sylvan section of the escarpment, is the village of Stanton. Stanway, Stanton, both names reflect the copious use of the underlying stone. Stanton owes its well-preserved appearance to Sir Philip Stott (1858–1937), an Oldham architect of northern mills who bought the village in 1906. Stott made his money not so much from his architect fees as from shrewd investment in the manufacturing mills themselves, and busied himself with sympathetic restoration of the buildings. Everywhere you will see his Art Nouveau lanterns, originally lit by gas (now using those inexpressibly ugly high-energy bulbs), superb alternatives to the usually mundane street lighting. The *Buildings of England* guide says that Stanton is 'architecturally one of the most distinguished of the smaller North Cotswold villages'.

Turning off by the village cross, with its medieval base and seventeenth-century sundial, brings you into a cul-de-sac that ends at a Tudor-style rectory and the church of St Michael. The church is Norman to Perpendicular, with some Victorian rebuilding, and the porch has a little attic above it, said to be a priest's room. On lifting the latch into the dim interior, I was assailed by the heady scents of wedding flowers and the polish that had been so lovingly applied to Sir Ninian Comper's furnishings, paid for once again by Sir Philip. Everything indicated that this is a well-loved and used church. Just to the west of the village is Wormington Grange, late Georgian with neo-Greek bits added, but look out for the neo-Tudor lodge on the road. I've got a thing about lodges, but this one is particularly appealing with its porch reaching right up to the roofline. Stanton must vie with many Cotswold villages for being the favourite postcard on a box of fudge, but thanks to Sir Philip it certainly looks proper as opposed to prim. You can still perceive, behind the pristine stone and roses, the ancestry of yeoman farmers, manor house servants and scurrying rectors.

◄ **OPPOSITE**
Stanton church

↙ **BELOW**
Wormington Grange Lodge

Going back to the Stow road at Stanway, travel eastwards and look out for the stone quarry on the left as you progress further up the steep wooded hill. A dead fox stared glassily up at me as I took a photograph. Cotswold stone is such a delightful, robust and characterful building source, the underlying geology unearthed to complement the landscape perfectly. Everywhere you will find quarries, either disused or very much active, carved out of clefts in the hills, buried in woods. If you're lucky, you'll come across someone rebuilding a dry stone wall, sleeves rolled up, jacket hanging on a pickaxe handle. This is no rough-and-tumble thrown-together walling, this is a true Cotswold craft. The walls themselves are battered, allowing wet to drain down the sides; typically the base is around 24 inches, the top 16 inches. Two types of stone will be used: 'face' for the outer surfaces, 'in-fill' for the inner. Running through it will be longer pieces called 'keystones', and the vertical stones on top are known as a 'cock and hen' finish. No mortar is used, which allows rainwater to run freely through the wall and not freeze.

Turning left for Cutsdean, where you'll find the Church of St James in a farmyard, a bend in the road brings us upon a reminder of a perhaps more reduced Cotswold staple: sheep. Up on a bank above the road is a nineteenth-century sheep wash, a stone-walled circular pool with a narrow ramp leading up out of it. An oak sluice gate controlled the flow of water brought from the River Windrush into the wash, where sheep were lowered in and prodded about by farmworkers until they were well and truly dunked, whence they would stagger up the ramp into a retaining pen. Sheep got filthy wandering about the hills, and a well-washed clean fleece was worth much more in the woollen trade that provided so much past wealth in the Cotswolds.

BAPTISM DOTH REPRESENT UNTO US OUR PROFESSION WHICH IS TO FOLLOW THE EXAMPLE OF OUR SAVIOUR CHRIST AND TO BE MADE LIKE UNTO HIM

Compared to even a hundred years ago, sheep are now low on the ground, as it were. Five thousand years ago, shepherds were doubtless watching their flocks from on top of the Belas Knap burial chamber above Winchcombe; Romans introduced the 'Cotswold Lion' sheep, and the medieval period saw Cotswold farmers become extremely wealthy from their wool-growing livestock. Once, 20,000 sheep would have been sold at a time at Stow Fair, and even the name Cotswolds is from 'cotes' (the buildings) and 'wolds' (the wide open spaces ideal for sheep rearing). Various enclosures and changes in agricultural practice diminished the trade, and Cotswold sheep, once exported all over Britain and indeed the world, are perhaps now largely confined again to these Gloucestershire and Oxfordshire hills.

From Cutsdean we can wander up to Snowshill, but it's worth making a detour back to the main road and through the village of Ford, with its excellent Plough Inn (don't get too distracted by the Donnington Ales, brewed just down the road), to where we can once again turn north for the village of Condicote. 'Quintessential' is a word I try not to overcook, but I suppose one could easily apply it here. The village green is enclosed by dry stone walling, a rusty pump leans in the shade of trees and the church of St Nicholas presides over the north side. This is twelfth century in essence, but everyone complains that it was hugely over-restored. Certainly William Morris would have had a fit, with all the plaster being scraped off the interior walls. However, there are Norman fragments if you know where to look, particularly around the south doorway. The trouble is I can get distracted by the more overlooked, possibly mundane, things in country churches. Here it was a framed baptismal roll, hung with picture cord in a dark corner. Simple, unremarkable, it looks like it was bought from an ecclesiastical catalogue in the 1930s, with a header illustration by Clare Dawson that has storybook children helping Christ out with the cross. It's so touching, and straight to the point, and I haven't seen one anywhere else.

ABOVE
Baptismal roll, Condicote

OPPOSITE
Snowshill Manor

▲ ABOVE
Snowshill

Snowshill could superficially be regarded as another Cotswold stereotype. Houses, cottages, pub and manor gather picturesquely around the church like choirboys around a vicar, with a steep rise that affords the classic Beautiful Britain view. Naturally it had to feature in a 'feel-good' film, *Bridget Jones's Diary* (2001), covered in manufactured snow to be all cosily Christmas for Bridget's visit to her cosily English mum and dad.

The Church of St Barnabas was rebuilt in 1863–4 by an architect who preferred to remain anonymous, but we do know who was responsible for the 1919 Arts and Crafts restoration of Snowshill Manor that dates back originally to around 1500. Charles Paget Wade, an eccentric architect and craftsman, housed here his eclectic collection of everything from Samurai armour to churchwardens' staves. Working on the Hampstead Garden Suburb he met Mackay Hugh Baillie Scott, whom he got in to sort out the Snowshill garden with what Wade called 'a series of outdoor rooms'.

A back road winding northeast out of Snowshill brings us temporarily into Worcestershire and to the top of Broadway Hill where the tower designed by

ABOVE
Broadway Tower

James Wyatt looks out over the Vale of Evesham towards the Malvern Hills. Built in 1797 by George William, 6th Earl of Coventry, it was erected to improve the view from his home at Croome Court to the west of Pershore. Broadway Tower is remarkably well preserved and brings together all the fashionable details of Norman style: round-headed windows, turrets, machicolation and battlements. James Lees-Milne, in *Worcestershire: a Shell Guide*, reckons you can see 13 counties from the top, but I expect it has to be on an exceptionally clear day. William Morris and his pals stayed up here once, and you can imagine the startled look on the otherwise impassive faces of grazing sheep as loud voices raised in Arts 'n' Crafts argument rang out from the open windows.

Once, you could descend into the town of Broadway via Fish Hill, but this is now closed off and you have to use the bypass. To be honest, I prefer to bypass Broadway too, the whole place having been turned into a manicured tourist trap, a living coloured postcard. There are of course some good buildings, notably The Lygon Arms Hotel (bought by the Spanish and so now called Barceló The Lygon Arms), but overall the effect is of a stage set, brushed down for the coach parties in the morning and told to put a cardboard welcoming smile on its face.

Far better is to turn right at the top of Broadway Hill after seeing the tower and follow the road back into Gloucestershire and over to Chipping Campden, turning left off the A44 where a tall signpost stands by the hedge. Pointing the way to places like 'Woster' and 'Gloster', this is a curious survivor from the days when the sign needed to be at a height that could be read more easily by those on horseback or sitting up on coaches. In the seventeenth century, this was on a main route over the Cotswolds from Winchcombe and Stanway via Snowshill, now just the winding lanes we have traversed earlier. Originally erected around 1669, the initials 'N.I.' stand for either Nathan or Nicholas Izod who lived nearby, and the mileages given should be regarded with a certain amount of scepticism. Two-thirds of the way down the hill, a little stone building with an ogee-shaped roof stands on the verge next to a field wall. You are on Conduit Hill, and this is the conduit, erected by Sir Baptist Hicks in 1612 to provide water for his almshouses we shall see down in the town next to the church.

Chipping Campden is undoubtedly one of the most satisfying English country towns; in both the quality of the buildings and their remarkable preservation, and the fine detail that can be enjoyed every few paces. The centrepiece is probably the Market Hall, with its five open bays and a rough stone floor where once the produce of the surrounding countryside was brought in for sale: poultry, cheese, butter and countless eggs. Again this amenity for Campden was provided by Sir Baptist, whose coat-of-arms adorns the north gable. His 'prodigy' house has now gone, razed to the ground by retreating Royalist troops in 1645, leaving only the outbuildings, telling garden earthworks and the stunning pair of lodges and gateway next to St James's Church, across the road from the almshouses that cost their benefactor £1000. (Look out for the other end of his waterworks, the conduit head on the terrace.) The entrance lodges must be among the first of such things in the country, a herald for what was to come at Campden House, with ogee-shaped domed roofs with finely ashlared detail. The big finials cleverly disguise the chimneys.

⬆ **ABOVE**
Signpost, Chipping Campden

◄◄ **OPPOSITE**
Gate lodges, Chipping Campden

◄◄ LEFT
St Andrew, Aston Subedge

❦ BELOW
Houses, Chipping Campden

The church of St James is a classic example of a Cotswold 'wool' church, with its soaring Perpendicular west tower. The money naturally came from those sheep, hefty bequests by wealthy merchants like William Grevel and William Bradway. We know their names, but precious little else. We don't know if they were good or bad, kind to their sheep or indifferent; all we know is that they wanted to assure themselves a place in heaven by getting some exquisite stone carving commissioned. There is therefore a heavenly host of detail to take in, but for its impact on the townscape try to be on Conduit Hill on a cold but bright winter's morning, and see the four gilded weather vanes on their pinnacles flash in the sun high above the surrounding rooftops.

Chipping Campden repays a slow stroll around the streets, particularly in late-afternoon light when the colour becomes richer and the detail crisper: a stone crown outside the old police station, the names of houses cut in English black letter on doorway quoins. We owe the look of the town to two far-sighted artists:

CR Ashbee, who moved the families of his Guild of Handicrafts here in 1902, and the motorcycling draughtsman FL Griggs. Ashbee influenced so much here, right down to typical Arts and Crafts lanterns, and Griggs became a passionate leading light in the foundation of the Campden Trust in 1929 that helped to conserve Chipping Campden's outstanding architectural legacy. His war memorial and wrought-iron signs can be seen in the town, but Frederick Landseer Griggs's pencil drawings will be well known to *aficionados* of Macmillan's *Highways and Byways* series of topographical books.

We can now work our way westwards from Chipping Campden towards the Cotswold Escarpment again, stopping to see the Church of St Nicholas above Saintbury, appearing to be literally clinging to the edge, and the equally well-positioned Gothick Church of St Andrew at Aston Subedge, with a sundial on the south wall. In this village, the influence of the Vale is obvious, particularly in Gardners Farm with its delicious mixture of Cotswold stone, half-timbering and brick. Hidden in trees half a mile to the east is a manor house built for Lord Saye and Sele in 1670: Burnt Norton, the inspiration for the eponymous poem in TS Eliot's *The Four Quartets*.

Following The Edge northeastwards, we arrive in Mickleton, Gloucestershire's most northern village. I first knew of it some years ago, when I used to make my way home across country this way from the west of England as a relief from the M5 motorway. It was always dark, and Mickleton took its place in a canon of villages (Wooler in Northumberland is another) that gave the appearance of having seen me coming, turning off the lights and then putting them back on again as my car went out the other side. An overworked and overtired imagination I know, but I was relieved to discover a different Mickleton in daylight. There still didn't appear to be very many people around, but there must be some ravenous carnivores because a well-stocked family butcher lines the outside of his shop with his mouth-watering signs offering wild venison, spring lamb, home-made faggots (oh yes) and pies of all descriptions.

On the High Street, Medford House is a handsome example of the gradual change from homely Cotswold Tudor to the more sophisticated and austere Queen Anne style, built around 1694 for Samuel Medford. I love the contrast between the honey-coloured stone and the well-trimmed front hedges, almost an illustration of a house. Behind is St Lawrence's Church, that has the interesting addition of a mid-seventeenth-century south porch that appears more secular than religious, a two-storey building embattled with pinnacles. Upstairs once served as a schoolroom. Down in the churchyard can be seen more symbols of the Cotswold reliance on sheep: gravestones with lambs lying down on them. Men and sheep. Inseparable in life, now together in the hopeful permanence of a country churchyard.

⌃ ABOVE
Church porch, Mickleton

◂◾ OPPOSITE
Gate pillar, Mickleton

⚘ BELOW
Medford House, Mickleton

And so to the last outlier of the northern Cotswolds, Meon Hill. Somehow this tree-topped hill, actually just in Warwickshire, has always been on the edge of my consciousness even before I first saw it. In certain lights, even on a bright summer's morning, there is an almost palpable sinister air about it. It may have something to do with an event that took place on its slopes on St Valentine's Day 1945. Charles Walton was a 74-year-old farm labourer who kept himself to himself, preferring to drink cider with his daughter at home in Lower Quinton rather than socialising in the pub. This, and his ability to charm birds out of the sky, naturally made his neighbours regard him as no stranger to the dark arts. On the 14th of February then, Walton went off to work on the side of the hill with his farm tools – a pitchfork and a trouncing hook. He failed to return home that evening and, on the alarm being raised, was found dead: the hook embedded in his throat, the pitchfork used to score a large cross in his chest. Everyone shook their heads and thought told-you-so witchcrafty thoughts, and obviously someone said they'd seen a big black dog wandering about the hill earlier. Robert Fabian of Scotland Yard came out of retirement to try to bring resolution to what is still an unsolved crime. Locals still won't talk about it, and like so many of these apparently unsolved mysteries everyone else hopes for a deathbed confession, but it's getting a bit late now.

⬆ **ABOVE**
Meon Hill from the north

I climbed Meon Hill early one sunlit April morning, following the 'Heart of England Way' from Upper Quinton. In fact I didn't get to the top. After wandering through the sheep pastures and under the backlit leaves of big chestnut trees, I heard on the breeze the sound of wood being chopped over to my right, similar to the erection of gallows at the start of the 1968 film *Witchfinder General*. Nervously rounding a hillock, I came across a farm lad working on some fence posts at the back of a blue tractor. I waved and approached him, hoping to God he wasn't reaching for a trouncing hook. We talked about the hill, and I asked him what he knew about Charles Walton. He looked down the hill and murmured, 'Not much', and then turned to me and said, 'They say there's lots of things whirl about on the top at night.' He paused and added, 'You won't catch me up there.' We both turned and looked at the tree-lined summit just as the sun started to flash over the edge and the sheep followed each other into the shadow of the final precipitous slope. I bade him farewell and started back down the hill, giving a slight shudder. Not because of the account of Charles Walton's gruesome demise, although that had obviously coloured my thoughts, but of something else. Something not understood.

MUD & OYSTERS
ESSEX ESTUARIES

I ONCE HELPED CREW a Thames sailing barge that embarked from the burnt-out end of Southend Pier. 'Crew' is probably one of my flights of fancy, as I'm now told that my main function appeared to be victualling the boat with beer. Setting off from London's Fenchurch Street Station, I expected that the run across Essex would be nothing but bungalows with taxicabs on the driveways and arterial roads suffocating in exhaust smoke. So it came as a surprise when the electric train pulled up at what appeared to be a country halt called Pitsea. Yes there was a dual carriageway out of one window, but to the south all I could see was marshland, and my first glimpse of an Essex creek of any significance that would finally decant into the Thames between the oil refineries of Canvey Island.

Essex is bordered on the west by its London and Hertfordshire neighbours, to the north by Cambridgeshire and Suffolk. Much larger than is perhaps realised, our perceptions of what is in fact a very rural county are inevitably clouded by the capital's overspill developments that reach out to Harlow, Brentwood and Ian Dury's *Billericay Dickie*. One glance at the map tells a very different story. From Shoeburyness to Harwich, the Thames Estuary opens out to the sea, and the tides start to run deep into the land

through a succession of estuaries: the Crouch, Blackwater, Colne and Stour. The fragmented margins of an English coast, widescreen vistas imbued with unexpected and sometimes eerie atmosphere typified by the lonely cries of birds on estuary mud, the snap of oyster shells opening in makeshift sheds and the ubiquitous pinking of wires against boat masts.

At the head of the Blackwater Estuary is Maldon. You will doubtless have seen the name on a box of sea salt in the pantry, and indeed the Maldon Crystal Salt Company is the sole survivor of what was once a thriving local industry. This part of the world is ideally suited to salt processing, the low annual rainfall being very good for maintaining high levels of salt in sea water. The Blackwater is consequently one of the saltiest in England, water being syphoned off from the middle of the river where the salt concentration is highest. After settling in large tanks, it's filtered and then boiled until the famous inverted pyramids of salt crystals emerge. I like this, such localised industry still producing for the kitchens and tabletops of the rest of the country. Maldon also contributed to the tradition of river transport for local needs, with 'stackies' – barges designed with shallow bottoms ideal for navigating the inland creeks with their cargoes of whole corn stacks.

Other roped and tarred reminders of Maldon's past dependency on maritime trade can be found down on The Hythe, where russet-sailed Thames barges are often moored up under the watchful gaze of the church of St Mary the Virgin. Here can be found the wonderfully evocative steam tug *Brent*, built in 1945 and once involved in dredging for the Port of London Authority. What a sight she must have been, going about her daily business, the prodigious funnel billowing smoke as she fussed about among the cranes and wharves of London docks, until one day arriving in the Blackwater and finally rounding Collier's Reach into Maldon. This is the ultimate sadness of places like this. A town whose quays were once the centres of working life, with everything else – shops, churches, pubs – existing as a life-support system, the quayside reduced now to a handful of sheds for the weekend boater (and thank goodness for that at least) and the odd spruced-up amenity for townsfolk and day-trippers alike. The ships and barges, once workaday visitors, are now in retirement on the quayside, with just the occasional day out into the estuary and the sea beyond. For the most part now Maldon appears to turn its back on the tidal Blackwater, other than to take in the view from an airy apartment designed in a pastiche of maritime vernacular.

▲ ABOVE
Steam tug Brent *at Maldon*

◄ OPPOSITE
Thames barges at Maldon

⚓ BELOW
Market Hill, Maldon

From Maldon, a road runs southeastwards to the estuary of the River Crouch, continually dog-legging with unexpected right-angled turns across an empty landscape of lonely farms and settlements with names like Copkitchen's, Good Hares and Snoreham Hall. And the inexplicable 'Carbuncle'. Just before Burnham-on-Crouch, a signpost points to the Dickensian-sounding Creeksea, and a private drive can be negotiated past the Hall (lawn being mowed with an Atco under pink cherry blossom) to a little church by the local golf course. Rebuilt in 1878, the architect F Chancellor used every material he could lay his hands on in the vicinity: stone, flint, brick and tile in a mad jumble of pleasing detail. Inside, a 1631 brass plate inscription starts off with: 'If any prying man, heere after come ....' The lane to Creeksea just peters out at a handful of boats on their trailers drawn up around the modest timber shed of the sailing club.

Burnham-on-Crouch is one of the most pleasing places on the Dengie Peninsula. Although quite isolated – Chelmsford is 20 miles away – the town's railway station remains open, missing the fall of Beeching's axe owing to the railway's proximity

to the Bradwell nuclear power station. The actual line now gives up at
Southminster. Like all of the Essex estuary towns, the river frontage always comes
as something of a surprise. Passing weatherboarded cottages, old bakeries and tea
warehouses, you slip down an alleyway and you're looking out across a broad
expanse of water, in this case over to Foulness. The buildings on the quayside
bring an eclectic sequence of styles and materials: whitewashed, colour-washed,
orange brick and painted boards. Ye Olde White Harte stands out not just for its
exterior, but also for its dark wooden-floored rooms looking out on to the bright
water opposite, an excellent place to sit with a glass of Crouch Bitter and a fat
prawn sandwich. New flats and conversions appear to have been achieved
sympathetically, comfortably at home with the corrugated iron boat sheds, and at
the eastern end is the classic 1931 Royal Corinthian Yacht Club by Joseph
Emberton. Brilliant white with cantilevered balconies and angled staircase lights,
one can almost hear the chink of ice cubes in gin and tonics just looking at it.

Before leaving the town, take a look at the little Rio Cinema. Burnham was one of
the very first places in the country to have such a thing. Originally the Electric
Kinema, after demolition in the 1920s it became the Princes Cinema, until being
dubbed the more exotic 'Rio' in the 1960s. Although boasting two screens — one
must be in the cleaning cupboard — it still has the jaunty air of a faded fairground

⬆ ABOVE
The Quay, Burnham-on-Crouch

➦ OPPOSITE
St Peter-on-the-Wall

attraction, which of course is where it all started. Lucky Burnham, to have this little picture palace still open on its doorstep rather than having to endure a popcorn-strewn multiplex.

Our road now turns to the north, up to depressing Southminster with its shuttered railway station at the end of the line. They've tried to liven things up a bit for the handful of commuters with a lively mosaic on the platform wall, but one is still tempted to carry on up towards Tillingham and the really remote northeast corner of the peninsula. The latter manor, for all its isolation, has been under the jurisdiction of the Dean and Chapter of St Paul's Cathedral in London since Saxon times, and the church, with its Norman porch and font, makes a picturesque grouping with the nearby weatherboarded cottages, reminiscent of the picture-postcard view of Clare in Suffolk.

The Bradwell power station looms in grey silhouette on the horizon, but on a corner of a cornfield near the entrance is a most unusual war memorial. The men of RAF Bradwell Bay, who in 1942–5 '... left this airfield to fly into the blue forever', are commemorated by a De Havilland Mosquito aircraft that disturbingly looks like a model aeroplane that's just unexpectedly nosedived into the ground.

So to the very end of the peninsula, passing a pub that says it's the last one before the North Sea. Down a track through wide fields where skylarks rise and fall on the breeze, the straight line of the horizon is interrupted by what looks like a big barn, which, remarkably, for centuries has been just that. Here was the Roman fort of Othona, which as it slipped into the mud was succeeded by the Saxons who built their chapel from the recycled Roman brick and stone. Dedicated to St Cedd, it survived by being used as a useful seamark and for agricultural purposes, until retrieving its original use as a chapel, now dedicated as St Peter-on-the-Wall. In all seasons and weathers, this is a rewarding walk across an Essex landscape: cool and shade after a hot afternoon stroll, welcome shelter after rainstorms that sweep across cropped fields and mudflats alike.

♥ **BELOW**
Rio Cinema, Burnham-on-Crouch

We have to go back down the peninsula to get round to the north side of the Blackwater, not forgetting to pick up a box of Bulls Eggs on a bend of the road by a row of coastguard cottages at Bradwell-on-Sea. The B1026 takes us from Maldon up through Goldhanger to Tolleshunt D'Arcy, where a green is overlooked by the magnificent orange brick D'Arcy House, one-time home of writer Margery Allingham, whose detective Albert Campion will be remembered from green-banded Penguin crime paperbacks. Feelings of mystery still fill the air as the road goes down to Tollesbury, past White House Farm behind trees, where Jeremy Bamber apparently murdered five members of his adoptive family in August 1985.

Tollesbury appears as an unremarkable Essex village, albeit with fading signs on gable ends and fresh bread put out in the window of a tiny bakery. However, in following the road to the end, the landscape once again opens up to the sea, bringing in this case a huddle of nautical buildings gathered around the channels and inlets of Woodrolfe Creek. First, the beautifully restored sail lofts on stilts with exterior ladders, built in 1902 to house the sails of J-Class (Jumbo) racing yachts during the winter months. Then, rounding the corner, one is met head-on by the atmospheric delights of rickety boat sheds and rusty oil-drum braziers burning offcuts of sea-soaked timbers, together with the sounds of hammering and good-natured sailing banter carried away on the breeze. At the end of one of the hards is the Woodrolfe Granary, a superb example of an Essex quayside store that now looks as if it might suddenly lurch sideways and collapse into the water. Grain would have been only one of many cargoes that found its way into this Victorian warehouse. The barges could equally have been carrying Newcastle coals, Kentish ragstone, Jersey new potatoes and roadmaking flint. Maybe the shed also saw the stacking-up of jam brought down from Tiptree on the wonderful but now extinct Crab and Winkle Line railway.

◄ **OPPOSITE**
A Tollesbury quayside

✎ **BELOW LEFT**
Woodrolfe Granary, Tollesbury

❦ **BELOW**
Bakers, Tollesbury

A walk out on to the Tollesbury Wick Marshes, crossing almost hidden inlets on little wooden footbridges, brings the sight of a red lightship moored among smaller craft rising and falling with the tide. You could easily think the ship arrived here from some dangerous shipping hazard out in the Thames Estuary, but in fact it's from South Wales, where it warned of the Scarweather Sandbank off Porthcawl. This eye-catching example of nauticalia now provides maritime holidays for children.

Back up through Tolleshunt D'Arcy again, where a crossroads is marked by a roundabout that serves as village maypole, signpost and weather vane, what better place for tea than Wilkin & Sons' jam factory at Tiptree? This is a very worthwhile detour on the way to the outskirts of Colchester; tea and scones with Little Scarlet strawberry jam and time to stock up with preserves and marmalades, all with those typographically classic Tiptree labels on the jars.

Colchester will need to be circumnavigated to reach our next ports of call, but another detour, off the B1025 and down a long lane through Fingringhoe, is worth it to see a later destination from across the tidal Colne – the river frontage of

↑ ABOVE
Virley Channel, West Mersea

↓ BELOW
Lightvessel 15, Tollesbury

⚓ ABOVE
West Mersea oyster shed

Wivenhoe. Carrying on southwards, the road crosses a causeway (called The Strood) on to Mersea Island. Winding through West Mersea, we are again given no hint as to what's to come, but soon another muddy shoreline of huts, yacht masts and motionless seabirds comes into view.

Coast Road is where you will find in abundance that Essex Estuary Essential: the oyster. Being boxed-up for London restaurants and bars of course, but here you will also find them in the more prosaic (and therefore so right) surroundings of the Company Shed eatery. No frills, airs or graces, the Shed offers the very best in English seafood. What you need to do is drop any thought of pretentious over-priced restaurant nonsense (one artistically placed sprig of rocket), buy your own bottle of wine and a good-sized loaf of bread, and settle down at a Formica-topped table and wait to be given your menu (fish, fish and fish), a corkscrew and a roll of kitchen towel. Expect to have yellow fish boxes moved to allow you to sit down, and don't be alarmed to see the lovely waitresses outside leaning up against boats having a cigarette. You can't book, the floor might be tidal and the service briskly efficient, but it doesn't get any better than this. It's only fresher if you eat off the deck of the boat.

You start to see why Colchester was so strategic to the Romans and just about everyone else who navigated up these estuaries and creeks, when you have to go back up to the ring road and down again to reach the east side of the Colne at Wivenhoe. You always know a village like Wivenhoe has been colonised when you see 'residents only' parking bays in the best bits and the website has 'Advice About Drugs' featuring prominently on the home page. You can see why when you look across at the river front from the quiet marsh opposite at Fingringhoe. The old village, so quaint with seafaring notions and boats almost nosing into the bar of the Rose & Crown, is in fact dwarfed on either side by blocks of wi-fi'ed apartments struggling to look at home with the Essex vernacular. We still get drawn to it, wanting there to be some kind of functioning vestige of how it was, hoping for a Thames barge to heave to with a haystack on it; and not really finding it, our vision starting to be selective, like mine when I photographed the waterfront from Fingringhoe, carefully editing out the flats.

◄ **OPPOSITE**
Wivenhoe from across the River Colne

BELOW
The Rose & Crown, Wivenhoe

▲ ABOVE
Beach huts, Brightlingsea

We're now on the right side of the Colne for Brightlingsea, reached through Thorrington and lodged on a creek just off the river. I first came here in the late 1970s with two friends keen to see a Thames barge race offshore. We conned a local into lending us his tiny boat for a fiver, victualled it with Hovis, cheddar and a case of Courage Director's Bitter, and then whirred out to the stately line of barges under sail in a strong southwesterly, weaving in and out of them like an annoying wasp around honey jars. We enviously raised our beer tins to those on deck, they raised their flutes of champagne, I was sick over the side. The end of the race was nothing short of breathtaking: the line of barges and Colchester smacks in full sail coming in from the steel-blue sea to the harbour, everyone who had a boat accompanying them, including a naval-hatted man with a pipe single-handedly sailing a little steamboat. All of this glorious maritime pageant of sail and steam lit by early evening sunlight.

Years later I couldn't believe that I would be invited to actually help crew one of these coastal workhorses, arriving in Brightlingsea at night and taken out to the sailing barge *Beric* in a dinghy. The race was fairly uneventful, even though I was in charge of dropping and pulling up the port leeboard, until as we were about to re-enter the harbour we were hit by a dramatic squall in a rainstorm and the whole thing listed to starboard and took on water. I sang 'For Those In Peril On The Sea' and lashed myself to the mast, but we very quickly righted and I promised to regularly empty my pockets into Lifeboat tins.

On our turn into Brightlingsea Creek I noticed a row of beach huts, and vowed that if I survived I would one day return to look at them with less saltwater in me. Much appears to have changed in the last quarter of a century, the waterfront is piled up with the ubiquitous rows of apartments and more appear to be on the way. The streets were empty, an old corner hotel with a cupola looking like reference for a surreal Chirico painting, so it was gratifying to see a large cone of gravel behind a dock wall and a crane of some sort working. Out on Westmarsh Point I found those beach huts, with their sometimes startling colour schemes, names like 'T'ut' and £15,000 price tags. I love how people have decorated them, that very English thing of perhaps being very comfortable in a crowd but still wanting to stand out now and then. One here has a bubbling seahorse stencilled on it in marine blue.

Can there be anything more infuriating when travelling in England than the nightmare of the 'restricted junction'? Having completed at enormous expense one of the most vital east-west routes in Britain – the A14 link between the A1 and the M1 – some bureaucrat didn't think it necessary to allow for traffic that might just want to go south on the M1. Here in Essex, I found another equally brainless example way out in the countryside as I tried to navigate from Brightlingsea to Harwich. Presumably, it was thought that no one from Clacton could possibly want to go to Harwich, so I found myself inexplicably driving virtually to Colchester before I could face the right way again. Locals obviously know a rat run involving a badger tunnel or something, but Harwich can be found if you go the right way down the A120.

⬆ **ABOVE**
Abandoned hotel, Brightlingsea

⬇ **BELOW**
Brightlingsea shed

PLEASE KEEP
DOORS CLEAR

In the late 1980s, my friend Mr Hooper and I formed a society called the Old Buffers. The idea was that everyone would dress up very smartly in business suits, overcoats and highly polished Oxfords, take a train somewhere and find pubs that had 'David Watts' by The Jam on a jukebox, and then try to get back to London the same day. Even now, only the two of us are in it (apart from notable guest appearances), but Harwich was our inaugural expedition. It nearly wasn't, because we discovered that the station where we had to change – Manningtree – had a *Brief Encounter*-style bar on one of the platforms. When we finally got there, we loved Harwich, a medieval grid pattern of streets on a very narrow peninsula sticking out from the northeastern tip of Essex. We discovered a lunchtime view across the harbour to Felixstowe docks in Suffolk, Trinity House yards filled with brightly coloured iron buoys, men driving ex-factory Maestros through the streets to ships, and seemingly a pub every few yards. Which suited us well enough.

Returning now, I'm pleased to report that nothing appears to have changed very much, except perhaps for the merciful absence of Maestros. I liked it even more. At a leisurely pace, you can walk up and down the parallel streets of a coastal town that still rings true to its origins, that still has that tangy feel of a working seaport – pilot boats moving in and out, the sound of steel hawsers being dragged over walled-off yards, Oriental sailors smoking outside pubs. The estuaries of the Stour and Orwell meet here, and everywhere are reminders of Harwich's intimate relationship with the sea. The gaily painted Pier Hotel with its look-out belvedere, the mid-seventeenth-century shipyard crane once operated by two human treadwheels in its timber housing, the Low Light sharing a promenade with beach huts. On a street corner, cream-painted public lavatories share a green with a red and white buoy and the yellow brick High Light that once housed carrier pigeons before the advent of the electric telegraph.

⋀ **ABOVE**
Church Street, Harwich

◂◂ **OPPOSITE**
High Light and buoy, Harwich

In King's Quay Street is another Essex cinematic delight, the Electric Palace. Norman Scarfe's 1968 *Shell Guide* tells of it being boarded up, the sad plight of so many cinemas. Not so now. Built for East Anglian showman Charles Thurston, it opened in November 1911, closed in 1956, but was restored and re-opened by the Harwich Electric Palace Trust in 1981 – one of the earliest of cinemas still projecting the latest films in a proper fashion. To one side of the building is a curious crane up by the roof. Thinking this was for heaving the latest blockbuster into the projection room, to my astonishment I found it is used for precisely that, 35mm film reels being somewhat heavy. It's not original, being put here at the cinema's restoration, but, in use several times a week, is an incongruous but fascinating addition to a cinema in a town full of cranes of one sort or another.

➤➤ OPPOSITE
Mistley Towers

❦ BELOW
Mistley Quay

Westwards from Harwich, the Stour Estuary narrows until our journey's end is met at Mistley and Manningtree. The river now becomes the centrepiece of Constable Country, but before the big sluice gate by Manningtree Station, the muddy tidal reaches are filled with everything from tiny plastic rowing boats to cargo ships anchored at Mistley Quay. Everywhere can be seen the impressive remains of the malting industry, still carried out in some quarters, while the rest have become apartments garnered under names like 'The Barley Store'. On my visit, my nostrils were assailed by a warm and oh-so-comforting smell that immediately took me back to my childhood and my mother's cakemaking. I had to find out what it was, and diving into a factory reception I was told it was indeed those essential food ingredients being processed. It warmed my heart too, that Mistley, perhaps much better known for Robert Adam's 1776 twin Tuscan-columned church towers (the church that connected them was demolished), should still be making something useful, and that ships were still mooring up under Essex cranes and old malthouses, swans slowly swimming by in quiet attendance.

⬆ **ABOVE**
Electric Palace cinema with film loading crane, Harwich

➤➤ **OPPOSITE**
Manningtree mooring

HEDGES & SIGNPOSTS
WILTSHIRE–DORSET BORDERS

THIS IS A comparatively small area, the very bottom left-hand corner of the tall rectangle that is Wiltshire. With close-knit dairy farms bordered by woods, it is perhaps more Dorset in character than the more recognisable Wiltshire – open plains, bare hills crowned with enigmatic clumps of trees. 'Chalk and cheese', as John Betjeman so brilliantly described it. Contained within a triangle formed by the A350 to the west, and the long-distance runners the A303 to the north and A30 to the south, only Shaftesbury is actually in Dorset. There isn't a useful label for this countryside, no 'Lakes' or 'Cotswolds'. Estate agents, naturally, have tried to dub it the 'cocktail belt', thinking of their Range Rover punters hurrying to pre-lunch Sunday drinks before the rabbit run back up the A303 to first homes in Notting Hill.

On numerous occasions I have arrived here to find the skies clouding over and to hear a distant rumble of thunder. So I've quite wrongly thought of it as decidedly spooky, particularly as every time I went to Tisbury I became convinced that everyone had taken in the washing and drawn the curtains. The lanes are narrow and either high-hedged or sunk between earthy embankments filled with hart's tongue ferns. The signposts are rusty and leaning at awkward angles and everywhere can be broodingly silent. There's a very palpable atmosphere here, with Fonthill and William Beckford's prodigious fallen tower still in the imagination on its hilltop, Old Wardour Castle and Teffont Evias romantically embowered in trees, and the crystal-clear River Nadder attempting concealment as it makes its way to Salisbury. Everywhere, stone cottages with comforting hoods of thatch sit hunched behind well-trimmed hedges as if also trying not to be noticed.

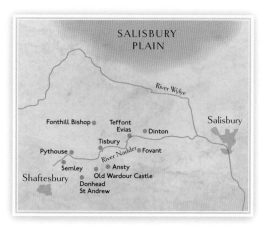

▲ **ABOVE**
St Mary's Church, Dinton

Before and after the roundabout at Amesbury, westbound on the A303, are two enigmas. The first is a development called, of course, Solstice Park, between the road and Boscombe Down Airfield. It's as though someone's decided to see how it will look if we ever colonise the moon. The chalk surface is impossibly scarred, there are developments of indiscriminate scale, and there's a Holiday Inn in case we want to go and have a holiday looking at it. I can't explain it, and really don't want to think too much about it. The other side of the roundabout is Stonehenge, with hundreds of people in cagoules standing staring at a collection of big grey stones, some of them even fallen over. In his book *Watching the Certain Things*, author Ralph Wightman remembers his father saying that it was so much better when it was just sheep grazing round it, and I have to agree. Nobody appears to be at all interested in the incredible and far more enigmatic domed barrows that sit out in the surrounding fields.

Travelling on over Berwick Down we arrive at Wylye, and turn south over the river that gives its name to the village, the town of Wilton and therefore Wiltshire. Up and over the downs, until a sunken lane descends steeply through banks of ferns to Dinton. The village lies on the southern slopes of the downs and above the

River Nadder before it meets with the Wylye at Wilton. A remarkably eclectic collection of buildings gathers around St Mary's Church which stands very proud with its crossing tower at its heart.

Opposite the recreation ground, there is a small National Trust car park, and from here a path leads through the trees to a stile that gives access to graceful parkland. Immediately to the right will be seen Hyde's House, an eighteenth-century remodelling of a sixteenth-century core and the birthplace of the first Earl of Clarendon. Unusual is the stone south elevation pediment with an *oeil de boeuf*, or 'bull's eye', window, set against a red-tiled mansard roof with dormers. I love dormers on big country houses, high above the more stately rooms below: Leo Colston at Brandham Hall on a hot summer's night in the film of LP Hartley's *The Go-Between* (1970), listening to a girl singing at a piano far below.

Across the road from the east end of the church is a house so exceptional it makes it into neither Pevsner nor the *Shell Guide*. Probably dismissed as an ugly curio of the late nineteenth century, Dinton Lodge has the look of an earlier house that has sprouted wavy eyebrow gables in every direction, and a south-facing upper-storey loggia with a classical parapet. Ringed with white-painted iron railings and front gate that have been given equal listing, I have seen nothing quite like it.

↟ **ABOVE**
Hyde's House, Dinton

♟ **BELOW**
Dinton Lodge, Dinton

↑ ABOVE
Teffont Evias: cottages, church and manor

Three-quarters of a mile west along the B3089 from Dinton is a turning left by a signpost leaning characteristically in the hedge. Round the corner is a scene so English it could make one drive straight into the small lake on the bend. I made a mental note that this could be a superb location for another Henry Fielding film, a classic grouping of an impressively steepled church, manor house and a pair of cottages, framed in woodland with a sheep pasture sloping gradually down to still water. This is Teffont Evias, and closer inspection revealed the church to be an early Gothic Revival by Charles Fowler in 1824–6, which ruled out my eighteenth-century fantasies. Oddly, the original dedication for the church was forgotten and so it was re-christened St Michael and All Angels in 1965. The churchyard is entered by a tiny bridge over a stream, a feature for many cottages and houses in the village, and in front is the seventeenth-century manor with the charming addition of Victorian towers.

I could have spent a lot of time lurking about here before being arrested, but our route takes us back up to the B road and through Chilmark (where quarries once

provided the white stone for Salisbury Cathedral) to Fonthill Bishop. A set of
farm labourers' cottages on the right may catch your attention – neat pairs built in
local stone with orange brick dressings and green 'estate' paint on the bargeboards
and doors. Turning left at the zebra-striped signpost on a triangle of green brings
us to something extraordinary. At first, we see two enormous piers each side of the
road, swaggering sentinels with bands of 'rustication' and a giant urn on each. A
low wall with big vases runs up to an equally rusticated arched gateway, a
triumphal entrance to the enigmatic estate of Fonthill. The gateway is naturally
attributed to Inigo Jones, but is thought to be mid-eighteenth century and
probably by the designer Henry Hoare of nearby Stourhead. It is perhaps curious
that the full effect of this stunning gateway was best seen by departing guests on
exiting, the sun falling for the most part on the 'wrong' side. This southern
elevation was quite rightly chosen as the front cover photograph for Timothy
Mowl and Brian Earnshaw's seminal book on country house lodges *Trumpet at a
Distant Gate* (1985).

⬆ **ABOVE**
Fonthill gateway

⬇ **BELOW**
Cottages, Fonthill Bishop

Fonthill will, however, always be indelibly associated with one owner: William Beckford (1760–1844). As a five-year-old, he took music lessons from an eight-year-old Mozart, and aged 10 he inherited the beautifully wooded 4900-acre estate, along with a very useful £1.5 million in cash (that's £165 million now). In 1786, Beckford wrote one of the first Gothic novels — *Vathek* — at one go over two days, and his thoughts turned to building something as memorable as the tower in his book. He dispensed with his father's house down in the valley and, with architect James Wyatt, had a vision of a 'Gothick' abbey on a hilltop half a mile to the northwest. With its prodigious 276-foot-high tower, it quickly became the most well-known folly in England. It was still not completed in 1800 when Beckford hosted a torchlit party in honour of Nelson and his victory at the Battle of the Nile. Imagine them arriving here, torches flaming in the night as a procession of horses and carriages thundered under the arch of the Fonthill Bishop gateway, and then the guests sitting down to a banquet by candlelight in the unfinished Abbey. Beckford sold up in 1823 and moved to Bath where he built another tower up at Lansdown. This still survives, unlike the Fonthill Abbey tower which, owing to very negligent construction, 'quietly subsided' (as James Lees-Milne has it) in 1825, chasing a servant down the length of a corridor as it fell.

William Beckford, and his tower, still haunt this park. As we go southwards, we pass the Beckford Arms, and a little further on the Tisbury Lodge, once heralding the mansion built around 1850 for the Marquess of Westminster that has also disappeared. Turning right in Newtown, we arrive at another estate, that of Pythouse, built in 1805 by Mr John Benett to his own design. On the right, just inside a wood, is a circular dovecote that is one of a number of secluded buildings in England that always bring to mind Walter de la Mare's exquisite poem *The Listeners*, with its opening lines: 'Is there anybody there?' said the Traveller, / Knocking on the moonlit door.' The fact that this patently isn't a dwelling takes nothing away from the notion. Deeper in the woods is a ruined chapel built by Benett for his wife Lucy, now behind steel fencing and with bushes growing up out of the roof. Nearby, I came across something equally alarming, probably the most ghostly scarecrow I've ever witnessed. Lopsided among the weeds of a patch of allotment, there was something fey about the stuffed pillowcase head and Miss Havisham gown. I hurried away, not looking behind in case the sightless apparition had uprooted and was squeaking and flapping behind me, reaching out twigged arms in supplication.

⌂ ABOVE
Pythouse dovecote

◄ OPPOSITE
Entrance pier, Fonthill

❦ BELOW
Pythouse scarecrow

Over the railway line we arrive at the village green of Semley, and another reminder of the builder of Pythouse with the Benett Arms. I once stayed here prior to an extensive photographic shoot at Old Wardour Castle, and after the first course at supper we heard a drum roll of thunder and then saw, through the round-topped windows, the green light up momentarily with eerie ignitions. We went outside, and looking towards the west saw lightning flashing virtually continuously behind boiling clouds, as if an alien mothership was about to come down for us. We ran about like children let out of school, going into the nearby churchyard to watch the Victorian tower of St Leonard's Church light up like a Hammer film set. All it needed was someone behind a tomb chest rattling a sheet of tin to make thunder, but fortunately we were called in for the main course before we could get electrocuted.

The churchyard has a curiously small monument to Lieutenant George Dewrance Irving Armstrong, who died serving with the Sherwood Foresters aged 36 on 5 August 1915. Designed by Henry Pegram, the plinth is surmounted by a bronze statue of a mounted soldier in a tropical helmet. Across the green from the churchyard is Church Farm and its range of outbuildings in scale with a farmhouse that still retains an appearance of small changes over many years. Evolution not revolution, a motto that some architects should have embroidered on their laptops.

▲ ABOVE
Church Farm, Semley

◀ OPPOSITE
Benett Arms, Semley

▼ BELOW
Churchyard memorial, Semley

We can now go slowly along the valley of the River Sem, past a lovely stone bus shelter, and then along a single-track road that winds up to Old Wardour Castle. Although only a short distance (as the ubiquitous crow flies) from the A30, this must rank as the most delightfully hidden English Heritage property. For me, it made a change to see the castle again in late summer afternoon sunlight, rather than staring gloomily at it from under big umbrellas while models confirmed their next assignments with mobile phones like housebricks. Towered over by cedars, and next to a lake where you'd expect the sword Excalibur to be suddenly thrust up out of the water, Old Wardour is a very extensive ruin. A 'licence to crenellate', that is: put embattlements on the parapets, was granted to Old Wardour in 1393. (Nearby, 'new' Wardour is the largest Georgian house in Wiltshire, an eighteenth-century mansion by James Paine.) The southwest corner is the most intact, the rest of the exterior is ruinous and reflected in the eighteenth-century grotto at the top of the surrounding well-mown lawn. Achieved with a Ransomes, I trust.

I came to a wedding reception here once, held in a big marquee under the cedars. I climbed up to the top of the castle and thought it a good idea to photograph the scene below from the vantage point of a narrow window. Unfortunately, my bulk got wedged into the opening and nobody did anything to help for laughing. Old Wardour's finest hour though, was in the Civil War (1642–51) when 25 Royalists, led by the elderly Lady Arundell, held 1300 Cromwellian troops at bay for five days. She finally surrendered after an honourable deal had been struck with the Parliamentarians, who then promptly and dishonourably broke it. Bloody Roundheads. They should film this stirring story here, as they did a portion of *Robin Hood: Prince of Thieves* (1991) when it was used as Kevin Costner's dad's castle. To the west, on the outer bailey wall, is a delightful Early Georgian Gothick summerhouse. From the castle, it looks like a one-storey building, from the lane below it's two storeys, the lower now housing the toilet block.

◄◄ **OPPOSITE**
Old Wardour Castle

✎ **BELOW**
Summerhouse, Old Wardour Castle

To return to our route, we have to retrace our steps down the narrow lanes and follow both the River Nadder and the railway line to Tisbury, at the heart of the countryside we are circumnavigating. This large village, or faded town, has a look about it of only slowly relinquishing its past. The railway station, opened in 1859, is almost intact in red brick and with a curved platform canopy of painted tongue-and-groove wood. The car park, along with the digital display panel, tells of Tisbury's easy connections to Salisbury, Exeter and London Waterloo – which is less than a hundred miles away. The line is single track here, trains having to wait on a loop to let each other through. As I wandered about the only platform, I could hear raucous shouts and laughter from The South Western pub opposite, and was gravely tempted, even though it was three o'clock in the afternoon. I can assure you that I walked by and up the main street instead, going into a delicatessen to re-stock on Dorset Knob biscuits. I told the delightful couple behind the counter about my previous experiences in Tisbury, waxing lyrical about closed doors and distant rolls of thunder. I thought they were going to say: 'What do you expect?', but instead they reassured me that Tisbury is alive and well and everybody buys fresh bread from them in the morning and then disappears to eat it in the afternoon. They challenged me to a pub crawl around their six pubs, and I promised I would return.

Wandering the streets, I found high on a wall the kind of link to Tisbury's past that I had hoped to find. A 'ghost' sign that still showed the name 'Randall' painted in red around a curved-top stone window frame, with 'plumber' and 'gas

& water' just about visible next to it. Some of the sign had tantalisingly faded even more, leaving just the odd intriguing letter. Another, more robust ghost, reminded the town that the Wiltshire Brewery's proprietor had once been 'Arnold Beckett'. The cut-out stone letters are still extant on the brewery premises, now turned into the obligatory apartments. They look out over the cruciform church next door that displays a tower restored after a lightning strike (told you) by, yes, Mr Benett of Pythouse. Rudyard Kipling's parents are buried in the churchyard.

⌂ **ABOVE**
Derelict workshops, Tisbury

✒ **BELOW**
Underwoods Electrical, Tisbury

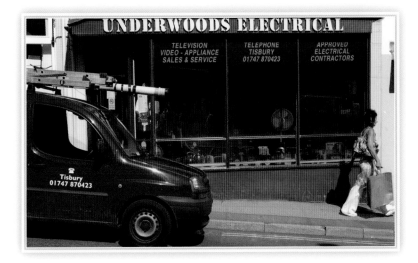

We can now drop down southwards to Ansty and make our way along the A30 to Shaftesbury. On a particularly awkward stretch of the road, I saw an old stone milepost under the trees and, after finding a convenient farm gateway to park in, I walked back to it along the road as early evening traffic careered by at high speed. The inscriptions spoke volumes: 'Sarum', the old and conveniently short name for Salisbury, and the equally milestone-friendly 'Shaston' for Shaftesbury. This gave me pause for thought, because 'Shaston' is Thomas Hardy's *nom de plume* for the Wessex town, italicised on the map in his novels to denote a fictitious name. It is in fact an old alternative name for the town, but I like to think that the lonely milepost caught Hardy's eye as he cycled by from Dorchester, perhaps on his way to research dairy maids.

Shaftesbury sits perched on a greensand escarpment, 700 feet above the Blackmore Vale that was once dotted with the kind of dairy farm so filmically described by Hardy in his novel *Tess of the d'Urbervilles*. If you've never been here, the first thing you have to do — just to get it out of the way — is to walk from the High Street to behind the 1820s neo-Tudor Town Hall. A clue as to what you will see lies in a giant fibreglass Hovis loaf on the pavement, and rounding the corner is Gold Hill, probably the most photographed street in England. Ridley Scott (*Alien*, 1979; *Gladiator*, 2000) shot Britain's favourite television commercial here in 1973; the baker's boy pushing his bike up the steeply-cobbled slope and then freewheeling back down again, cut to a brass band playing Dvořák's *New World Symphony*. Another director, John Schlesinger, got here first though, using Gold Hill to even

more stunning effect in his Hardy film *Far from the Madding Crowd* (1967); shooting the precipitous street both ways — Sergeant Troy's mounted troop in red tunics clattering downhill, the tragic Fanny Robin in rags crawling up as rainwater ran down the gutters. Gold Hill does have everything for a photographer: stone cobbles, a row of cottages like a staircase, pastoral countryside as a scenic backdrop. All you need is a couple of long-suffering householders to light coal fires.

The high retaining wall on the west side of the street holds back the old Abbey precinct, once the preserve of Benedictine nuns in the thirteenth and fourteenth centuries. By the time of Henry VIII's Dissolution there were only 56 of the holy sisters left, and now very little remains but flowerbeds with an awe-inspiring view. Far less photographed in Shaftesbury is architect Andrew Trimen's mid-nineteenth-century Congregational Church in Mustons Lane. Trimen was the Congo's architect of choice. Impressively Corinthian with its portico of columns holding up a pediment, I can only assume that the Shaftesbury congregation are either now very few in number or have rolled off down Gold Hill, as I was somewhat alarmed to see that it's now 'Amore: ristorante pizzeria'. Very sadly, we can't expect beautiful buildings like this to still be places of worship, but considering what could have happened here the exterior has survived virtually intact, except for 'Amore' etc blocking out the fanlight. A problem of usage will increasingly burden those responsible for buildings like this (incidentally Grade 2 Listed), and as Amore wasn't open for me to have a *quattro stagioni* I can't report on the interior. I suppose we should be grateful that it's not turned into a tyre-fitting bay or tanning salon. At the end of Mustons Lane, a gimlet eye will follow you from an upper-storey window on the corner.

From Shaftesbury we can either descend into the Vale towards Blandford Forum, or return up the A30 towards Wilton and Salisbury. This way we can make a detour through the Donheads, turning left in Ludwell and dropping down first to Donhead St Mary, past the beautifully proportioned Parkgate Cottages, and then over the Nadder to its sibling Donhead St Andrew. It was here that I took proper notice of the street nameplates, characterfully cast in iron with mid-blue backgrounds: thought given to material and letter style, and perfectly at home

◄ **OPPOSITE**
Amore pizzeria, Shaftesbury

❦ **BELOW**
Street sign, Donhead St Andrew

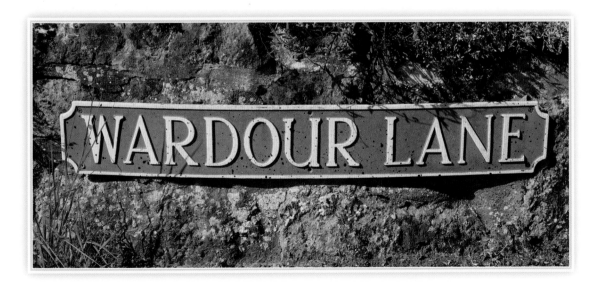

against Wiltshire stone walls. This local distinctiveness is what can be so intriguing about England. The differences between counties, the sudden unfamiliarity of ordinary things greeting us as we arrive at new destinations. I remember the pleasure of seeing how the buses looked on holidays: green Southdowns in Sussex, red and cream Devon Generals. Or the breweries – Bullards in Norfolk, Fremlins in Kent, Harveys in Sussex. So much of this local diversity is now under threat that we must put our hands up and say 'Hang on a minute' when whey-faced bureaucrats do things like destroy traditional signposts, or tell us we should stop using county names when we address an envelope.

Back on the A30, the main road now shadows the downs to the south that rise steeply up to wooded crests, only a field or so away. White Sheet Hill, Swallowcliffe Down, Sutton Down and then Fovant. Here on the hillside are a set of graphic depictions cut into the chalk, six army cap badges looking like they're pinned on an olive drab uniform. Fovant, together with the neighbouring villages

of Compton Chamberlayne and Sutton Mandeville, became a vast training and transit camp for the British Army in the First World War. Thousands of soldiers were processed through here, with shooting ranges, a hospital, camp cinema and a branch line serving it off the London to Exeter railway.

Many of the soldiers, of course, never returned, and their comrades remembered them for posterity by carving out their badges from the turf in 1916. Hard thirsty work on a 30-degree slope, but during the Second World War they were allowed to grow over so as not to provide a navigational aid to enemy aircraft. Weather and cattle grazing added to their deterioration, but after the war the local Home Guard turned themselves into an Old Comrades Association that eventually became The Fovant Badges Society. Not all could be saved, but here are those that were, a remarkable memorial on a Wiltshire down.

Some years later, this hillside was put to another, somewhat more prosaic use. A local dairy farmer came up here in the 1930s and inscribed huge letters on the grass with strong fertiliser that grew into the legend 'Drink More Milk'. The slogan was

apparently still visible many years later, like 'Marples Must Go', surviving on an M1 motorway bridge until at least the early 1990s. Ernest Marples was Minister of Transport from 1959 (when he signed off the construction of the motorway) until 1964.

We come to the end of our short journey, but only a little further along the road is Wilton, once the county town of Wiltshire before Salisbury stepped in. Wilton is well worth a walk round, quite apart from the Earl of Pembroke's magnificent house and Palladian bridge over the Nadder. Take time to look at the Italianate Romanesque Church of St Mary and St Nicholas on the main road as you come in. Looking like it's been plucked from a Tuscan grove of cypresses, this is, as even Pevsner had it, a 'tour de force'. If you're leaving the town for Salisbury on a late summer's evening, you will also be treated to the sight of the magnificent cathedral through the trees, the white Chilmark stone of the glorious fourteenth-century tower and spire catching the last of the day's sun, perhaps a ghostly apparition from a medieval fantasy.

FISH & TIN
NORTH CORNWALL COAST

THE ATLANTIC COAST of north Cornwall stretches from Marsland Mouth above Morwenstow to Cape Cornwall by St Just. In my book, anyway. Rugged, sea-scoured and inhospitable in places, this is the untamed edge of a county that has seen its local farming, fishing and mining subjugated by a terrifying influx of tourism. Where once isolated granite homesteads clung to the cliffs and wind-blown fields, an incongruous mass of white- and cream-rendered bungalows gather around the over-popular hotspots. Locals migrate to the nearest towns as house prices rocket, and second homes wait for the key in the door at weekends, high days and holidays.

Constant and unforgiving is the sea, blue-green masses of saltwater heaving under a fogbound Pendeen Watch, waves thundering into caves under Tintagel, tides flowing ceaselessly in and out of Port Isaac. Inland, unexpected mists suddenly gather around the ancient stones and fougous of Penwith, bleak landscapes are pinpointed with cowering trees bent back from westerly winds. A country of deserted tin-mine chimneys, Methodist chapels and lost saints. A self-styled separate country that wants to stand proud from the rest of England, but resigns itself to the fact that the four-wheel-drive from Putney is as important to its survival as the folk memories of serious mining and fishing. The electricity wires so abhorred by John Betjeman, perhaps the area's most famous 'incomer', may have replaced the oil lamps, Dayglo surfboards the fishing smacks, but there is still much that reminds us why we fell in love with this southwestern outpost of England in the first place.

Very soon after crossing the border from Devon, a signpost points to Morwenstow, Cornwall's most northerly parish. After going through a village called Shop (where I don't think there is one, oddly), a high-hedged lane leads past The Bush Inn to a cul-de-sac by a church perched in a cleft above the cliffs. St Morwenna and St John the Baptist is Norman, very dark and gloomy inside, and coming round one of the pillars you may be confronted by a red-faced cleric who will frighten the life out of you if you're not expecting it. This is Morwenstow's most celebrated incumbent, the marvellously eccentric Rev RS Hawker (1803–75), presented here in effigy, at least on my visit.

Stephen Hawker was a remarkable man. Clergyman, poet and antiquarian, he wrote the Cornish anthem 'The Song of the Western Men', the one that goes: 'And shall Trelawny die? Here's 20,000 Cornish men will know the reason why.' When he arrived here in 1834, there hadn't been a vicar in residence at Morwenstow for over a hundred years. The parish was stuffed full of smugglers and wreckers who thought nothing of leaving drowning sailors to the sea, but Hawker instituted Christian burials for those unfortunate enough to be washed up on the rocky shore. The figurehead of *The Caledonia*, wrecked in 1842, can be seen high up on the church wall, and a ghostly replica out in the churchyard where nine of the 10-man crew are buried.

'Parson' Hawker dressed in a claret-coloured coat, blue fisherman's jersey, pink hat and long sea boots. The only thing in clerical black were his socks. He once dressed as a mermaid, and quite properly excommunicated his cat for mousing on a Sunday. The Harvest Festival, as we know it, was introduced by him in 1843, and all were welcome. Which doubtless included his nine cats and large pet pig. Hawker's memorials are all around. The vicarage has its chimneys fashioned in the likenesses of his previous church towers, the kitchen chimney is a model of his mother's tomb.

One of the great joys here, though, is to walk out on the coastal path. As I went into a field of newly turned hay, the scent of it reached me at the same time as the sound of the waves crashing against the rocks far below. As the path reaches the cliff edge, there is a little stone stile and a short steep slope down to a tiny building that is the National Trust's smallest property. This is Hawker's Hut, and here he watched the restless sea and pondered over the lost souls of sailors. He also puffed away on a pipeful of opium. The hut has graffiti-scored seats on three sides and a stable-type door, and, although doubtless heavily restored over the years, it doesn't excuse the National Trust for using shiny Pozidriv screws in the hinges. Hawker married his first wife Charlotte when he was an undergraduate and she 21 years his senior. His second wife was a 20-year old Polish girl he married when he was 60, who bore him three children. He converted to Roman Catholicism on his deathbed.

↑ **ABOVE**
Rev RS Hawker

↙ **BELOW LEFT**
Hawker's Hut, Morwenstow

↓ **BELOW**
Figurehead of The Caledonia *in Morwenstow church*

Boscastle is the meeting place of two fast-flowing streams and the two geological formations of Cornwall – the clay country of the north that is Devonian in character, and the granite that epitomises the rest of the county to the south. The water courses became thunderously full on 16 August 2004, when Boscastle and nearby Crackington Haven were inundated in an event that was reckoned to have a one-in-400-year chance of occurring. We will all be familiar with the newsreels of torrents of brackish water carrying cars along like bathtime toys under the taps. Some say that farming practices such as uprooting hedges and trees further up the valley contributed to a much bigger run-off of rainwater, but whatever the causes, Boscastle was very fortunate not to have experienced any loss of life. So the ice-cream shops and Witch Museum survived, and certainly the little town appears to have rebuilt and renewed itself very successfully.

This is a classic Cornish harbour, a narrow channel between high cliffs with rectangular white and cream buildings contrasting very artistically with the dark greens and browns of nature. Two stone jetties (one was destroyed by a mine in the Second World War) saw coal and iron coming in from Wales, slate and cereals going out, but inevitably the arrival of the railway at Camelford, in the late nineteenth century, soon put the trade into terminal decline. The Victorian tourist

◀◀ OPPOSITE
Tintagel Castle

▼ BELOW
Boscastle

had already discovered Boscastle, and of course the railway helped it along in becoming a holiday destination. Fortunately, it never became a Padstow or Newquay, and in the stillness of a quiet late summer afternoon, the past is still discernible behind the witch's amulets and clotted-cream ices.

Tintagel suffers from Arthuritis. Here, the dedicated followers of Uther Pendragon wait for their master to return, to transform himself back from a red-beaked chough perching on the castle walls into King Arthur, to at last lead his people to deliverance. So they bide their time outside the taverns, some shaven ready for battle and displaying their allegiances with Celtic tattoos, their idol reduced to a five-foot plastic effigy that blocks the pavement. In the interregnum they can have their aura photographed or tuck into what's probably called a Lancelot Pasty. (The Guinevere is smaller and more dainty.)

Away from the throng of the main street and up on the hill is the church, so gloriously dedicated to St Materiana. Like all Cornish coastal churches, it appears hunkered down against the westerly winds in a treeless landscape. It's as if the stonemasons got so far up shaking scaffolding and thought, 'Actually, I don't think a hundred-foot tower's such a good idea after all.' The graveyard is full of Victorian Celtic crosses, and of course they say that, when Uther returns, non-mortal campanologists will ring out a welcome. A path leads down to the cliff edge which affords spectacular views of the ruined Tintagel Castle, and an equally awe-inspiring prospect of the immense King Arthur Hotel on the opposing headland that in silhouette (only) looks like Camelot has indeed been rebuilt. We've got the twelfth-century Geoffrey of Monmouth to thank for the Arthurian connection, but recent archaeology has more or less disproved it. It's just a pity that Uther didn't leave more tangible evidence like Excalibur hanging up at the back of Merlin's Cave.

Don't try to drive down into the old village of Port Isaac. The narrow roads are impossibly steep and there's nowhere to park. St Austell Brewery drays need to get down unhindered, and, oh yes, coastguard Landrovers. Far better to leave your car at the top, where the car parks look out over the immense bay that stretches from Varley Head to Tintagel. Port Isaac is, we now have to acknowledge, 'Port Wenn', the home of television' s *Doc Martin*, the irascible medic with an unfortunate bedside manner; and roadside manner, seaside manner, you name it. The little fishing village is generally delightful and unspoilt, and the programme does it full justice. The only evidence of filming would appear to be the now easily removable signage, so that The Old School Hotel, for instance, can quickly revert to being the Old School. The Doc's surgery exterior is prominent on the other side of the harbour, along with a typically Cornish version of a Methodist Chapel (1846) where they must have sung 'For Those In Peril On The Sea' with particular fervour.

Many of the houses and cottages have walls hung with pale greeny grey Cornish slate and tiny gardens sheltered from Atlantic storms by whitewashed walls. The harbour itself is similarly protected by enveloping cliffs, tides flowing in right up to the Town Platt where portable boats and beer barrels are deposited, and out again to the jetties leaving larger boats leaning on their keels. Fishing is still vital here, with a cheery shop selling fresh crabs and lobsters along with equally fresh culinary advice. I like Port Isaac, and do hope that television tourism doesn't take it over too much.

▲ **ABOVE**
Port Isaac, Town Platt

➤ **OPPOSITE**
Port Isaac harbour

Along the coast westwards, Port Quin is sad and almost neglected by comparison. In 1698, all the men of the village were lost when their fishing fleet foundered in a storm, and the place never fully recovered. The wives and children moved away, the cottages fell into ruin, pink valerian and willowherb took over. A handful of cottages were repaired and are now let out by the National Trust, who incidentally own 40 per cent of Cornwall's coastline. But there is still a very melancholy air even on the brightest day. I came here once and found a gloomy man chipping away at a granite wall to make a recess. 'Are you making room for a wall-mounted post box?' I enquired patronisingly. Chip, chip. Without looking up he replied, 'No. Rabies noticeboard.' Chip, chip.

Up on the hill above the tiny harbour is a Regency Gothic towerlet, perched on Doyden Point. Apparently there are only two rooms and a cellar, the latter amenity giving rise to the rumour that it was built for someone to drink themselves stupid without interruption. Footpaths pass all around, and it's very soothing to lie back on the grass (at a suitable distance from the very sheer cliff edge) and hear the white-edged green sea surging across the dark rocks below.

Trebetherick is where poet, writer and broadcaster Sir John Betjeman had a home, as did his father before him. A hedged lane winds its way down to Daymer Bay, and from here it is a short walk across a golf course to the tamarisk-shrouded St Enodoc Church. It was once shrouded in sand, just the thirteenth-century spire (unusual for Cornwall) revealing its position in the dunes. Until it was dug out and restored in 1863, a priest was lowered down through a hole in the roof in order

◀◆ OPPOSITE
Port Quin doorway

❦ BELOW
St Enodoc Church, Trebetherick

to recite a service, necessary to keep it open. On a corner of the churchyard is a wooden shack that I always thought was originally used as a store for the corpses of sailors drowned in wrecks on the notorious Doom Bar across the nearby mouth of the Camel Estuary. Betjeman was buried just by the lych gate on 19 May 1984, his coffin carried by bearers across the golf course in driving rain.

Down the road is Rock, which has never really appealed to me, it seemingly being filled with Boden-clad youths shouting about what they're going to do in their gap years, 'txtng' mates in Putney and throwing up fruit-flavoured vodkas. They probably think that Betjeman is a Dutch lager. We will continue down to our crossing point of the Camel and continue heading west. A now dismantled railway ran up the estuary, not once deviating from the banks of the River Camel. In *First and Last Loves* (1952), Betjeman described the line: 'Green Southern Railway engines came right into the brown and cream Great Western district of Cornwall ... and we are at Wadebridge, next stop Padstow. The next five and a half miles beside the broadening Camel ... is the most beautiful train journey I know.'

When Betjeman wrote that, the little port of Padstow was a remote, quieter place and they caught exceptionally large prawns where the town drains fell out into the Camel. Not so now. The streets can be unbelievably crowded, everyone shuffling at a snail's pace from ice-cream parlour to fudge emporium and queuing for exotic fish 'n' chips. I saw a sign that said 'Special Today: Rick Stein's Fruit Cake' and imagined a Dundee with a layer of kippers in it. It's sometimes too difficult to look down into the harbour for the soft-shoe shuffle, but I did catch a glimpse of a sailing ship, the beautiful wooden Baltic trader *Ruth*, and up in the town the Spar supermarket still has a window above the door with the legend 'Tobacconist' in

◀◀ OPPOSITE
Port Quin tower

🔖 BELOW
Padstow old trade

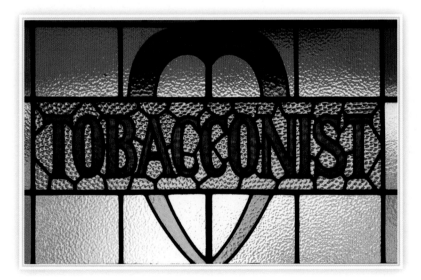

coloured glass. On May Day, a man in a huge black tent-like skirt rolls around the town frightening women.

Northwards we can take a cul-de-sac lane to Lellizzick Farm and walk across fields to the cliff path that goes up to Stepper Point. On the horizon will be a tower, much like a Cornish engine-house chimney, but this is in fact a daymark, used to aid navigation into Padstow through the narrow channel into the Camel by Doom Bar. We can look down into the estuary from high in the fields, beaches on both sides framed by blasted trees. On the way up to the daymark we will pass Butter Hole, probably one of the most deeply impressive and beautifully unspoilt coves on this north coast. There's no way down, and I expect the only visitors will either come in from the sea or abseil down like commandos.

ABOVE
Across the Camel to Daymer Bay from Lellizzick

OPPOSITE
Daymark on Stepper Point

BELOW
Padstow new trade

◄◄LEFT
Island House, Towan Beach, Newquay

↙ BELOW
Huer's Hut, Newquay

Mmm. Newquay. I was going to say it's best to avoid it unless you happen to have a penchant for surfers' Lycra, giant Australian pubs painted bright green, and signs everywhere saying 'No Worries'. All this, and more, is to be seen in Newquay. There are, of course, stuccoed Victorian terraced streets of homely B&Bs and up at Pentire, high above Crantock Beach, it appears to be wanting to emulate the seriously high-end real estate of a Cannes or Nice. Which it can't, really. But two curiosities are worth seeing.

One is the extraordinary 1910 house on top of a tiny island sitting on Towan Beach, connected to the mainland by a suspension bridge. Sir Arthur Conan Doyle is said to have stayed in it, as a guest of Oliver (spark plug) Lodge. It's apparently

ABOVE
Crantock Beach

a great place to watch dolphins from, and the three-bedroomed house was recently on the market for £750,000. Considering that at the time of writing a five-bedroomed house in Newquay (and not on an island) is upwards of £1,750,000, this seems a bargain. But you may have to put up with empty 'Ratzpiss' bottles being thrown up at you from beach 'barbies', and you'll only own the island down to the mean high-water mark.

Round the corner up towards Towan Head is the Huer's Hut. I forgot the name and how to get there, so went and alarmed an old lady by asking her where Newquay's Huer House was. It's a little fourteenth-century white-painted building with an outsize chimney and outside staircase, perched on a cliff edge, and is where the huer lived and worked. It was his job to watch out for shoals of pilchards arriving in the sea below, staining the water red with their presence. He would then cry 'Heva! Heva!' to alert the fisherfolk below, and would direct the boats to the shoal. Why 'heva' I don't know, I suppose it carried better on the coastal wind than 'Pilchards! Pilchards!'. The huer would also use two bushes as a semaphore to signal other news to ships like 'The captain's got a new baby', or 'The bosun's wife's run off with a surfer'.

In typical Cornwall style, another little lane runs for two miles out of St Agnes and down to the sea at Chapel Porth. This was a very recent discovery for me, and I have to say it is one of the most delightful beaches I have seen on this stretch of coast. I urge you to come out of season, even if it's only September, and in the early evening as I did. Hopefully, a low sun will create fantastical contrasts between the outcrops of rocks and the deep black shadows of the caves, and the tide will be out sufficiently to enable you to walk round the miniature headlands. But beware. The waves crash relentlessly up the shore, preceded by wide pools of water that careen over the sand and can catch you unawares. I got well and truly soaked getting the photograph opposite.

The engine house 200 feet up on the cliff once served the Wheal Coates Mine, opened in 1872. Here are lodes of particularly good-quality tin, but a massive beam engine was required to pump water out of the deeper sections which lay far under the sea. The mine finally closed in 1914, but the remaining buildings have been preserved by the National Trust. I can think of no better place than Chapel Porth to sit at the mouth of an inviting cave watching the encroaching waves while tucking into a Hedgehog from the little shop. That's vanilla ice cream topped with clotted cream and chopped hazelnuts – but watch those tides.

➤➤ OPPOSITE
Wheal Coates engine house

❦ BELOW
Beach and caves at Chapel Porth

I like St Ives. Even though a seagull once tried to steal my breakfast from my table (I got my own back by giving him a piece of toast with mustard on it), and the council charge you £3.50 to park your car in the middle of the night. Everything they say about the light is true. No wonder artists packed themselves into trains to

get down here: Sickert, Turner, Whistler, Nicholson, Hepworth, Heron, Hodgkins, Frost. Bernard Leach made pots, Alfred Wallis drew ships in pencil and painted on any old bit of cardboard he could find.

Poster artists loved it too. The views are stereotypical 1930s railway advertising – cream and grey cottages curving round a harbour with a lighthouse and bobbing fishing boats, and just where you want it a church tower as a focal point. St Ives divides itself into two – a morning side where the rising sun will light the harbour, and an evening side where sunsets can be watched from

Porthmeor Beach. I love getting up early in the morning, while there's nobody about, and wandering along to Smeaton's Pier where fishermen are turning up in salt-battered pick-ups loaded with nets and creels. A blackboard is chalked-up with weather conditions and it's good to see fishy activity still going on in the shadow of the rust-stained lighthouse. But as Betjeman says in his *Shell Guide*, St Ives 'has gone in more for pictures than pilchards, and for tourists instead of tin'.

This is a town of rich texture: steep alleys, tiny courtyards and always a glimpse of the Atlantic through archways. Steps up to cottages, steps down to the sand. A palette of cream, blue greys and silver with a brushstroke of treacly brown for the fifteenth-century St Ia's Church. The fish cellars are now garages for steeply parked Mercedes, salting sheds are now hung with pictures of salting sheds, but The Sloop Inn keeps faith with a history reaching back to the fourteenth century (drink and eat at the long tables in the black wooded bar). St Ives must be seen on foot, but you can still arrive here by a train that runs round from Lelant Saltings and Carbis Bay.

❦ **BELOW**
St Ives harbour, morning light

The landscape alters abruptly as soon as we take the coast road westwards. Here is where a film location manager would set a series on prehistory called *The Birth of Man* or similar. We have entered the Land's End Peninsula, or Penwith as I prefer to call it: moorland, granite, gorse; and the standing stones, fougous and quoits that tell of pre-Christian ritual. It's not difficult to think of families in lonely slate-roofed cottages still sitting down to Stargazy Pies (the ones with fish heads sticking up out of the pastry), before taking a scrofulous child out into the fog to cure it by dragging it naked through holes in rocks. I once came past a farmyard near Zennor to find a goose, a cat and a dog sitting in a row in the middle of the road. I stopped, they walked to one side. After I'd gone by, I looked in my driving mirror and saw them reconvene. I fully expected to find Rupert Bear hiding behind a hedge.

Turning right in Pendeen, a lane goes down to the Pendeen Watch Lighthouse, one of my favourites. The cliff is high so the light tower itself doesn't have to be; the lamp house sits above a row of cottages where once the keepers lived with their

❦ BELOW
Pendeen Watch Lighthouse

families. Trinity House holiday lets now, the light is controlled by telemetry from just about the furthest point eastwards from here: in Harwich, Essex. What's happening to the safeguarding of our coast? Also in Essex, I read of complaints that the coastguard was being moved 14 miles inland because of a lack of volunteers.

The lighthouse arrived here because shipping was unable to see either the Longships or Trevose Head lights due to high cliffs, and many ships foundered on the sunken and exposed rocks below. The light was only commissioned in 1900, and after they had detonated the cap of rock in order to give a level platform. The foghorn which echoes around the coves and headlands is now sadly an electronic device that looks like a dirty wedding cake, instead of the characterful dual black horns that are still extant. What a gloriously sonorous and melancholic sound they must have made. From the steep paths of the headland, we can look across to the mine chimneys of Levant and Higher Bal clinging to the cliffs opposite, our next port of call.

❦ **BELOW**
Zennor, Penwith Peninsula

Cornwall was probably once the most mined area in the world. Geologically, fissures opened up in the granite when it was still cooling, allowing more molten rock to rise up from the fiery depths of the earth. In these rocks were minerals that crystallised as they cooled: tin, copper, iron, lead and zinc. Sometimes gold (very little) and silver (quite a lot). The nature of the fissures meant that mining had to be done vertically, so for each mine a separate vertical shaft was sunk, unlike in a coal mine where one shaft could service numerous horizontal galleries. Each shaft needed to be continually pumped dry, so engine houses were built to accommodate huge beam engines using the best steam coal imported over the sea from Wales. The Levant Mine has a fully restored and working steam engine in separate housing to the main engine house, it was once used to service the main shaft and to take miners down to work instead of the usual time-consuming ladders.

Copper was first mined at the Levant and, when that became unprofitable, tin mining took over. Lumps of rock were brought to the surface and crushed, the result being suspended in liquid so that the heavier specks of tin would sink to the bottom. One per cent of tin was average, three exceptional. It simply didn't make enough money, and one by one the mines closed. However, thanks to the self-styled 'Greasy Gang' and the National Trust at the Levant Mine, you can see how it all worked, and get just a glimpse of what it meant to be maybe 2000 feet below the surface in pitch black, with just candlelight to guide the pick and shovel.

➺ OPPOSITE
Higher Bal engine house

❦ BELOW
Levant Mine engine houses

The end of Cornwall for me is Cape Cornwall, not Land's End which has been turned into a dubious tourist attraction where you can either be photographed next to a signpost with your home town inserted into it, or drive away quickly in the opposite direction. Cape Cornwall may be a few yards short of the 'Most Westerly' statistic, but it is infinitely more rewarding. Four miles north of Land's End in the parish of St Just you can still watch huge Atlantic breakers exploding over rocks, but you can also climb up the Cape (the only 'Cape' in England) and lean against the old mine chimney that now serves as a memorial to the generations that once worked the Cornish mines. For a long time, this was considered the 'land's end', and it's here that the waters of the Atlantic divide, currents flowing either northwards into the Irish Sea and the Bristol Channel, or south into the English Channel.

◀◀ LEFT
House painting, Cape Cornwall

❦ BELOW
Boat painting, Cape Cornwall

There are those, inevitably as this is Cornwall, who want to see more 'tourist infrastructure' here, so thank goodness for the rigorous opposition of the National Trust who own Cape Cornwall. Yes there's a car park, and you can buy an ice cream or a can of pop from a little caravan, but it's still possible to be alone and wander about among the lobster creels and leaning rusty sheds that seem about to topple over into the sea. I was very tired after my journeys down from Morwenstow, which seemed such a long way back up the coast. I sat down on a very big egg-like rock to contemplate the sea breaking on the shore, and very slowly toppled backwards. I couldn't stop myself, and ended up with my legs in the air as a gull on a nearby shed stared balefully at me with its implacable grey eyes before turning away.

BELLS & WHISTLES
HIGH LEICESTERSHIRE

HIGH LEICESTERSHIRE is not 'high' as in the Pennines or Cheviots, but mountainous when compared to the flatlands that extend off to the east. It is more often described as 'rolling uplands', English pastoral at its very best. Essentially east Leicestershire, it forms a very rough diamond, with the extremities map-pinned clockwise by Leicester, Melton Mowbray, Oakham (just over in Rutland) and Market Harborough. It has the River Welland as its southeastern border, the River Wreake its northwestern, with the rise of the limestone escarpment as an eastern frontier. There is nothing between these hills and Russia, and old farm labourers would once tell you that the east winds 'blow straight through from the Urinals'.

This is a country of small villages of brick and stone, isolated farms and mellow country houses behind stands of chestnuts and limes. Often the only sounds will be a far-off tractor or combine, melancholy church bells marking the hours, and shotguns going off. The area is traversed by railway lines long abandoned, but they still continue to serve as an ideal matrix with which to plot the landscape. The gentle hills once echoed to the lonely blasts of whistles, skeins of white exhaust smoke marking the progression of trains making their way through the shallow, hidden valleys.

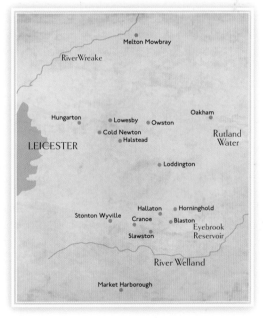

◄ **OPPOSITE**
Main Street, Slawston

➤ **ABOVE**
Bargeboarded porch in Hallaton

⬆ **ABOVE**
Lord Morton's Covert near Cold Newton

I must have first set my somewhat unappreciative eyes on High Leicestershire from a railway carriage in the 1950s, an impatient child wondering why the holiday special hadn't reached the seaside within minutes of leaving the now extinct Belgrave Road station in Leicester. Instead, we were all in for the long haul before this same train would finally let us out at a remote tile-hung station in Lincolnshire, a handful of miles from our weather-bleached bungalow looking out over the cold North Sea. But all this was some time away, probably after the enamelled sandcastle bucket had frequently been put to unmentionable utility.

Once the train had noisily emerged from the glass and iron canopy into the early Saturday morning sunlight, it ran through the shrubbed and tennis-courted Leicester suburbs until negotiating the first cuttings, embankments and viaducts of the Great Northern Railway (GNR) that took us out into the fields. Would I have noticed bleak Ingarsby Hall from the little station, or Jacobean Quenby Hall on its tree-crested rise? No, not until my first faltering bicycle rides would I start to take in these folds of land, green fields spotted with Border Leicester sheep, neatly layered hawthorn hedges in the cold early months.

I would seek out my eldest brother Roger, who worked on a farm at Hungarton, in a dip below Quenby, finding him lurking in a ditch with a menacing billhook or driving a little grey Ferguson pulling a muckspreader. In his pale brown overalls and matching flat cap, he always reminded me of the all-purpose worker that drove my agricultural Dinky Toys. He once took great delight in telling me to stand in a trailer half full of manure only for him to let out the clutch so violently that huge muddy divots showered and ruined my brand-new gaberdine school mackintosh.

The Quenby estate is still announced by red-painted field gates with a white top rail, but only recently did I discover the same idea on neighbouring demesnes: blue and white around Lowesby, black and white for Ingarsby. It is a very rural, worked-in country, planted with fox coverts by the hunts and given names that paid homage to, say, a local huntsman – Lord Morton (a wood planted in the nineteenth century in an old stone quarry) – or to act as a reminder to the local populace of where they could end up if transported for not making a pork pie properly: Botany Bay. At first, the gentry had objected to the railway companies even daring to suggest that they would invade these hallowed steeplechasing acres, but soon came to realise that hoofing horses around England was a much easier proposition, let alone being able to fill wagons with their local ironstone or Stiltons. There are still remnants of a direct telephone line put into Oakham signal box for a pre-war Lord Lonsdale to summon up his own set of horse boxes out of a siding in order to go hunting back on his family's Westmorland estate.

⬆ **ABOVE**
'Q' for Quenby farm gate

⬇ **BELOW**
Quenby Hall near Hungarton

Beyond Quenby, the line passed under Cold Newton, a handful of cottages in an exposed position that must have given rise to the name. My farming brother once lodged in Hungarton with a remarkable character called Freddie Green, whose family had lived in every one of a row of six or so Cold Newton cottages. Starting at one end, they moved into the next dwelling as soon as the predecessor became overrun with mildew or rats. After they had vacated the last one at the other end, the whole row just fell into the ground. I remember seeing it as just a rectangular patch of nettles, the sure sign of previous human habitation.

The gated road to the north of Cold Newton passes through the farmyard of what was once the manor that stood at the heart of a much larger, now deserted village. A higgledy-piggledy marlstone farmhouse, that looks as if it has grown organically out of the soil, is surrounded by abandoned machinery and blue-and-white Lowesby gates. The humps and hollows of the lost village can still be seen in the open fields, and one gets the feeling of looking out over a medieval landscape, particularly in early-evening light with sheep grazing around isolated clumps of thorn. I talked to the tenant of Manor Farm, who confirmed my worst fear that it is true that the new owners of the halls and granges really do complain about mud on the road spattering their Mercedes and BMWs, and gag at the beastly smells emanating from stockyards. We looked at each other in mutual despair, the unheard sound between us that of a metaphorical 12-bore having cartridges slid into it. On a more positive note, he did tell me that when he was a boy in Lowesby, the whole school would be let out into the playground and surrounding lanes if the foxhunt came anywhere near the village.

The muddy road leads round to the front of the farm and over Skeg Hill to Lowesby, with its late seventeenth-century Hall and hair-raising stories of hunting occupants and their loud red-faced guests. One December night in 1838, the third Marquis of Waterford wagered 100 guineas that his horse could clear a five-barred gate set up in the dining room. The feat was accomplished, with the horse only just grazing its nose on the fireplace. After one drunken post-hunt party in April 1837, the Mad Marquis and his friends attempted to daub red paint on buildings in Melton Mowbray, the origin, we are told, of the phrase 'painting the town red'.

Our railway curves round to Lowesby station, the red-brick remains of which are now sensitively converted into a dwelling. The derelict station was naturally a source of great interest: the old booking hall and waiting rooms, a separate lamp room which must have leaked tantalisingly with the scents of oil and paraffin, and a signal box now marooned in a farmyard.

❦ **BELOW**
Manor Farm, Cold Newton

The embankment here was a favourite haunt of blackberry pickers, and one can easily imagine a bowl-full being given to a train crew just before the guard gave a shrill blast on his Acme Thunderer. I don't doubt there was also the covert reception of a couple of glassy-eyed rabbits caught on the embankment to be secreted away behind stacks of newspapers and parcels in the guard's van. From here, the line joined with a far-flung outpost of the London & North Western Railway (LNWR) at Marefield Junction, and very soon passed through John O'Gaunt — named after another foxhunting covert — from where a dairy once sent three or four tankers of milk to London *every* day. The last trains to run from Belgrave Road were allocated solely to the dairymen, part of a rural initiative to try to keep workers from migrating to Leicester. This line continued up to Melton, but our tour of High Leicestershire now leaves the holiday special ('Are we there yet?') and takes another imaginary train southwards back to the junction and on down towards Market Harborough.

Over to the left towards the Rutland border is the isolated village of Owston (pronounced 'Ooston'). I'm always skulking about here, parking up under the trees outside St Andrew's Church. Parts of this church, namely the nave, north aisle and tower, are the last remnants of an Augustinian abbey founded in the twelfth century. Across the fields can be seen Owston Woods, the last of the original forest that at this time would have covered the landscape as far as the eye could see from the tower. Shades of RL Stevenson's *The Black Arrow* perhaps, old Appleyard felled among his cabbages by a bowshot singing out from the woodland fringes. Nobody's taken a pot-shot at me yet, as I've walked up the grassy path among the superbly lettered slate tombstones, under trees where a noisy parliament of rooks build high in the uppermost branches, but only time will tell.

🌲 **ABOVE**
Snowdrops, Owston

➤➤ **OPPOSITE**
Viaduct near Marefield Junction

🌲 **BELOW**
St Andrew's Church, Owston

⬆ ABOVE
Oxey Farm near Loddington

◄ OPPOSITE
Lowesby Hall (1707)

Below the Roman camp of Whatborough, at 755 feet the highest hill in High Leicestershire, Tilton-on-the-Hill's station was also a mile away from its hilltop village, with the hamlet of Halstead in-between. As soon as the line was sanctioned and planned, fears grew among the villagers that the arrival of itinerant navvies would bring drunkenness and brawling into the local pubs, so a facility was built for them near to the proposed station.

The Salisbury Arms continued as a station inn, and in the mid 1970s I had my introductory pint in its remarkably bucolic surroundings. The drinking companion who first took me there once photographed five generations of the Vickers family standing or sitting outside, everyone from a babe in arms to the 90-odd-year-old matriarchal Mrs Vickers. As much farmhouse as pub, the Salisbury consisted of just one room, lit by a single lamp that illuminated the bottles and glasses behind the bar. Here Mrs Vickers dispensed our libations, wiping a tumbler on her flowered apron if your female companion wanted a gin and tonic, her spectacles reflecting the fire in the grate. The lavatory facilities were alarming, at least for the girls, who were reluctantly allowed to ascend the stairs into the gloom of the upper floor. We boys were sent outside to a tall hedge against the road. On one curious occasion, I asked Mrs Vickers if she had any cigarettes on the premises and she shouted, 'Lynley, cigarettes!' Twenty minutes later her son appeared with

20 Player's No 6. He'd either got the tractor out or cycled up to the machine in the Tilton pub. Eccentric doesn't adequately describe Lynley. After closing time, he would go and mend gates in remote fields by moonlight, and one evening introduced me to a hen held under his arm, a very alert fowl that wouldn't release an egg gripped in a yellow vice-like claw. I once drove by the pub as Lynley arrived at the double farmyard gates on his red tractor and, with an eye on an early doors' drink, stopped to ask if he wanted me to open them. His reply was drowned out by the horrendous noise of his simply driving straight at them, splinters of wood flying skywards where they mingled with a blue cloud of exhaust smoke. The Salisbury has sadly gone, now a private house after a brief spell as what I suppose was an early manifestation of a gastro pub.

Below the pub, the railway burrowed between the hills of Colborough, with its high crown of birch trees and row of tall Scotch firs at the western end, and Robin-a-Tiptoe with a tall story attached. The latter is a long barrow-like eminence where an attempt was made to hang a local sheep rustler. His height was such that his toes just touched the ground and he was released by his fellows after the inept administrators of justice had piously departed down the steep slopes. After a cutting below lonely Oxey Farm, passengers would have looked straight down on to Loddington church, a westering sun shadowing both train and headstones on the churchyard that sits at the top of a sheep pasture just outside the village. Loddington Hall was once a ruin we trespassed in, now the headquarters for a Game & Wildlife Conservation Trust project. A previous incumbent excelled himself while returning here from the hunting field. His wife had asked him to bring back some treacle from the grocers in Tilton and, on being told that they had no container to put it in (the viscous liquid being dispensed from a barrel), he promptly told them to fill up his top hat, which he carried home under his arm for four miles.

◀ LEFT
The Salisbury, Halstead

➤ OPPOSITE
Wet and dry, Eye Brook at Loddington

To the south, a blue brick viaduct crossed the Eye Brook: a pleasing local landmark once seen across the fields until ruthlessly detonated for hard core a few years ago. The station and cottages at East Norton were next to the main A47 road that keeps to the high ground between Leicester and Duddington, the escape route for more Saturday seaside journeys made in a convoy of red-and-black Midland Red coaches. Once the bat-infested East Norton tunnel was negotiated (later a good place to comfort frightened girls), the line began its gentle descent into the Welland Valley.

Hallaton was once an important agricultural centre, and its station reflected this status with cattle docks and numerous cottages. Cows still ruminate next to brick railway huts, perhaps hearing the ghostly lowing of their antecedents being loaded into trucks. Many will know of Hallaton for the extraordinarily violent Bottle Kicking that takes place over the fields between the village and its arch rival Medbourne on Easter Mondays. Violent, but good natured. I have had 18-stone blokes crash into me during their quest to gain possession, and have always heard them say 'Sorry!'. This is truly 'Olde England', with a hare pie sliced up by the vicar on the church steps and the 'bottles' (in reality wooden casks) paraded through the streets.

◄ OPPOSITE
Hallaton Bottle Kicking, hare pie cutting

❦ BELOW
Hallaton village green

There are much quieter pursuits in Hallaton. Go and take a look at St Michael and All Angels Church, one of the finest in High Leicestershire, with a carillon of bells in the tower that plays things like 'Old Hundredth' on the hour, or just a bar or two on the quarters. Before you leave, take a closer look at the eastern exterior wall. Here can be seen the base of a glass bottle set in among the stones. Apparently, the rector next door gave a big bottle of beer to men repairing the wall on an exceptionally hot summer's day, and as a merry jape they mortared in the empty. Up on the edge of the village on the corner of the Allexton road is the village cricket pitch. I can think of no better prospect from any other ground in

↑ **ABOVE**
Wall bottle, Hallaton church

↖ **ABOVE LEFT**
The old Estate Office, Horninghold

➤➤ **OPPOSITE**
Cricket match, Hallaton

↙ **BELOW**
The Thatched Cottage, Horninghold

↟ **ABOVE**
Farmworkers' cottages, Stonton Wyville

the county, the field giving on to classic Leicestershire landscape views to the north and east, with Horninghold church spire just peeping over a wooded fold of land.

A short gig drive from Hallaton station is the remarkable estate village of Horninghold. Once little more than a thirteenth-century church and a seventeenth-century farmhouse, in the 1880s Thomas Hardcastle, a wealthy Lancashire cotton merchant newly resident at nearby Blaston Hall, began improving the village with a post office and a handful of cottages. He turned the farmhouse into a Tudor-style manor and, prior to the First World War, his son and the architects Goddards of Leicester created a model village. The houses and hunting boxes were immediately occupied by Hardcastle's mates, and Hallaton station saw an Edwardian heyday of hunt traffic. In its maturity, these houses and cottages are a beautifully eclectic mix of building styles, vernacular Arts and Crafts and Cosy Cotswoldesque surrounded by chestnuts and copper beeches.

South of Hallaton, the railway line divided again, a right-hand fork crossing the Welland at Welham as Market Harborough approached, the left-hand making for Medbourne where it followed the Welland Valley to Stamford. A triangle of lines was formed by a baseline link between the two, again following the willow-bordered river and passing through a delightful little limestone station next to a row of poplars that served yet another village nearly a mile away called Ashley. My young boys think it's named after them, and of course I haven't disabused them of the notion. The tracks from Hallaton to Harborough ran below Slawston Hill, a gorse-strewn whale-backed height more Dorset than Leicestershire. A post windmill once crowned the hill, the last manifestation of which was repaired or reconstructed by the Fernie Hunt as a landmark, a wooden variant on the steeplechasing spires and towers that rise up into sightlines in every direction.

From the high embankment below Slawston, you would have had a magnificent view to the west past the long rise of Langton Caudle to Crossburrow Hill, an ancient site dividing Cranoe – with its delightful little iron and limestone church on its steep rook-haunted hill – from cul-de-sac Glooston and the slightly eerie Stonton Wyville. Here, a narrow lane goes into the tiny hamlet from the road to Tur Langton, a few yards from an eighteenth-century watermill with a rare, at least for round here, mansard roof. Towering firs glower over it. Stonton itself is just a tiny church hiding in yews next to a seventeenth-century manor house, which itself has the embanking of medieval fish ponds as a neighbour. A handful of houses sit scattered behind the trees and hedges, including a terrace of cottages in red brick with typical Leicestershire diapered blue brick crosses let into the upper-storey wall.

For some unexplained reason, the church was a curious magnet for us in our youth, a place to visit in the dark after we'd been thrown out of local pubs. We'd say, 'Let's go to Stonton', and whoever got there first would hide in the pitch black among the Victorian pews. Of course, we'd jump out on the others with bloodcurdling yells. One night, we cautiously opened the door and a stack of hymn books flew from their shelf in front of us with a furious clatter liked disturbed pigeons. We fled, not to return for some time. It's a wonder that with all this going on, the recumbent effigy of Edmund Brudenell didn't harrumph and sit up crossly on his 1590 tomb chest.

The Brudenells have always held estates in the surrounding countryside. Between Cranoe and Hallaton is Othorpe House, sitting gloomily isolated among dark trees above yet another lost village. Returning home at night, I always look up the hill to see if there's a light winking in and out of the trees like a poacher's lantern, its isolation adding drama to the landscape, although only half-a-mile from my village. Rumour has it that when that most famous Brudenell – Lord Cardigan of

➸ **OPPOSITE**
St Mary Magdalene, Stapleford

⤷ **BELOW**
Saxby rectory

the Charge of the Light Brigade – went off to the Crimea, his bailiff thought that his master would never survive, so he rifled the coffers and built himself Othorpe. I would like to have been a nineteenth-century fly-on-the-wall to hear his stuttering explanation on Cardigan's return. From this rise, the occupants of Othorpe must have looked out down into the valley and noticed the trails of smoke betraying the presence of a train crossing the Welland, just prior to joining the main line within earshot of the barking Fernie Hunt kennels in Great Bowden. Followed by the slow clanking into a bay platform at Market Harborough's magnificent Queen Anne-style station.

Sadly these branch lines have gone, the embankments and cuttings now just the haunt of badgers and foxes, sniffing the cold air where once they caught the whiff of steam. From Market Harborough, you can still make your way to Leicester, from where you can take a cross-country train that follows the Wreake Valley up to Melton Mowbray, perfect on a spring day with high clouds reflecting in the river. From here, the little train will run very close to Brentingby and Wyfordby before looping around Stapleford Park, where the fierce 1846 Battle of Saxby took place. The seventh Earl of Harborough's estate workers pitched in against the Syston and Peterborough railway navigators who were determined to drive the tracks straight through the parkland. The Earl hated foxhunting and railways, the latter prejudice almost certainly because of his interests in the Oakham Canal. Man-traps were set in the woods, heads were bludgeoned and the railway was sent packing, forced into what is still known as 'Lord Harborough's Curve'. From here, the line drops down into Rutland at Whissendine, before arriving in the county town of Oakham.

This is very obviously my own patch; the pastoral, hidden acres that I have known since an infant and continually returned to after roaming about the English counties that I love so much. Deserted drovers' lanes billowing with creamy cow parsley on a May morning, woods and spinneys busy with rooks, evening sun lighting red brick barns. The bleat of sheep carried on a late-afternoon breeze, the hot breath of cattle exhaled in frosty yards. An unspoilt, very English working landscape, once able to be seen from the comforting dusty carriage cloth of a forgotten train; once a landscape to lose oneself in after leaving a country station, the silence closing in from the undulating pastures.

➽ OPPOSITE
Still on the move, railway track and farm bridge near Hallaton

BIBLIOGRAPHY

John Betjeman (ed), *Collins Guide to English Parish Churches*, Collins (London), 1959

John Betjeman and John Piper (eds), *Shell County Guides*, Faber & Faber (London), 1934–84

Nikolaus Pevsner, *Buildings of England Series*, Penguin / Yale University Press (London / New Haven), 1951–74

Philip Wilkinson and Peter Ashley, *The English Buildings Book*, English Heritage (London), 2006

INTRODUCTION

Bartholomew's Road Atlas of Great Britain, Bartholomew (Edinburgh), 1951

WG Hoskins, *Rutland*, City of Leicester Publicity Department (Leicester), 1949

WG Hoskins, *Touring Leicestershire*, City of Leicester Publicity Department (Leicester), 1948

David Milner (ed), *The Highways and Byways of Britain*, one-volume compilation reissue, Macmillan (London), 2009

HV Morton, *In Search of England*, Methuen (London), 1927

Michael Pitt-Rivers, *Dorset: A Shell Guide*, Faber & Faber (London), 1966

Nikolaus Pevsner, *Buildings of England: Leicestershire and Rutland*, Yale University Press (New Haven, London), 1984

Various authors, *Vision of England* series, Paul Elek (London), 1940s/1950s

SQUIRRELS & GRAPES
SOUTHWEST CUMBRIA

HV Morton, *In Search of England*, Methuen (London), 1927

Norman Nicholson, *Portrait of The Lakes*, Robert Hale (London), 1963

AW Wainwright, *Pictorial Guide to the Lakeland Fells*, Frances Lincoln (London), boxed set, 2007

Doreen Wallace, *English Lakeland*, BT Batsford (London), 1940

BOOKS & MAGPIES
HEREFORDSHIRE & SHROPSHIRE

Irwin Dermer and Tony Meeuwissen, *The Witch's Hat*, Andre Deutsch / G Whizzard (London), 1975

AE Housman, *A Shropshire Lad*, The Richards Press (London), 1933

Kilvert's Diary, Vols 1 and 2, Jonathan Cape (London), 1938

Fiona MacCarthy, *Eric Gill*, Faber & Faber (London), 1989

SPB Mais, *Highways and Byways In The Welsh Marches*, Macmillan (London), 1939

John Michell, *The View Over Atlantis*, Garnstone Press (London), 1972

Edward Osmond, *A Valley Grows Up*, Oxford University Press (Oxford), 1956

Iain Sinclair, *Landor's Tower*, Goldmark / Granta (Uppingham / London), 2001

Alfred Watkins, *The Old Straight Track*, Garnstone Press (London), 1970

FLINT & SAMPHIRE
NORTH NORFOLK

Jane Hales, *The East Wind*, Veal (Wisbech), 1972

Richard Ingrams and John Piper, *Piper's Places*, Chatto & Windus / The Hogarth Press (London), 1983

Richard Mabey, *Food for Free*, Collins (London), 1972

HV Morton, *In Search of England*, Methuen (London), 1927

Nikolaus Pevsner, *The Buildings of England: Norfolk 1: Norwich & North-East*, Yale University Press (London and New Haven), 1997

Nikolaus Pevsner, Bill Wilson, *The Buildings of England: Norfolk 2: North-West & South*, Penguin (London), 1999

SHEEP & SHINGLE
ROMNEY MARSH & DUNGENESS

Peter Ashley, *Unmitigated England*, Everyman (London), 2006

HE Bates, *Colonel Julian and Other Stories*, Michael Joseph (London), 1951

Fay Godwin and Richard Ingrams, *Romney Marsh and the Royal Military Canal*, Wildwood House (London), 1980

Rudyard Kipling Collected Verse, Penguin (London), 1983

Rudyard Kipling, *Puck of Pook's Hill*, Macmillan (London), 1933

Philip Larkin, *The Whitsun Weddings*, Faber & Faber (London), 1964

Walter JC Murray, *Romney Marsh*, Robert Hale (London), 1982

John Newman, *The Buildings of England: West Kent and The Weald*, Penguin (London), 1980

John Piper, *Romney Marsh*, King Penguin (London), 1950

Russell Thorndike, *Doctor Syn*, Wildside Press (Maryland), 2009

WALLS & WOOL
NORTH COTSWOLDS

TS Eliot, *The Four Quartets*, Faber & Faber (London), 2001

James Lees-Milne, *Worcestershire: Shell Guide*, Faber & Faber (London), 1964

MUD & OYSTERS
ESSEX ESTUARIES

Clifford Bax, *Highways and Byways in Essex*, Macmillan (London), 1939

Norman Scarfe, *Essex: Shell Guide*, Faber & Faber (London), 1968

HEDGES & SIGNPOSTS
WILTSHIRE–DORSET BORDERS

WH Auden, *A Choice of de la Mare's Verse*, Faber & Faber (London), 1963

Thomas Hardy, *Tess of the d'Urbervilles*, Macmillan & Co Ltd (London), 1912

James Lees-Milne, *William Beckford*, John Murray (London), 1990

Timothy Mowl and Brian Earnshaw, *Trumpet at a Distant Gate*, Waterstone (London), 1985

Nikolaus Pevsner *The Buildings of England: Wiltshire*, Yale University Press (New Haven and London), 1971

Ralph Wightman, *Watching the Certain Things*, Cassell (London), 1951

FISH & TIN
NORTH CORNWALL COAST

John Betjeman, *First and Last Loves*, John Murray (London), 1969

John Betjeman, *Cornwall Illustrated: Shell Guide*, Architectural Press (London), 1934

BELLS & WHISTLES
HIGH LEICESTERSHIRE

WG Hoskins, *Leicestershire: The History of the Landscape*, Hodder & Stoughton (London), 1957

RL Stevenson, *The Black Arrow*, Cassell (London), 1918

INDEX